RAMBLING ROUND IRELAND

About the Author

At the start of his rambles, Peter Lynch was the Deputy Director of Met Éireann in Glasnevin, and by the time he completed them he had become the Met Éireann Professor of Meteorology at University College Dublin. He lives in Glenageary, County Dublin.

RAMBLING ROUND IRELAND

A Commodius Vicus of Recirculation

Peter Lynch

The Liffey Press

Published by
The Liffey Press
Ashbrook House
10 Main Street, Raheny,
Dublin 5, Ireland
www.theliffeypress.com

© 2010 Peter Lynch

A catalogue record of this book is
available from the British Library.

ISBN 978-1-905785-91-9

Printed in Ireland by Colour Books.

CONTENTS

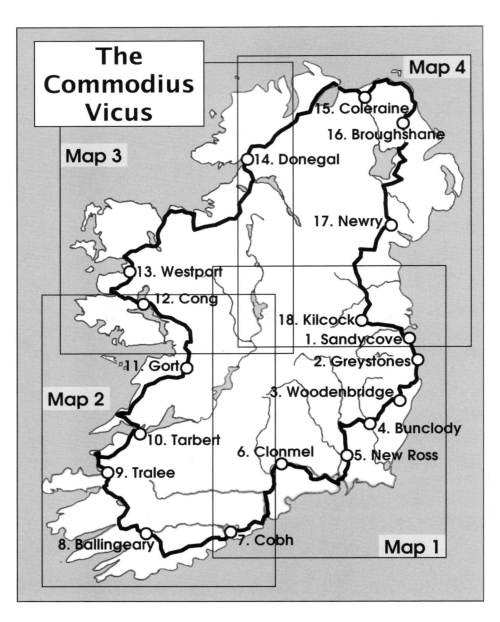

The route of the 13-year Commodius Vicus of Recirculation.
Approximate total distance 1,200 miles.
Average speed: ¼ mile per day, a blistering pace!

PREFACE

riverrun, past Eve and Adam's, from swerve of shore to bend of bay, brings us by a commodius vicus of recirculation back to Howth Castle and Environs.

Finnegans Wake – James Joyce

EVERYWHERE IN IRELAND THERE IS SOMETHING of interest or beauty or wonder. It might be a spectacular landscape, or some fascinating industrial curiosity, or just a conversational encounter with one of the gentle people of the country. This is the story of a journey around Ireland, on foot over many years, and of the little adventures that befell the rambler on his way. While the land became inundated with mobile phones and iPods, and the Celtic Tiger roared briefly before slinking back to his lair, this happy wanderer hobbled onward round the coastal counties, soaking up the landscape (sometimes literally) and enjoying the company of chance-met people. This generous journey – this commodius vicus – was part pilgrimage, part adventure travel, part educational tour and part Zen experience, but above all it was enormous fun.

It was great fun rambling round Ireland. Sometimes I was alone, more often with friends. Nothing bad happened: no muggings, no robberies, no accidents, no serious mishaps; indeed, nothing at all, really, yet it was a wonderful adventure. Almost everyone I met was pleasant and the one or two exceptions were a source of innocent merriment. Each day brought new and interesting things to see. I was in no hurry;

just as well, since it took thirteen years to circumambulate the country. There was only one rule: the rambles should all join up to form a continuous circuit of Ireland. A few stages were done out of sequence and a few in reverse direction, but together they formed a complete route around the island. The acme would have been to follow the shoreline. But with our convoluted coast (mathematicians call such curves fractals) this would require an indefinite time to complete, so I chose a less wiggly but more practical route as shown on the map on page *vi* above.

The stages of the Commodius Vicus were undertaken over a long period. The descriptions relate to conditions when I visited each area. Subsequent changes have resulted in inevitable anachronisms. Thus, for example, if the pound was the currency when I passed, prices are left in pounds, not converted to euros.

Those readers who enjoy the book may also want to visit our website, www.ramblingroundireland.com.

Acknowledgements

Many people helped me on my way, but special thanks go to the following: My fellow-Hillpigs and walking buddies, Mark Draper, Frank McKenna and Tom Murphy, for their delightful company, uproarious humour and outrageous disregard for convention.

All who provided accommodation and/or hospitality, especially Mick and Lorna Kelly (Corrofin), Step and Annette McNamee and family (Gilroe), Denis Bloomer and Audrey Corr (Westport), Rory, Lucy and Sadhbh Breslin (Newport), Ciara and John Mark Dick (Skreen) and Johnnie and Deirdre Matthews (Hackballscross).

Hendrik Hoffmann, for assistance with the conversion of computer files. Conor Sweeney, for help with map preparation. Jonathan Williams, for reading an early draft and for giving me valuable advice. Maeve Garrett, for reading a later draft and for pointing out numerous errors. All remaining blunders are deliberate, to keep readers alert.

David Givens and all at The Liffey Press who, in defiance of Jonathan Swift, have made a silk purse out of a sow's ear.

My sons Owen and Andrew for coming along part of the way. Also, Owen for helping to set up a website and Andrew for digitally enhancing the photographs. My beloved wife Cabrini, for tolerating the whole bizarre escapade with forbearance and understanding.

The plain people of Ireland, for their kindness and hospitality.

Dedication

> *Al ĉiuj kuij helpis min kiam mi mem ne povis*
> (To all who helped me when I could not help myself)

This book is dedicated to John, Brian and the late David Ellis, with thanks for their enterprise in setting up an unofficial scout patrol, The Kestrels, long ago, and for the inspiration that this provided to me at a formative stage of my life.

I also recall with gratitude the voluntary service of Peter and Noel Curran, Freddy Wright, Eddie Hearns and the other Leaders in the 17th St. Begnet's Troup in Dalkey.

All author royalties from the sale of this book will go directly to Scouting Ireland.

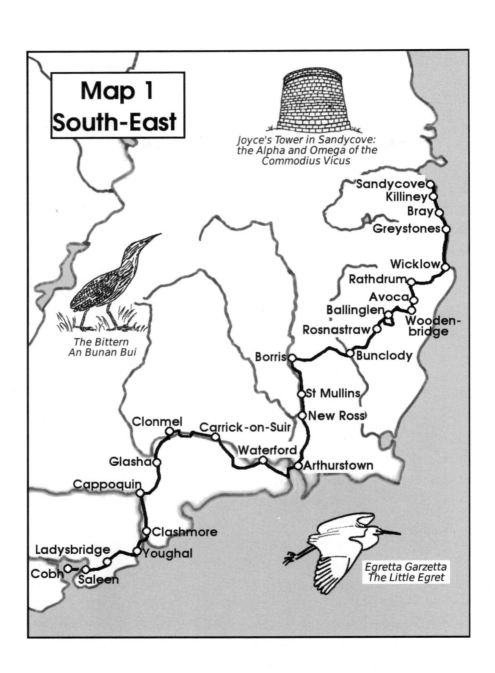

Map 1
South-East

Joyce's Tower in Sandycove:
the Alpha and Omega of the
Commodius Vicus

Sandycove
Killiney
Bray
Greystones

Wicklow
Rathdrum
Avoca
Ballinglen
Rosnastraw
Wooden-
bridge

The Bittern
An Bunan Bui

Borris
Bunclody

St Mullins
New Ross

Clonmel
Carrick-on-Suir
Waterford
Glasha
Arthurstown
Cappoquin

Clashmore
Ladysbridge
Youghal
Cobh
Saleen

Egretta Garzetta
The Little Egret

Chapter 1

THE COMMODIUS VICUS COMMENCES

*'Billy Pitt had them built,' Buck Mulligan said, 'when
the French were on the sea. But ours is the omphalos.'*

Ulysses – James Joyce

THE OMPHALOS, A SACRED STONE AT DELPHI, marked the centre or na-
vel of the world. This image was used by Joyce when, in the opening episode
of *Ulysses*, he had Malachi Mulligan describe the Martello tower in Sandycove in terms of it. Joyce's Tower, the opening scene of one of the greatest
journeys in literature, seemed the ideal starting point for an odyssey.

The notion of a walk around Ireland had been in the back of my mind
for some time, but I had never given it serious consideration. One sunny
Sunday morning, the first day of December, 1996, I arose to find a spider
in the bath. Overcoming a mild arachnophobia, I transferred him to the
window-sill. Perhaps this gave me a sense of omnipotence, or perhaps
something heard on the radio as I ate breakfast triggered thoughts of
travel. 'Sunday Miscellany' was playing, with its characteristic hotch-
potch of diversionary tales: Isambard Kingdom Brunel; a Lady on her
London accent; Megalithic Crannogs in Lough Gara. An orchestrated
version of the Beatles' 'Girl', and 'A Lovely Bunch of Coconuts' on a barrel
organ punctuated the spoken pieces. One item, on the Maritime Inscription, the forerunner of An Slúa Maraí in which I had served as a youth,
may have caused a wanderly synapse to fire: join the Navy and see the
world! Whatever the reason, I decided that now was a good time to start.
Thus, I set out on a journey of over a thousand miles without preparation
of any kind. I had no equipment, no training and inadequate knowledge.

However, it was to be quite a learning experience, and all needs would be met along the road.

As my house is about ten minutes from the Martello tower, I decided that the omphalos would be the official starting point. So, after breakfast I ambled down to Sandycove. A cold front had passed through during the night and the air was crystal-clear with a fresh north-westerly breeze. A few cargo ships lay at anchor in the bay, saving dues by delaying their entry to the port. The shamrock-emblazoned funnel of the cross-channel ferry Isle of Inisfree drifted across the northern horizon. A flock of oystercatchers rose suddenly, startled by my arrival and emitting their alarm-call, 'bi-dee, bi-deee'. At Otranto Place I stopped at the stone erected on the centenary of Joyce's birth. In 1983, a tree was planted here by the Cathaoirleach of Dun Laoghaire Corporation, who did not pass up the chance to have his name included on the inscription. A few lines from *Ulysses* are carved on the stone:

> ... *he gazed southward over the bay, empty save for the smokeplume of the mailboat, vague on the bright sky-line, and a sail tacking by the Muglins.*

Not the most apposite choice, as it contains an uncharacteristic Joycean gaffe: from Sandycove Point, the observer would have to have directed his gaze eastward, not southward, to spot the smokeplume of the Holyhead-bound mailboat. An even more notorious blunder occurs a few pages earlier, when Joyce has Stephen and Buck Mulligan 'looking towards the blunt cape of Bray Head that lay on the water like the snout of a sleeping whale'. The cetacean simile makes it clear that no other headland was intended; yet Bray Head lies behind Dalkey Hill and is quite invisible from Joyce's Tower.

I passed around by the little Sandycove Harbour; a lifeboat was based here as early as 1803, one of three around Dublin Bay and arguably the earliest organised lifeboat service in the world. The original lifeboat-house is now part of a private residence, Neptune House. Passing Geragh, formerly the home of the architect Michael Scott, built like a ship in the stark international style of the 1930s, I came to the Martello tower. As hinted by Buck, William Pitt the Younger was Prime Minister at the time the tower was built in the early 1800s. It was one of a chain of seventy-four such defences built around the coast to repel a possible naval attack by Napoleonic forces. As the invasion did not occur, the tower never saw military action, but its role in literature has ensured it abiding fame. In September 1904 Joyce stayed for about a week at the tower with Oliver St. John Gogarty. The opening scene of *Ulysses* takes place on the gun platform at its top. The tower is now the Joyce Museum, open during the summer months and containing a collection of memorabilia of the author and some first editions of his works.

The yelps and hoots of a few intrepid swimmers drifted up on the wind from the Forty Foot bathing place. This name is the source of several theories, the most probable being that the 40th Foot Regiment was based in the the nearby battery, which was built shortly after the tower and manned by a garrison of thirty-six men. There has been a long tradition of bathing here, originally reserved for men only. The Sandycove Bathers' Association, formed in 1880, made many improvements to the amenity. For the last thirty years or so men and women have shared this excellent swimming place.

Stage 1: Sandycove to Killiney

Warm sunshine merrying over the sea,' wrote Joyce, but Bloomsday was in June. On this fresh December day, I was reluctant to emulate the hardy swimmers' early-morning plunge into the scrotum-tightening sea, so I clambered down to the rocks and began my odyssey. A small fishing boat, piled high with fish boxes, plied its way homeward. Further offshore, the huge new car ferry, the HSS, was easing its way into Dun Laoghaire. I hopped along from rock to rock, heading south-east towards Bullock Harbour. There are large areas here where the rock has been cut down to a level plane. There was extensive quarrying of granite along the shore between Sandycove and Bullock in the eighteenth and early nineteenth centuries. Many holes, notches and grooves can still be seen in the rocks: fingerprints left by the quarry-men. These granite rocks are the northern extremity of a large body of rock, the Leinster Granites, extending in a broad strip from Dublin Bay south-westward through the Wicklow Mountains, Mount Leinster and the Blackstairs, as far south as Kilkenny. This granite is a fine building material and has been used since early times for the many castles and churches in this area and, more recently, for the Martello towers. Sandycove and Bullock harbours were built by the Ballast Office in the mid-eighteenth century, to transport the stone across the bay to build and extend the Dublin quays. The durable granite was used for Dun Laoghaire Pier, the South Wall in Dublin, and numerous elegant houses in the neighbourhood of Dalkey.

At Bullock I had to climb through a garden and over a high wall to drop down onto the quay. A Dublin Port and Docks Board notice, warning that swimming was forbidden in the harbour entrance, was superfluous on this occasion. A handful of small boats danced merrily in the clear water, but most boats were on dry land for the winter. Bullock Castle, standing in a commanding position over the harbour, was built by the Cistercian monks of St. Mary's Abbey in Dublin, to protect their fisheries. They had another castle and a large farm at Monkstown. Bullock Castle is finely built and in good repair but is not open to the public. It is owned by the Carmelite sisters, an American order who run Our Lady's Manor, a retirement and nursing home, with buildings in a range of styles of increasing ugliness as one moves eastward. Whatever about its benefits to the residents, the Manor has a gloomy, oppressive, almost overpowering effect on the harbour, doing little to enhance its attractiveness.

I carried on up the steep hill from the harbour, past the site where the Shangri-La Hotel once stood. This was one of a number of local hotels of character which are now gone, others being the Cliff Castle, the Coliemore and the Khyber Pass. I passed another Martello tower, with access blocked by a high steel gate. Several fine houses along this road back onto the rocky shore, which is nice for the owners, but of no earthly use to the rest of us. There are strong arguments that the foreshore should be accessible to all. Certainly, a path around the coast of Ireland would be an enormously valuable amenity, and even an approximation to this ideal would be of huge benefit to the country.

At the top of the hill, I came to St. Patrick's Church, a noble granite building with a solid elegance, standing on a rocky outcrop. This was built by the Church of Ireland in 1843. I peeped in and saw that a church service was being celebrated, although celebration was not the mood induced by the hymn, whose doleful minor key negated its theme, 'Rejoice, rejoice'. A little further on I came to Loreto Abbey, another beautiful cut granite building, erected just one year before St. Patrick's. It is an impressive building with a spectacular setting overlooking Dalkey Island, and is still used as a convent school. At the end of a lane behind the school, a well-constructed tunnel leads to Lady's Well, in the grounds of Carraig-na-Greine. The owner of the house, Charles Leslie, built it sometime around 1850 so that he would not have to suffer the indignity of seeing the plain people of Ireland trudging across his land, laden with buckets of water. The tunnel is about six feet high, enough to walk upright in comfort. Near the well, it branches, with the right fork leading to Lady's Well, and the left one continuing eastwards. Exploring it as boys, we convinced ourselves that this passage led under the sea to a smuggler's lair on Dalkey Island. In fact, it is to another exit, although I could not find just where it surfaced. Sadly, the tunnel is now bricked up. I hope that some day access to it will be restored, for it is a source of wonder and adventure and historical interest.

At the top of the lane I saw the ruin of Carraig-na-Greine beyond a hockey pitch. A notice said 'Trespassing Strictly Prohibited', but I took no notice of it. This course of action was to be repeated on many occasions. There are too many of these signs, and in this case another notice indicated that work in progress was funded by FÁS, and included local contributions. I reasoned that if I were contributing to the work I ought to have a right to oversee it. The house is another fine granite building, just one storey and basement, but was in a derelict state, and with an uncertain future.

Coliemore Harbour was build around 1868. It is a beautiful little harbour, thronged with small boats on summer days. At the diminutive harbour, a few divers were entering the water. Across on Maiden Rock the seabirds, mostly gulls and cormorants, luxuriated in the morning air. There were about twenty boats on the slip but, apart from the scuba divers, the water was deserted. The view across to Dalkey Island is one much favoured by amateur painters, and is often seen reproduced in the art-shop windows of Dalkey village. From time to time, a coronation is held, crowning some local big-wig as King of Dalkey Island. This old custom has a long tradition and is good fun. The King has a long and illustrious title, and he is crowned with great pomp and circumstance, and ferried out in glory to the island.

A tourist map of the neighbourhood stood in a display case beyond the harbour. Coliemore Park and Sorrento Park were marked, the former also known as Dillon's Park and the latter, very occasionally, as Dowland Park. I climbed the hill, below a statue of a sailor which stands on a rock at Nerano, overlooking the island. At Dillon's Park I found a sculpture of two goats, made from concrete pasted into a wire mesh frame which was rusted and broken. Billy stood looking for his brothers on the island while Nanny reclined beside him. They were the worse for wear, though there only a few years (they have since been patched up). I followed the goats' gaze across to Dalkey Island, where three ruins stand, St. Begnet's little church to the west, a Napoleonic battery to the east, and a Martello tower crowning the highest point of the island. There is a freshwater well below the tower, which is surprising for such a small island. Begnet was a local saint who lived in the seventh century. His feast day is celebrated on the 12th of November.

Growing up near here, we had many happy days fishing, or just messing about in boats. The currents in Dalkey Sound can be strong, and we often had a tough job pulling back to Bullock Harbour against the tide. The island is a wonderful place to spend a sunny afternoon, and there are boat trips from Coliemore Harbour during the summer months. Frank Mitchell, the late renowned naturalist, wrote in his book *The Way that I Followed* that Dalkey Island was the chief treasure-house of his archaeological career. He carried out several excavations on the island and found a wealth of artifacts, some dating back over 5,000 years, indicating human presence here over a remarkably long period.

I followed a path from the park around to Sorrento Point, to enjoy a breath-taking view of Killiney Bay, with the whale-like Bray Head visible at last. However, the way forward was fenced off so I returned and crossed over to Sorrento Park to find a recently-restored mosaic depicting John Dowland (1563–1626), an Elizabethan poet and lutenist. Here I rested for a while, drinking in the panoramic views. On nearby Beacon Hill there was a Coast Guard Station in earlier times, now used for private residences. A tiny red-brick hut on the hill served us as a scout den for a time. Below the park is Sorrento Terrace, in a most spectacular setting and comprising eight fine houses built around 1845. The end house, whose grounds include Sorrento Point, was sold for almost £6 million shortly after I passed.

I carried on round to the Vico Road. The source of the name is uncertain, but it is sometimes associated with Giovanni Battista Vico (1668–1744), a famous Neapolitan philosopher. He formulated a Law of Cycles, which sought to reduce the entire course of history to a threefold succession of phases: theocratic, aristocratic and democratic – or divine, heroic and human. He saw these exemplified in government, language, literature and civilisation. Joyce was much taken with this philosophy, and once commented to a friend, 'my imagination grows when I read Vico'. The cyclicity of human affairs was fundamental to the structure of *Finnegans Wake*. The redolence of the phrase 'commodius vicus of recirculation' in the opening sentence of the book appealed to me, and I decided to adopt it for my Hibernian circumambulation.[1]

The Ramparts was, like the Forty Foot, formerly a men-only bathing place. It is very popular, and now more egalitarian too. This neighbourhood has an Italian flavour, with Killiney Bay often compared to the Bay of Naples. Many houses here have Italianate names: La Scala, Milano, Mt Etna; the last is particularly apt, as it stands over the railway tunnel and must suffer volcanic sounds and tremors as the trains run beneath. I passed the Cat's Ladder, a steep flight of steps up to Shaw's Cottage, where George Bernard Shaw lived for eight years of his youth around 1870. He later wrote with only slight hyperbole that 'I lived on a hilltop with the most beautiful view in the world'.

Taking the path down across the railway I came to White Rock beach. Huge granite bulwarks, fifty feet high, support the railway here. In a cliff cave nearby, Flann O'Brien's wonderful scientist hero De Selby fabricated his unique concoction DMP (named, ironically, using the acronym for the Dublin Metropolitan Police). The water was too high to walk around the White Rock. A man with an Alsatian told me the tide was falling, but there was no need to wait as I climbed across the rock easily. Behind the granite outcrop is another slate-like green rock, schist, I recalled from school geology. Robert Warren, a former owner of Killiney Hill and sur-

---

[1] Here I invoke Humpty Dumpty in *Through the Looking Glass*: 'When *I* use a word, it means just what I choose it to mean – neither more nor less.' Thus, a commodius vicus is a generous journey; and 'vicus' rhymes with 'like us'.

rounding lands, was compensated for facilitating the building of the railway by being provided with a private bridge and platform, which can still be found above White Rock.

On Killiney beach the pattern of footprints in the sand near the water's edge conflicted with the Alsatian-man's hypothesis about a falling tide. Just beyond White Rock I came to the ruins of the White Cottage. I remember spending happy days on the beach and having lemonade and ice cream in what was at that time a tea room. There were also pop dances in the White Cottage in the swingin' sixties. The nearby Court Hotel, formerly a private home, is a curious amalgam of gables and conical towers. It was a pleasure to visit this friendly and comfortable hotel[2] for refreshments before catching the train home. At Killiney Station I bought a single ticket back to Glenageary, from a surly, grumpy ticket-man, who didn't know his luck. On such a beautiful day there were plenty of reasons to smile. I had come, with digressions, about five miles in two hours, representing half of one per cent of the full circle. It was a good and pleasant start.

Stage 2: *Killiney to Bray*

Two weeks later, at Glenageary Station, I picked up the free *Commuting Times*, and read good news about the Blue Pool, which was to re-open soon as a fitness centre. Another article dealt with rail delays due to wheel-slip caused by leaf-falls. Does this not happen every autumn, I wondered? The 10:53 DART brought me to Killiney. The bright sunlight as the train emerged from the railway tunnel under 'Mt Etna', made the views of Sorrento Point and Killiney Bay more glorious than ever.

At Killiney Station, I stood on the foot-bridge for a while, soaking up the scene. Heavy showers were bubbling up over the mountains but, with luck, they would stay there. The sea was sparkling in the morning sunshine. Opposite the station and beside the Court Hotel stands a house with a beautiful roof, made from ceramic tiles of the most exquisite deep-blue colour. The air was clear, with the details of Dalkey and Killiney hills sharply delineated. The 'castle' on Dalkey Hill was a telegraph tower, built in 1807, from where communication with navy ships in Dublin and Kil-

---

[2] The Court Hotel has since gone the way of the Coliemore and the Khyber Pass.

liney bays was possible using semaphore signalling. Messages could be relayed from here to the chain of Martello towers.

I passed the ticket office, where the unsmiling attendant sat reading a magazine. A hundred years ago a travel writer observed that 'There are civil and obliging railway officials in Ireland, but there are also railway officials – and not a few of them, but very many – to whom civility and courtesy are words without meaning.' *Plus ça change, plus c'est la même chose*. The writer was none other than William Bulfin. Bulfin cycled around the country about a hundred years ago and wrote about his travels in his eccentric and idiosyncratic book, *Rambles in Éirinn*. If I may write in the style of Myles' Catechism of Cliché: Bulfin never disguised the fact that his sympathies lay with the cause of Irish independence, when lesser men were content with the role of time-server and sycophant. He applied his stirling qualities of mind and lofty intellect to the national cause at a time when it was neither profitable nor popular.

Bulfin's book bears the stamp of his individual perspective, with its outspoken contempt for any tendency towards Anglicisation, and is un-balanced and bigoted in places, but it is interesting for all that, especially since the Ireland about which he wrote has vanished forever.

The obelisk on Killiney Hill was built in 1742 at a time of severe hard-ship and suffering. The landowner, Col. John Mapas, organised the con-struction to provide employment for the poor. A smaller obelisk, with a hexagonal base, stands on the hillside nearby. Bulfin was concerned that 'All is not lovely on Killiney Hill. A monument stands there which is an architectural monstrosity and a vainglorious abomination.' He considers whether to call it 'a freak, a nightmare, a horror or a phenomenal heap of ugliness'. He saw no merit in the fact that Col. Mapas had organised the erection of the obelisk to provide a source of income for the poor when times were hard.

Bulfin visited the obelisk on an autumn Sunday on his way to Luggala in Wicklow. By a curious turn of history, he had stopped on his way at the Martello tower in Sandycove to visit some literary men who were 'creating a sensation in the neighbourhood'. He describes the three men without naming them, but they can be no others that the three who appear at the opening of *Ulysses*. One, an Oxford student and a strenuous Irish

Nationalist who spoke Irish at the slightest excuse, was Samuel Chenevix Trench (the insufferable Haines in *Ulysses*). The second was 'a wayward kind of genius, who talked in a captivating manner, with a keen, grim humour'. This was Oliver Gogarty. Of the third, Bulfin wrote only that he was 'a singer of songs which sprang from the deepest currents of life'. Joyce, of course, was renowned for his excellent tenor voice, in the same league as John McCormack. Evidently, Bulfin was ambivalent about Joyce, for he wrote that 'The other poet listened in silence, and when we went on the roof he disposed himself to drink in the glory of the morning'. Since Joyce spent only six days at the tower we can, with a modicum of sleuth-work, fix the date of this meeting to be Sunday, 11th of September, 1904. There is a delightful serendipity in the incident, and in the appearance in 1907 of a perspicuous and perceptive description of the distinguished residents of the tower, many years before the publication in 1922 of *Ulysses*.

The large Killiney Hill Park was a deer park in the seventeenth century. It was opened to the public as Victoria Park in 1887 by Prince Albert. It is a delightful resource, much used and appreciated by the citizens of south County Dublin. On the hillside stands Ayesha Castle, among the most spectacular and exquisitely sited houses in the district. It is built in the style of a Norman castle, complete with battlements, out of local granite. Named for the heroine of Rider Haggard's novel *She*, it is owned by the singer and composer Enya. Another splendid house nearby, Temple Hill, is the home of Bono, of U2 fame. Further south is the familiar hump of Carrigolligan, more popularly known as Cathy Gallagher, and the chimney of the old lead works at Ballycorus on the hilltop nearby.

I walked a few hundred yards up a laneway opposite the station, to the old ruined church of Killiney. The name is from Cill Iníon Léinín, the church of the daughters of Lenin. This was not Vladimir Ilyich, but a St. Lenin, who presided over a religious settlement here in the early seventh century. Returning to the sea by Military Road I came to a large notice: 'Killiney Coast Protection. County engineer: P.A.F. Dullaghan, BE, C Eng, DIP, FIEI, MICE, MIPI.' Surely, Neptune would fear to do battle with one so highly qualified, although the penultimate acronym would hardly inspire terror. On the beach below the cliffs, a bulwark about four metres high, of cavity blocks and earth, has been constructed. As it becomes overgrown it may provide a solid line of defence against the ravages of the sea, though I suspect that Neptune will win in the end. Two castellated granite houses stand near the beach here and just beyond is another Martello tower, converted into a private home with the addition of two extra decks. A Mr Enoch, who carried out the conversion when he was owner, wrote a short pamphlet about these towers. He refers to this particular one as Enoch Tower.

Two small streams run down the beach beyond the tower, the Deansgrange River and the Shanganagh River. I hopped across them without difficulty. The course of the old railway is evident here. It originally ran close to the sea-shore but due to continual attack from the waves it was moved inland to a new alignment in 1915. A notice on the beach cautioned 'WARNING: Sewage Outfall Pipe. Keep Clear'. Over the nearby sewage pumping station, someone had thoughtfully placed a wind-sock, a nice touch, warning the growing number of residents hereabouts of possible pongs. There were once two more Martello towers between here and Bray. Both ended up in the sea, thanks to the coastal erosion which continues to this day.

Should I continue by the cliff-top or by the beach? This sort of question, which I would call Frost's Dilemma for reasons to be made clear, would recur frequently during the Commodius Vicus. I met a man with two dogs, and asked him whether the tide was coming in? 'A little,' he said. You can't beat local knowledge! He advised me to keep to the beach and avoid the cliff-top, which he said was deeply undercut and might be dangerous. Another corporation notice – local authorities are masters of notification – read 'Keep Clear: Falling Debris', so it might be dangerous below, too, I thought. Indeed, the remains of an old brick wall, hanging precariously from the cliff, told its own story of ongoing coastal erosion. I strolled along the sand, enjoying the soothing tranquility of the gently breaking surf, the swell at regular five-second intervals coming from an apparently calm sea.

A grey wagtail bounced busily about, keeping me company for a while. Apart from that, there was little wildlife to be seen. It is said that the remains of an ancient village, Longnon, marked on old maps, can be seen offshore at exceptionally low spring tides. I have never seen it, nor have I met anyone who has, but Peter Pearson recounts reports of sitings in his book *Between the Mountains and the Sea*. However, the closeness of the name to long-gone makes me suspicious that there may be a hoax underlying the story of Longnon. Or perhaps, like Brigadoon, the village comes to life briefly and on rare occasions. Although there has been considerable 'development' in this area, several stately houses remain, among them Shanganagh Castle, now an open prison for the rehabilitation of young offenders.

The railway was extended from Kingstown (Dun Laoghaire) to Bray in 1854. An inland route, the Harcourt Street line, joined the coastal line at Shanganagh Junction just below Shankhill village, both opening on the same day in 1854 and running on the same line from the junction to Bray. The Harcourt Street line was closed in 1958, definitely one of the most shortsighted political decisions ever made. Although I was only eleven at the time, I recall the controversy about this foolish and myopic decision, and my father's less-than-favourable remarks about Todd Andrews, the chairman of the Irish transport company, Córas Iompair Éireann, who was responsible for the closure.

As I continued around the country, I was to find many more derelict railways. At the foundation of the State there were almost 3,500 miles of railway. The total has now fallen to under 1,500, less than 45 per cent of the earlier figure. Most of the closures occurred in the 1950s and 1960s. It is understandable that where lines were losing money, services had to be reduced or stopped. It is incomprehensible that so many lines were abandoned, rails lifted and land sold. Of course, hindsight is 20–20, but foresight was totally absent in those who allowed this devastation of such a valuable national resource to take place. Let us hope the tide is turning: there are plans currently to invest significant sums in the railways. The electrification of some lines must be seen as progressive, and perhaps the long-promised Lúas will appear one day.[3]

The weather had been gradually deteriorating, and I arrived in Bray in a heavy drizzle. A shambles of warehouses marked the town's boundary. A notice on the river bridge warned: 'Fly Fishing Only'. I walked out

---

[3] As indeed it now has.

the short North Pier. The brown water of the Dargle flowing from the harbour mouth was carried northward in a long sweep of floating fresh water: the shitbrown river on the snotgreen sea. A dozen swans were cruising about on the murky waters of the harbour. Huge sewage storage tanks stood nearby; the contents are pumped to an outlet several miles out in the bay. At the Harbour Bar – O'Toole's, a good Wicklow name – I asked for a hot lemon drink. 'Would you like ice in it?' asked the bright young barman.

I walked out the South Pier. The lighthouse that stood at the end of the pier was destroyed in 1957 by Hurricane Carrie. The brown/green water contrast was even clearer from this side. The division was sharp on the left side, more diffuse on the right, for some deep fluid dynamical reason beyond my ken. The pavilion of Bray Sailing Club, overlooking the harbour, was full of merry-makers. Martello Terrace juts out curiously at the end of the Esplanade. James Joyce lived in Number 1, and it was here that the acrimonious Christmas dinner party, described in *A Portrait of the Artist as a Young Man*, took place, when the question of Parnell versus Holy Mother Church gave rise to heated emotions.

Another Martello tower, again converted to a residence, was the last I should see for some time. The 'National Aquarium' – what justification for the adjective? – is on the sea-front nearby. A sign indicated Sunday opening in winter, but the door was closed. So, I walked up to the station, via the quaint, old-fashioned passage-way called Albert Walk, and took the train home.

Stage 3: Bray to Greystones

There is little evidence of early settlement at Bray, which developed rapidly during the nineteenth century. The town sprang up after the arrival of the railway, and was modelled on the English south-coast resorts. Indeed, it became known as the Brighton of Ireland, and was a lively and attractive place in its heyday. A painting by Erskine Nichol shows the seafront in 1862, with fine Victorian houses and a Martello tower by the shore. The construction of the esplanade further enhanced the resort, which expanded as sea-bathing grew in popularity.

After the chaos and confusion that tends to surround the Christmas festivities, it was pleasant to escape the domestic milieu with my son, Owen, for the next stage. We took the DART to Bray on a hazy day. The weak December sun was struggling to break through a thin veil of stratocumulus as we walked along the esplanade. The sea-front was rather shabby and dilapidated, the grass was in bad shape, the deserted bandstand had a forlorn air and litter blew about on the breeze. We passed the lifeguard hut and a granite boathouse near the funfair. The whole impression was of a place that had known better times. As we climbed the path up the side of Bray Head, the view back to the esplanade was more impressive. Certainly, Bray was nicer from a distance. From near here, a chairlift used to carry visitors up the side of Bray Head to the Crow's Nest, near the summit. I recall that it cost a shilling for the return trip, or 9 pence up and 3 pence down. I once took the trip with my girlfriend: I offered to pay the down-fares if she would pay them up. She didn't agree to that deal, but she did agree to marry me.

We took the path on the sea side of the railway. This was not as convenient as the more established path on the land side, and required some walking on the railway tracks (the line has since been electrified and this is no longer a reasonable option). A notice over a tunnel read 'D.S.E.R. I.S.O. Gauge', indicating the original name of the railway, the Dublin & South-Eastern Railway. An old whitewashed bathing hut stood on the strand below. The cliffs were reinforced in several places with heavy-duty wire mesh to minimise rock falls. We came to an oven-like brick structure on the old track, perhaps used when the new line was being cut. A number of gull-like birds flew about the cliffs. I took them to be fulmars, as they glided brilliantly, with hardly a wing-flutter.

We had to walk through a few short tunnels and one about fifty yards long. Then we came to an old tunnel parallel to the new railway. Beyond it, the line has completely fallen away so that the old 'permanent way' no longer exists. It is a very curious and striking sight, two tunnels side by side, one without any possibility of use. They reminded me of a pair of spectacles belonging to a one-eyed man. The route chosen for the railway, around the vertiginous east side of Bray Head, meant the construction of three tunnels and five viaducts over ravines, very like the structures built by Brunel in Devon and Cornwall. The Earl of Meath would not allow the line to pass through his land on the western side of the hill, forcing the construction through this difficult and precipitous terrain. The line was completed remarkably quickly, in about one year, under the excellent engineering skills of William Dargan. There was a derailment in 1867 at The Ram's Scalp, the second viaduct. Fortunately, the train fell to the landward side so that only two people were killed; had it gone the other way, it would have plunged 100 feet into the sea, with many more fatalities. Storms have continually battered the rocky headland, undermining the cliffs, so that no fewer than four deviations have been necessary. The scene of the accident was close to the Brabazon Tunnel, and the course of the old railway disappears, dropping straight into the sea beyond the tunnel.

At Cable Rock we had to clamber up to the path above the line. Beyond this, the path was seriously eroded in places. At the outlet of a stream we had to hang on to a fence and swing over a precipitous drop to get across. The muddy path was only a foot wide here, and quite dangerous. The evidence of coastal erosion was even clearer further on, where we counted no fewer than four parallel fences, each having become defunct as the path was moved further and further back from the encroaching sea. Near Greystones, we climbed down to where a stream flowed through a long tunnel under the path, and trudged down the shingle of North Beach towards the town. Six travellers' caravans were parked on the path near Greystones. A notice told of the fish to be caught: Plaice, Cod, Flounder, Ray (in summer) and Whiting (in winter).

A solitary small fishing boat (WT 108) lay high and dry on its beam end in Greystones Harbour. We passed round by the tiny inner harbour to the eponymous outcrop of grey stones. The defunct railway tunnel we had walked through earlier was clearly visible as a hole in Bray Head. We passed a pleasant little sandy cove nestling amid the grey rocks and continued along the sea-front to the station, where we caught a No. 184 bus back to Bray and the train home.

Chapter 2

A Walk in the Garden

Still south I went, and west and south again,
Through Wicklow from the morning till the night,
And far from cities and the sites of men,
Lived with the sunshine and the moon's delight.

'Prelude' – J.M. Synge

THE NEXT VENTURE WAS A FOUR-DAY excursion from Greystones to Woodenbridge, a walk in the Garden of Ireland. Synge's lines are particularly apt: I was heading south to Wicklow town, then west to Rathdrum, then south again through the Vale of Avoca. My reading material consisted of Bulfin's *Rambles in Éirinn*. I set out on a glorious July morning, taking the 08:45 DART from Glenageary to Bray. A sign at Bray Station indicated the possibility of egress for the old and infirm through a gate on the east platform: to exit, they must call the station attendant on an intercom to request him to open the gate. Wondering how efficiently this arrangement worked in practice, I adopted a hunched, decrepit posture, pressed the button and spoke in a quavering voice; but there was no response. Only a little behind schedule, the 09:20 train left for Greystones, along the beautiful stretch of line that I had walked earlier with Owen. At Greystones a sign at the east platform gate read 'Absolutely No Exit From Station Here'. I exited through this gate, along with the other passengers.

Stage 4: Greystones to Wicklow

A ridge of high pressure over Ireland with a cold front slow moving off the west coast promised a bright dry day. Fortunately, a thin veil of high cloud lasted through the morning, protecting me from the harshness of the summer sun as I marched southwards towards it. I took a short path to the beach, to start the walk to Wicklow, about twelve miles away. After a brief stretch on the beach, there is a path more or less beside the railway, making easy going all the way. I passed the golf links and came to a spot marked on the map as Cobbler's Bulk. Here I met a man exercising his four collies and we chatted for a while. The dogs looked sprightly, with lustrous coats. He told me how he walks them for three hours and gives them just one meal each day. I asked about the path south and was assured that it should be trouble-free, and that the area around 'The Breaches' was particularly rich in wildlife.

For ten miles, from Ballygannon just south of Greystones to Wicklow town, a long shingle ridge – the Murrough – stretches along the coast. It is well above high water level and forms a continuous barrier between the Irish Sea and the low marshes behind it. The shingle was deposited by the sea when the water level was higher after the last Ice Age. It is capped by a layer of sand held in place by marram grass and other dune vegetation. The name Murrough is from the Irish word *murbhach* for a salt-marsh. The railway runs along the Murrough, and rows of large concrete blocks chained together have been placed on the sea side of the track in several places to minimise coastal erosion.

The sandy turf of the Murrough was like Dunlopillow under foot. The graffiti on an old block house gave a commentary on Irish society: 'Property is Theft', 'Anarchy is Order' and 'You are all Walking Abortions'. Fortunately, this last was followed by a little smiling face! At the twenty-mile marker, a northbound goods train passed me with six buff-coloured sausage-shaped wagons carrying Anhydrous Ammonia. It was coming from the IFI fertiliser factory near Arklow, and going to another sister plant near Cobh. It is a consequence of the decimation of the national railway system that this daily train, carrying hazardous chemicals, had to travel right through the heart of Dublin, there being no other practicable rail route available.

There is a forlorn platform at Kilcoole station, where a single train stops each morning, allowing people from the neighbourhood to commute to Dublin for work. A mile or so further on, I came to Kilcoole Marshes, separated from the sea by the Murrough. The sea enters the marshes through a narrow channel in the railway embankment, known as The Breaches. This channel blocks up occasionally in winter, causing extensive flooding of the marshes. Swans were plentiful here, and a heron sat frozen at an unlikely angle, looking like a harmless branch but poised to kill. A variety of wading birds frequent the tidal salt-flats. On the beach, a large section of the dunes was fenced off to allow the little terns to nest undisturbed. These are among Ireland's rarest breeding birds; they winter on the West African coast. A flock of them darted about noisily overhead. The tide was flooding in under the railway at something over ten knots, as a gang of railway-men worked on maintenance of the line.

After mile-22 the direction of the coast changes from South-by-east to South-by west. This is Six-mile Point, the distance being from Wicklow. The old Newcastle station house stands here, now a private home. I took the road inland for a mile or so to Newcastle, and lunched at The Bridge Inn in the village. At a small airfield by the road from the coast, a large notice displayed the conflicting messages 'Welcome to Aviation. Private: Members Only'. Newcastle could fairly be described as unremarkable, and the detour added three miles to my journey.

Heading south, another road gave access to the coast again. I stopped near the 24-mile marker and had a swim. The beach was almost deserted here, the sea smooth and warm, rejuvenating me for the last five miles. But although Wicklow Head was now in sight, those few miles seemed never to end. The headland, the easternmost point in the Republic, loomed in the afternoon haze, never getting any closer, as I trudged mile after mile along the now monotonous sand murrough. The cloud had evaporated and a scorching sun burned down. My short pants left me dangerously exposed, and my legs became quite severely sunburned.

Broad Lough, the tidal estuary of the Vartry River, appeared on my right. Nearing the town I passed increasing numbers of locals out for a stroll. The path led eventually to the north pier and outer harbour of Wicklow. Duffy's Circus was in town, generating a buzz of excitement and activity. I hobbled past the big top and along the river to the Bridge Tavern where I checked into a room and collapsed onto the bed, exhausted and badly burned. I had done about fifteen miles in seven hours, including stops. My room-with-a-view cost £17.50 and overlooked the Vartry River, which joins the sea at Wicklow Harbour after flowing down through the Devil's Glen from the reservoir near Roundwood. The Bridge Tavern was the birthplace of Capt. Robert Halpin, a famous mariner of the last century. His most memorable achievement was the laying of the first transatlantic cable from Valentia to Newfoundland. A monument to Capt. Halpin stands in a small square further up the town.

The town of Wicklow boasts a long history. St. Patrick is said to have landed here in 432 AD to begin his mission to Christianise the country. The Irish name of the town, Cill Mantáin, means the Church of Mantain, who was a disciple of Patrick. The English name is from Vikingalo, the place of the Vikings, who established a settlement at the river mouth at the end of the eighth century. While not the most beautiful town, Wicklow has some features of particular interest. South of the Halpin statue, the main street has a unique split-level structure, with the two-way traffic on each level often causing mild chaos. Further down the street stands the Billy Byrne Memorial, commemorating Byrne, Michael Dwyer and other heroes of the '98 Rebellion. Billy Byrne was born in 1775 into one of the last great Catholic landed families in Wicklow. He fought in the vanguard at Arklow and at Vinegar Hill. Captured in 1799, he was found guilty of being a rebel leader and was hanged at Gallows Hill, half a mile from Wicklow on the old Glenealy Road. For the bicentenary of the 1798 Rebellion a year-long calendar of events was in preparation, with many celebrations and commemorations in Wicklow and Wexford. Wicklow Gaol was under renovation and would open as a museum shortly after my visit to the town. Wicklow played a vital role in the Rebellion, holding out for longer than anywhere else. Michael Dwyer was the leading Wicklow rebel, fighting on for several years. Dwyer finally gave himself up after the failure of Robert Emmet's uprising in 1803 and was deported to New South Wales. The Military Road, from Rathfarnham, south of Dublin, to the Glen of Imaal, cutting right through the mountainous heart of the county, was the first purpose-built road in the county. It was constructed

by the authorities specifically to combat and capture Dwyer and his com-
rades-in-arms. There were five barracks along the route – at Glencree,
Laragh, Glenmalure, Aughavanagh and the Glen of Imaal, each manned
by a captain and 100 soldiers.

Over 30,000 rebels died during the rebellion. Government losses were
minuscule by comparison, as rebel pikes were no match for musket and
cannon. Hundreds of rebels were transported to penal colonies in Australia. They are honoured with great pride by their descendants today.
The rebellion, far from leading to the independence of Ireland, led more
or less directly to the dissolution of the Irish Parliament by the Act of
Union in 1800.

After a snooze at the Bridge Tavern, I took a short stroll around the
harbour. There were about a dozen fishing trawlers and an assortment
of pleasure craft. On the promontory south of the harbour stands the
ruin of the Black Castle. Originally built in 1178 by the FitzGeralds, who
were given the lands by Strongbow, it has been destroyed and rebuilt
several times. The present ruins date from the time of Cromwell. The
harbour has been a focus of maritime activity for at least a millennium.
I finished the day with a meal at the Bayview Hotel. It stands on the
split-level main street, without much view of the bay. I enjoyed a mixed
grill while watching a television programme about the sale of bad meat
by Tesco's.

Stage 5: Wicklow to Rathdrum

After the usual generous breakfast, I checked out of Bridge Tavern
and headed for the tourist office, where I got some information
about Capt. Halpin, and about other points of local interest. I bought
supplies – some fruit and biscuits, and Lucozade NRG for energy – and
started up Friar's Hill, heading westward. There was an enjoyable view
back over the Broad Lough, with the Vartry flowing down to the harbour.
The quiet road was bordered with grassy banks festooned with a variety
of wild flowers, bright purple and golden in the morning sun (I had not
yet learned to identify wild flowers beyond daisies and dandelions). At
first, the going was good and I drifted effortlessly along. After a while,
the morning became hotter, my pack seemed to become heavier, and my

shoes were hot and heavy and hurting now. I rambled on pretending not to notice these minor problems.

The road I was following crossed the main Wexford Road, the N11, at Ballynabarney, and continued westward, following the ridge south of Glenealy. I was high on the side of a broad open glen, with Carrick Mountain on the other side. Above Glenealy, at another crossroads, the road became a track, leading through a deciduous forest to an area marked on the map as a nature reserve. I did not see much in the way of fauna: whatever animals lived there were probably resting in the noon-day heat. The wood was silent and serene and it was nice to be in the shade for a while, with the dappled sunlight flickering through the leafy canopy. I passed an old ruined house as the path sloped down to Deputy's Pass. Here I came to a stream, the nascent Potter's River, which runs down the valley to the sea at Brittas Bay. It was said to have run red with blood when Deputy's Pass was the scene of an ambush of British troops in 1798. Deputy's Pass is a narrow v-shaped valley formed by outflowing meltwater after the last Ice Age.

I took off shoes and socks to wade across the stream, greatly enjoying the refreshing feeling of the cold water on my sore feet. As a boy scout I had often drunk from streams, and lived to tell; but nowadays, with such widespread use of chemicals, more care is needed for survival. A short path led to the road, where I sat on a grassy bank to rest and drink some NRG. Two French ladies stopped their car to ask directions to Glendalough. I told them the way and let them go before realising that I should have asked for a lift to Rathdrum and resumed the walk later in a fresher state. Joining the main Rathnew–Rathdrum road, I followed it towards the latter town. Now the day was really hot. My feet were in bad shape and my head ached. The traffic whistled by, blasting me with wafts of hot air.

A crazy idea occurred to me: the railway would be easier and quieter going. Climbing up, I followed the line for a mile, with increasing nervousness. The track curved between overgrown banks, with no view forward or backward. I feared a train would come upon me without warning. As I rounded a bend, the sight of the bright DayGlo jackets of a gang of rail workers further down the line induced me to quit the track. Slithering down a brambly incline to the road, I heard the thunder of a lone locomotive screaming past above me. It is illegal to walk on the railway; I was beginning to see why. Back on the road, the traffic was heavier than ever and the day hotter. Walking on a busy road has nothing to recommend it. I later learned that there is a way from Glenealy to Rathdrum through the forest to the north of the railway.

The river Avonmore flows south past Rathdrum in a deep valley, spanned by the railway on a beautiful viaduct. I climbed slowly up the steep hill to the town, and found the Cartoon Bar on the east side of the square, where two pints of lemonade revived me. The walls of the bar were covered with witty caricatures by the cartoonist Terry Willers. I learned that this bar was the headquarters of the International Cartoon Festival, held each June Bank Holiday.

The lady in the tiny tourist office next door to the Cartoon Bar was most helpful to me in finding a place to stay the night. Before leaving the town, I visited the other pubs on the square – The Woolsack to the north, the Railway Bar on the south side and Morgan Mackey's opposite the Cartoon Bar on the west side.[4] In the little Anglican church nearby, brass plaques bore the names of men who were probably rich landowners and important dignitaries long ago. On the Arklow road I found my B&B about one kilometre out of town. Collapsing onto the bed, I slept for two hours in the hot afternoon. Showering and bathing my footsore frame, I struggled back to the town for an evening meal at The Avondale Restaurant.

Stage 6: *Rathdrum to Avoca*

Charles Stewart Parnell, one of the leading Irish statesmen of the nineteenth century, was born at Avondale in June 1846, at a time when the country was in the throes of the famine. He spent much of his life here. He was regarded by many as Ireland's uncrowned King, and was celebrated in song as the Blackbird of Sweet Avondale. Parnell entered the House of Commons in 1875. The policy of his Home Rule Party was to highlight Irish issues by obstruction and filibustering. A Protestant landowner himself, he mobilised the Catholic Church in demanding land reform and Home Rule for Ireland. He was for a time imprisoned in

---

[4] On a recent visit, I found two of these three pubs in an advanced state of dilapidation.

Kilmainham, and from there he conducted an effective land-rent strike, breaking the vice-grip of the rackrenting landlords. He fell in love with Kitty O'Shea, the wife of Capt. William O'Shea, a former member of the Home Rule Party. When Capt. O'Shea's demand for £20,000 was refused by his wife, he filed for divorce, naming Parnell. In those Victorian days the big crime was to be found out, and the scandal effectively ended Parnell's political career. The Catholic bishops took a dim view of his affair with Kitty and turned against him, accelerating his downfall. He died shortly afterwards of pneumonia at the tragically young age of 45, having wedded his beloved Kitty only four months previously.

Taking the road south at the cross below the town of Rathdrum, I headed for Parnell's home. The road followed a ridge west of the Avonmore River. Far away on the opposite hillside I saw clouds of dust, thrown up by the heavy lorries carrying loads of gravel from a quarry in the valley. I came after a half hour to the gate of Avondale. Avondale House and Forest Park are open to the public. There are over 500 acres of magnificent woodlands, with miles of secluded river and forest walks. There is a wide variety of wildlife and over ninety species of birds have been recorded here. The Park is the cradle of Irish forestry, with a huge range of trees, both native and exotic species. The total refurbishment of the house, in the style of the 1850s, was completed in 1991, the centenary of Parnell's death. I took a tour of the house and watched an interesting audio-visual presentation outlining Parnell's life and career.

Passing through the majestic woods of Avondale, I followed the course of the river through beautifully wooded country to the boundary of the estate. Eventually rejoining the road, I passed an old shed with an ancient petrol pump, and several wrecks of old ambulances. Someone had a curious taste in collectables. I came to a junction near Lion's Bridge just above the point where 'the bright waters meet'. A castellated bridge, which spanned the Avonmore River, was washed away by Hurricane Charley in 1986, and has been replaced by a concrete bridge. High on the hill above stands Castle Howard, a large fortified house originally called Cronebane Lodge, built for a mining boss during the troubled seventeenth century. Many famous people have stayed there, Thomas Moore and Walter Scott amongst them. Near the top of Cronebane Hill, not visible from the valley, there is a large glacial erratic known as the Mottee Stone. Apparently its name derives from the French word *moitie* for 'half', as it marks the half-way point between Dublin and Wexford. But I suspect this theory; after all, everywhere is half-way to somewhere! I could not face the climb on this occasion, but drove up the hill on a later visit to the area. The stone must weigh about 50 tons so, if Finn McCool really threw it here from Lugnaquilla, as legend maintains, the other stories about him may also be true. At all events, metal rings allow easy access to the top of the stone where the climber may rest whilst enjoying a splendid panorama.

Shortly, I came to the Meeting of the Waters. It could have been said not so long ago that Thomas Moore's lines are too well known to need quoting, but 'Moore's Melodies' are not played on MTV and are seldom heard now that 'The Walton's' programme is gone:

> There is not in the wide world a valley so sweet
> As that vale in whose bosom the bright waters meet;
> Oh! the last rays of feeling and life must depart,
> Ere the bloom of that valley shall fade from my heart.
>
> Yet it was not that nature had shed o'er the scene
> Her purest of crystal and brightest of green;
> 'Twas not her soft magic of streamlet or hill,
> Oh! no, – it was something more exquisite still.
>
> 'Twas that friends, the beloved of my bosom, were near,
> Who made every dear scene of enchantment more dear,
> And who felt how the best charms of nature improve,
> When we see them reflected from looks that we love.
>
> Sweet vale of Avoca! how calm could I rest
> In thy bosom of shade, with the friends I love best,
> Where the storms that we feel in this cold world should cease,
> And our hearts, like thy waters, be mingled in peace.

Moore did not overstate the beauty of the Vale of Avoca. I lingered awhile in the little park where a monument to 'Ireland's National Poet' stands, listening to the lapping water. It is a true marriage, where two rivers mingle to form a new one. Here, the Avonmore, coming from Lough

Dan and above – joined on its way down by the rivers from Glenmacnass, Glendassen and Glendalough – combines with the Avonbeg from Glenmalure to form the Avoca River.

Between 'The Meetings' and Avoca village, the remains of the old copper mines are evident on both sides of the valley, with tall brick stacks still standing proud amidst the huge ochre spoil heaps. Avoca is among the best mine-sites in Ireland. Several ruins of engine-houses, with their distinctive Cornish chimneys, remain. At White's Bridge, I crossed the river and passed under the railway bridge, where I found two large ore-bins and a timber stockade for containing the spoil. Above me stood the ruin of the Williams engine-house, named for the Williams brothers of Cornwall who operated this mine through the nineteenth century. A Marian Cross erected in the early 1950s stands high on the hill above.

On the opposite side of the valley, the Ballygahan engine-house can be seen. Behind it there is a magnificent drystone arch, which carried the mine railway. The arch cannot be seen from the road, but is well worth the effort of a detour. It is possible, if slightly difficult, to drive to the top of the valley on the west side, following the 'Red Road' which goes up from beside Moran's Garage. The view down the Vale from the hilltop is breathtaking. The mine railway, built in 1847, was the earliest railway in County Wicklow. There is some uncertainty, but it is also claimed that the first steam engine in Ireland was installed at the Avoca mine. Most of the engines were used to pump water out of the mines, allowing access to levels below the water table. Power to haul the ore wagons of the railway was also provided by one of these massive beam engines. Iron was mined at Avoca for thousands of years. Lead was discovered below this and was worked until about 1750, when large copper deposits were discovered. Sulpher, zinc, silver and gold have also been mined here. The mine works, now abandoned, are in no way ugly, but possess a strange and slightly extraterrestrial beauty. There were plans to establish a mining heritage centre in Avoca to ensure that what remains is preserved. I looked forward to visiting it.

A short walk of a mile or so brought me to Avoca. The town was overrun with visitors. It is the scene for filming *Ballykissangel*, an incongruous TV programme about a most improbable English curate in an Irish village. Bus-loads of tourists from England visit the town, stretching the resources to the limit, but the locals seem to bear the inconvenience with patience and good humour. There is no tourist office here, but the butcher, Isaac Lett, made several phone calls when I asked him if he knew of a B&B, and eventually fixed me up, refusing any reward. Thanks, Isaac! I stayed at Riverview House, an old constabulary barracks overlooking the town from across the river, and managed by May Byrne. I had come only a few miles, but was quite exhausted. Clearly, I needed to get fitter if the grand Commodius Vicus was ever to be completed. My feet were in poor shape: I had been walking in light town shoes and the tarmac roads had resulted in severe blistering. It was becoming obvious that a pair of sturdy walking boots wouldn't go astray.

Stage 7: Avoca to Woodenbridge

After a fry-up in May Byrne's, I set out from Riverview House at about nine o'clock, moving slowly southwards. Still stiff and blistered, every movement was accompanied by twinges of pain, and I didn't expect to get too far. Crossing the river to Avoca village, I turned right, up a hill and then down to the gateway of the Ballyarthur Estate. A number of signs warned me to behave: 'Game Rights Reserved', 'Dogs on Lead', 'Lands Poisoned'. A broad trail led me through the wooded estate. The old and new churches south of Avoca enhanced the view across the river. Rabbits scurried to and fro across the trail. I came to a large fenced-off enclosure with a multitude of fledgling game-birds, pheasants as far as I could tell. At a notice reading 'Roaming Guard Dogs', my pulse and pace quickened as, grasping my stout stick tighter, I sped south, all aches forgotten in my fearful flight from the fangs of the fierce mastiffs. I followed the trail to the golf course at Woodenbridge, and then onto the beautifully spongy turf by the river bank, around the course to the footbridge and level crossing.

By now, the aches and pains made further progress so unattractive that I decided to catch a bus home. But which way? I could go north to Dublin for a DART home, or south to Arklow for a train. The bus south was due in an hour, so I decided to head that way. Anyway, my intention at this point was that the Commodius Vicus would bring me through

Arklow and on down the east coast, so it was useful to have a preliminary look around the town. With an hour to kill, I hobbled down through the golf course a few hundred metres to another 'Meeting of the Waters', the junction of the Avoca and Aughrim rivers. It was interesting to see the contrast in the colour of the two banks below the confluence of the rivers: on the east side the stones were stained a bright copper colour, on the west they were a clear silvery-grey. Returning to the bus stop, I sat on a wooden bench, basking in the sunlight and resting my bones.

At Arklow, I had several hours to wait, but there are things to see in this town. I found the railway station and slept on a hard bench for an hour, then to the Maritime Museum, where a kind and helpful woman showed me around. Arklow has a long maritime tradition. The name is of Viking origin, but records of the town go back much further. It was Menapia on Ptolemy's second century map of Ireland. Four generations of Tyrrells built boats here, from 1864 to the 1990s, Asgard II being one of their better known achievements. There has been a lifeboat here since 1826, one of the oldest lifeboat stations of the thirty-six around the coast.

Chapter 3

Into the Croghan Valley

Two roads diverged in a yellow wood
And sorry I could not travel both
And be one traveler, long I stood
And looked down one as far as I could
To where it bent in the undergrowth ...

'The Road Not Taken' – Robert Frost

AT WICKLOW TOWN I HAD VEERED west to reach the Vale of Avoca, thereby missing a chance to continue along the coast. At Woodenbridge, I faced Frost's Dilemma once again: two roads diverged, and a choice was required. The Vale of Avoca continues from here down to Arklow and I considered travelling this route and then on down the coast of Wexford. There would be much of interest to see along this coast and I had a map of Wexford showing a path all along the coast. But a dashed line on a map is no guarantee of a walkable path. I was also concerned about the lakes on the south coast of Wexford, Tacumshin and Lady's Island Lake among them. I felt sure that it might not be too easy to traverse the south side of these and suspected that long detours might arise. The alternative choice, the road westward up the Aughrim River, looked equally attractive. It would bring me by way of Aughrim, Tinahely and Shillelagh to the River Slaney at Bunclody and then I could cross the Blackstairs to the Barrow valley. I opted for the latter route although inevitably such a choice raises the question of what is missed. The fact that there had been an old railway from Woodenbridge to Shillelagh along the Croghan Valley was a further attraction of the westward route.

South of Aughrim rises Croghan Mountain or, more precisely, Croghan Kinsella, the southern-most outpost of County Wicklow, standing on the border of Wexford. The Goldmine River flows down the northern flanks of this mountain to meet the Aughrim River at Woodenbridge, where both flow into the Avoca. The valley of the Goldmine River was once a rich source of the precious metal. It is believed that the beautiful gold ornaments in the collection of the National Museum were made with metal mined here. There are many hundreds of gold artifacts in the museum, dating mostly from the Bronze Age, some of them quite large and heavy. From time to time rumours spread of gold strikes, and in 1935 there was a minor 'Gold Rush' to this area. It is likely that the gold deposits were in a thin seam that has now been fully worked out, but hopes of an El Dorado never quite fade.

Stage 8: Woodenbridge to Ballinglen

I parked my car at the hotel in Woodenbridge. Just a few metres down the road stands the bridge where the old railway from Woodenbridge to Shillelagh passed under the road. This 16.5 mile branch line opened in 1865. It was busy for many years, but the service was suspended in 1944 and the line was fully closed in 1953. I was hoping to follow the track of the railway, but it was completely overgrown and impassable. So, reluctantly, I followed the R747 north-west to Aughrim, soon passing a trout farm. In some places there was a welcome grassy verge, but mostly it was tarmac. With my new boots, walking felt like floating on a cloud. I wondered how anyone could have been so stupid as to try to walk around Ireland in town shoes. The lapping waters of the Aughrim River flowing beside the road were a soothing accompaniment as I drifted along. Stopping by the river for refreshment from my haversack, the idea occurred to me to cross to the other side and try to find the railway track. But the woods looked dense there, and the river was wide with no obvious way to ford it. Further on, the road crossed the river and the course of the railway, which was indeed impenetrably overgrown.

Near Aughrim, a path took me across a small footbridge to a hugh derelict mill. This was once the main flour mill for a large surrounding region, the railway serving as a vital means of transport. But centralisation to much larger mills in the main cities spelt the end of such enterprises. A local priest whom I met nearby told me that there were plans to renovate this building and make it into a hostel. Let's hope this works out. Winding my way around the mill, I came out on the road opposite the Catholic Church. I lit a candle there for my wife Cabrini, who is a great believer in candle-power. It was pleasant to sit in complete peace and silence in the church. Moving on to the town, I stopped at the first pub, O'Tooles, and massacred two pints of Cidona. The barman, seeing I was a rambler, told me many things about the Wicklow Way. He spoke of how a local athlete, Mick Rice, had covered its entire eighty miles in twenty hours. If this is true, it is also remarkable. I find it hard to do four miles per hour on the flat for three hours. Mick Rice must have literally run up and down the slopes of the circuitous and precipitous 'Wiggly Way'.

After buying some supplies, I headed south-west from Aughrim. The plan was simple: to follow the railway line to Tinahely. Kevin Cronin gives an account of this walk in his book *Off the Beaten Track*. Though it had been published only a year or so before, I found the guidance in it unreliable. Parts of the track were accessible, and the walking there was most enjoyable. I was following alongside the Derry Water, a river that rises on the north slopes of Croghan, and flows north-eastward down the valley to where it joins the Ow River near Aughrim to form the river with the name of that town. But there were also places on this section that were completely impassable. It was necessary to abandon the track and take to the road more than once. In the afternoon heat the flies were everywhere. By the time I reached Ballinglen Station, I was hot, thirsty and exhausted, and my legs were in shreds from thorn-cuts and barbed wire scratches.

The old Station House at Ballinglen was occupied by an artist by the name of David Wilcockson. He showed me around his studio, and kindly allowed me to poke around the station and take some pictures. The platform survives, as do some inconsequential bits and pieces from the railway days. I hitched back to Woodenbridge, getting a lift from the first car that stopped – thank you, anonymous driver and family! Recovering my car, I returned to Avoca to meet Masie Caswell and her daughter Margaret, the hospitable proprietors of a B&B, The Arbours. Immediately upon my arrival, Margaret offered me tea and made me feel completely at home, very much part of the family. I felt very comfortable here and was assured that I was welcome to sit in their living room to read or watch TV. The weather forecast on this Saturday evening assured us that the following day would be fine; fair, dry weather through the country, with light winds and good sunny spells – ideal weather for walking.

Stage 9: Ballinglen to Ballinglen

The next morning, Sunday the 3rd of August, 1997, I was awoken by the sound of heavy rain. All indications were that it was 'down for the day'. A hapless forecaster from Met Éireann was bravely attempting to explain what transpired to be the most serious forecast failure for many years. For the August Bank Holiday, the busiest holiday of the year, multitudes pour out of the cities, heading for the beach with their children, buckets and spades and the family mutt in tow. Many stay in makeshift caravans among the dunes. I thought of these unfortunates, trying to keep young children amused while huddled indoors away from the pouring rain. They would be angry with the weather and angry too with the weatherman who had promised them sunshine. I also knew that, since among my responsibilities at Met Éireann was the development of computer models used to aid in prediction, I would certainly be participating in a major enquiry upon my return to work.

The holiday storm produced torrential rainfall in the south-east of the country, with particularly bad flooding in the village of Blackwater in Wexford. All the computer models – Irish, British, French and German – failed to produce an adequate warning of the storm. What went wrong? The ultimate cause of the failure was inadequate observational data over the North Atlantic. The storm originated from a small disturbance east of Newfoundland. It intensified rapidly, as it raced across the ocean, into a deep depression. Although the satellite imagery indicated a disturbance, the growing energy of the storm was not realised until it hit the coast of Ireland, after the Saturday evening forecast had appeared. It is possible, with hindsight, to trace the development backwards in time, but only after the later observations are available. We have since studied this storm in great detail and have come to understand the causes of the forecast failure. But the awful truth is that such occasional failures

– forecast 'busts' – are an inevitable consequence of the chaotic nature of the atmosphere. We struggle to reduce their frequency and severity but we cannot hope to eliminate them entirely. For forecasters, the silver lining in this particular cloud is that, since weather forecasts will never be completely accurate, weather forecasters will never be entirely dispensable.

I left Caswell's, hoping to walk from Ballinglen to Shillelagh, but continuous heavy rain dampened any prospect for the moment, so I scouted the trail by car. Checking the condition of the old railway line I found that Kevin Cronin's description was over-optimistic: the way appeared quite impassable. The tarmac road was unattractive, so I decided that I would follow a route through Coolalug Wood, south of the road, if ever the weather cleared.

I drove to Carnew and had brunch in a grimy chipper in the company of a sodden hitchhiker on his way to Gorey. Convincing myself that the rain was clearing, I returned to Ballinglen and, leaving the car at the Campus Garage, I climbed a wooden gate to a forest trail. I noticed that the upper left-hand beam of the gate was missing. The path brought me to Coolalug Wood, my goal being Tinahely. I had no compass, and the heavy overcast left no mountain view to guide my way. As the trail seemed to veer continuously to the right, I took off to the left, along a row of tall oak trees. The way was rough and blocked by brambles and ivy as thick as my arm. Finally, reaching an open field, I skirted it until I came to a trail which I was sure must bring me to Tinahely. Ahead appeared a wooden gate, the upper right-hand beam missing, the mirror image of that I had climbed earlier. My fears were confirmed when, reaching the gate, I saw my car parked across the road. I had come full circle, swirling like the weather in a wild cyclonic gyre. Rather than disappointment, I felt great relief not to be floundering around somewhere in the woods without a clue of my whereabouts. I resolved to buy a compass as soon as possible.

As the distance walked was about the same as I should have covered to Tinahely, the temptation was to consider that journey done. But I soon realised that this kind of cheating would bring the Commodius Vicus to naught. I would have to return again to the fateful gate and start over. I drove to The Meetings, the pub in the Vale of Avoca, for a bite to eat. The pub was jammed to the doors with holidaymakers trying to escape from the weather. Children ran about wildly while their parents tried to cheer themselves with a sup. A wizened woman of wavering voice was wailing 'The Rose of Tralee' to the largely oblivious, semi-ossified audience. The squeeze-box accompaniment was out of tune too, but not in the same direction as the dreadful Diva. Perhaps the one positive aspect of karaoke is that the backing is true to key so that at least the 'in between' parts are bearable.

Stage 10: Ballinglen to Rosnastraw Bridge

About a month later, I returned to Ballinglen for a second go at Coolalug Wood. I stopped on the way for lunch at Lawless's Hotel in Aughrim, a delicious turkey and ham dish worth every penny of its £5.00. The road between Aughrim and Carnew is called Holt's Way. General John Holt was born at Redcross in 1756. After his farm was burned by the Fermanagh Militia in May 1798, he joined the rebels, soon earning a reputation for leadership. He masterminded several successful attacks on government forces and, despite being twice wounded, managed to avoid capture. However, when it became clear that the long-awaited French support for the Rebellion was not coming, he reached settlement terms and was exiled to New South Wales as a free man. Eventually, he was granted an absolute pardon and returned to Ireland in 1814, surviving a shipwreck on the Falkland Islands en route. He died in 1826 and is buried at Monkstown, County Dublin.

I drove to where I had earlier ended (and begun!) my inadvertent circular loop, and parked at the Campus Garage opposite the dreaded gate with the broken limb. The garage owner assured me that he had no problems with me leaving my car there. I climbed the gate and headed once more for Coolalug Wood. I recognised the line of trees I had walked along the previous time. A fine drizzle started. With poor visibility I still had trouble keeping a sense of direction. I had bought a compass, but had forgotten to bring it! Indeed, I lost direction once more in the forest, and spent a half-hour floundering about. It was hard to believe that I would ever get around Ireland at this rate. I was greatly relieved when I finally found a dilapidated trail leading to the Derry Water. Unable to cross, as the river was in spate after all the rain, I followed upstream and skirted a turnip field. Coming to a road, I had no idea where I was until the pattern of roads at a junction allowed identification on the map: I was at Coolalug Bridge. A hill road led me on to the main Aughrim to Carnew road at Rosnastraw Bridge, a curious asymmetric bridge over a little stream. The rain was teeming down now and, as I had managed the 'Grand Traverse' of the forest, I decided to call it a day. The first driver to come by stopped and brought me back to my parked car.

After visiting Annacurragh Church I returned to Lawless's Hotel and ate a trout dinner served by the ever-courteous staff. Princess Diana's funeral was showing live on TV with Elton John singing about England's Rose (to the tune of Norma Jean). In a carefully measured and sharply focussed eulogy, Diana's brother, Charles Spenser, pounded the paparazzi who had hounded the Princess to death. He made it clear that his family, Diana's 'blood relatives', would not let the Windsors destroy the spirit and spontaneity of her children. I returned to Caswell's in sombre mood, as the bleak day darkened in a dismal drizzle.

Stage 11: *Rosnastraw to Bunclody*

I left Caswell's at 9.00 o'clock next morning and drove back to Rosnastraw on the Aughrim–Carnew road, where I parked the car and set out from where I had stopped the previous day. There was great joy in setting out on this fine, sunny morning. The countryside was bathed in an aura of peace, with a pleasing twittering of birdsong. The tarmac felt soft under my boots and my haversack was a featherweight on the back. I climbed the hill to the west from the bridge, heading for Bunclody. I passed a triangle with an old pump at a road junction, after which a grassy verge made the going pleasant along the bird-loud road to Tomnafinnoge Wood.

Tomnafinnoge Wood is the last remnant of the great Shillelagh Oak Forest. Timber from here was used in the fifteenth century for the construction of King's College Chapel in Cambridge, and later for Westminster Palace in London, for St Patrick's Cathedral and Trinity College in Dublin and for buildings in Holland and France. The forest once covered many thousands of acres but was heavily exploited and is now greatly diminished. The fatal onslaught on Wicklow's forests began in the six-teenth century when the land was 'planted' with English Protestant set-tlers. Vast areas of forest were cut for building, iron smelting and ships for the navy and merchant marine. The cut logs from Shillelagh were rafted down the Derry and Slaney Rivers to the sea at Wexford. Queen Elizabeth I introduced a policy of forest clearance with the dual purpose of providing timber for ship-building and of flushing out the rebel Irish. As wooden ships had a lifetime of only a few decades, there was a vora-cious demand for timber. Tomnafinnoge Wood grows on deep fertile soil in the valley of the Derry River and is dominated by oak and beech, with an understorey of holly and hazel. A few sika deer graze in the wood. Following a protracted campaign to save it from destruction, the wood is now in public ownership, with Wicklow County Council having overall responsibility for its management and preservation.

The plantation of Wicklow with English settlers in the sixteenth and seventeenth centuries dispossessed the local familes of O'Toole and O'Byrne, who became tenants on their own former lands, with mainly ab-sentee landlords. The largest of the Wicklow estates, about 80,000 acres in 1838, was that of Coolattin. I stopped for a spell to talk to a little old man sitting on a wall, who told me something of the history of Coolattin Park. He said it belonged to the Earls of Fitzwilliam, and the last one was killed long ago in an air crash in Paris with Margaret Kennedy.

On down the hill I strode, as the road became a path, an avenue of magnificent oak trees. I soon came to a little bridge with a big name, Livingstone Bridge, where a duck and her duckling family scurried across the path. Across the bridge I met a group of duck-shooters in Land Rov-ers, who were concerned that I would trample through the forest and frighten the ducks before they could blast them to kingdom come. I as-sured them that I would stick to the trail; I had no wish to be mistaken for a drake. Passing the large mansion, Coolattin Park, I skirted the golf course and followed the drive to the main road.

Another large house with huge block chimneys stood opposite the gate of Coolattin. From here a magnificent rustic trail led south, crossing a small road and then passing straight through the middle of an enor-mous field of barley. I sat under a spreading oak in the middle of the field and had some lunch. It was necessary to follow the tarmac road for a mile or so, until I found another track, south of the Carnew–Bunclody road. This high trail afforded a beautiful view back to Croghan and, as I rounded a wood, Mount Leinster appeared ahead. I was now on the Wicklow–Wexford border, one foot in each county. A glorious trail wound down the hill, with delightful rolling country to north and south, bathed in the gold of the gentle September sunshine. A young farmer was busy in his tractor cutting hay. He was using the sunny Sunday weather to make up for time lost in the earlier storms. I had to join the road again for the last mile or two to Clonegal, crossing the bridge over the Derry River from the quaintly named Watch-House Village. This name derives from the guard-house that stood here in the bad old days. The road was much busier then with traffic south from the railway at Shillelagh.

Clonegal is a beautiful place, with nice stone houses beside the Derry River, which comes down from Lugnaquilla through Tinahely and Shillelagh, and joins the Slaney just below the village. A stroll up a beech-lined avenue brought me to Huntington Castle. On the site of a Kavanagh stronghold in Norman times, the castle is a slightly dilapidated but fine example of Jacobean architecture. It has featured in a number of period films. Here the Right Reverend Hierophant, Olivia Robertson, presides as Arch Priestess of the Fellowship of Isis. The castle has attracted many famous visitors with interests in the occult. In former times, W.B. Yeats, George Russell and Oliver St. John Gogarty were regular visitors. The Fellowship is said to be the largest pagan organisation in the world, with members in nearly 100 countries. In the castle basement there is a genuine Egyptian temple dedicated to the goddess Isis, and visitors come from far and wide to participate in ancient rituals.

I bought some food in the village, and some Vaseline to treat a case of the dreaded crotch-rash which was worsening with every step. I headed southward for a stiff slog over a hill, and reached Bunclody after about another hour on tarmac. There were no buses of any use so I hitched back, getting a lift from two girls who were off to a 'trad session' in Hacketstown. They dropped me at a junction two miles from Carnew. Those two miles were hell: the rash was now glowing angrily despite liberal globs of Vaseline that sizzled upon application.

Having taken some refreshment in Carnew, I stood on the road northward to hitch a lift to Rosnastraw. After an hour, as I began to despair, a local whom I had seen in the pub stopped and offered me a lift. He was heading home to Coolboy. While reasonably sober, he was certainly 'over the limit'. I asked was he not worried about being stopped by the Guards. 'Ah no! Sure they all know me here.' The difficulty of picking up a lift on a quiet road, and the uncertainty as to the state of the driver, made me resolve never to hitch again. But I knew that such resolve was unlikely to be sustained. Regaining my car, I repaired to Lawless's Hotel for tea, but the hotel was overflowing with crowds from the Wicklow football final, so I headed on home and crashed out for a twelve hour sleep, having walked about 22 miles that day.

Chapter 4

UP THE AIRY MOUNTAIN, DOWN THE RUSHY GLEN

The yellow bittern that never broke out
In a drinking bout might as well have drunk;
His bones are thrown on a naked stone
Where he lived alone like a hermit monk.

'The Yellow Bittern' – Thomas MacDonagh

Stage 12: *Bunclody to Borris*

I SET OUT FROM BUNCLODY ON EASTER Monday 1998, a beautifully clear and crisp-cold day. The Good Friday Agreement on the future of Northern Ireland had been signed in Belfast just three days before, and there was a general atmosphere of euphoria. I was planning to cross the mountains to the Barrow River and follow it 'down the rushy glen' to the sea. My goal for the day was to reach the town of Borris, on the other side of the Blackstairs Mountains. 'Plan A' was to climb a series of successively higher peaks, from Black Rock Mountain to Mount Leinster (795 metres). However, the thought of an accident alone on the hillside in such freezing conditions was unappealing. The light snow-cap on Mount Leinster persuaded me to adopt 'Plan B', to follow the quiet road to the Nine Stones, where I would not be out of touch, and where the option to take a road to the TV mast atop Mount Leinster would be available if desired.

Uphill I went, crossing from Wexford back into Carlow at the Clody Bridge. The road to the north of the mountains was quite unfrequented.

Primroses lined the verge and I sailed along to the sound of the birds. The glen was a golden glow of gorse. The Clody River flows down a broad valley framed by a crescent of hills with Mount Leinster at its crown. On the arrival of a snow flurry, I took to the forest and followed a rough track parallel to the road. When both flurry and track expired, I slid down the bank to recover the road, getting gorse-gashed in the process. The golden glow was not so glorious now. Soon the road was joined by the South Leinster Way. This putative walking trail is, at least for this stretch, nothing more than the road that was always there. But the further sections, beyond Borris, are more justifiably described as a way-marked trail, following the Barrow River to Graiguenamanagh, and then crossing Brandon Hill and onward to the Suir Valley.

Nearing Corrabut Gap between Croughaun to the north and Mount Leinster to the south, I followed the road up to the pass to enjoy a fine panorama of Carlow and Kilkenny. Returning one hundred metres or so, I took the road over the north flank of Mount Leinster. Grassy verges made the going easy now and, with the ever-present threat of rain or snow, the forests beside the road were reassuring. A heavy fall of soft hail arrived just in time for me to stop for lunch. I retired to the trees to enjoy a sandwich and a drink. The hail easily penetrated the dense canopy of conifers, but bounced harmlessly off me. I listened to the radio news as I munched my sandwich. A group of pot-holers, who had been trapped several hundred feet below ground in Galway, had been located and brought safely to the surface. I felt relieved for them, and also at not having taken the mountain trail in these conditions, causing a call-out of the mountain rescue team.

As I left the forest, an old billy-goat who had been squatting among the trees rose and followed me. An assiduous study of *The Beano* in my youth had given me a deep knowledge of goat-lore: Billy-goats, when not eating the contents of clothes-lines, rush up behind old men and butt them over fences. I hurried up the hill-road faster than I would have liked. The goat seemed repeatedly to lose interest but each time I peeked back he caught my eye and trotted after me. Eventually, I lost him, and soon reached the Nine Stones, at the pass between Mount Leinster and Sliabh Bawn. After the quiet road it was a surprise to find this spot so busy. Here were parked about a dozen cars; it is a popular spot for day trippers, and on this Bank Holiday a group of hang-gliders were preparing to fly. A sign marks the road to the top of Mount Leinster giving the height of the mountain and of the TV mast (122 metres) at its peak.

The road to the summit did not tempt me. It was another stiff 350 metres to the top, and I would have had to come back the same way. Following the road westward and downhill, I heard behind me the un-mistakable sound of an animal's foot-fall: Billy had sauntered over the pass to seek me out. I shouted abuse, but this just seemed to encourage him. At last, a car came up the hill and stopped, and the occupants threw something edible to Billy. The truth dawned: all he had wanted was one of my sandwiches. I escaped downhill, soon crossing a cattle-grid which, perhaps, might have deterred the goat, but by now he was paying more attention to his new friends and I saw him no more.

Brandon Hill loomed ahead, at a magnetic bearing of 240 degrees (I had not forgotten to bring my shiny new compass this time). This is the highest point in County Kilkenny. To the left was the flank of Sliabh Bawn, which must take its name from the many outcrops of white quartz. The South Leinster Way is on the tarmac road until it joins the Barrow beyond Borris. The glen here is rich in ancient monument sites. On the map are marked crosses, megalithic tombs, holy wells, cairns and rock art. This last intrigued me, so I asked a chance-met local about it.

> *Me*: 'Nice Day, isn't it?'
>
> *He*: ''Tis, begor!'
>
> *Me*: 'Do you know anything about the rock art hereabouts?'
>
> *He*: 'Rop art, is it?'
>
> *Me*: 'No, rock art.'
>
> *He*: 'Rot art?'
>
> *Me*: 'No, rock art. See, here it is, marked on the map.'
>
> *He*: 'I haven't me glasses.'

You haven't your hearing aid either, I thought unkindly. But he was kinder, and told me where to find an old cross nearby. I soon found the farm where the rock art was indicated on the map. The owner, Peter Rose, welcomed me and showed me the specimen of rock art on his land. It had been found down the river valley and moved here for better accessibility. The rock was something under a metre in diameter, roundish, with a carved pattern of uncertain significance. He marked it out in chalk and, together with his father and a friend, we chatted about its possible provenance and purpose. It seems it is about 4,000 years old. We thought it could be a primitive map or diagram of the local landscape, the two concentric circular patterns representing a Rath. But this is wild speculation. Peter told me about a number of other antiquities in the area. He also showed me another stone, a horseshoe-shaped quern used long ago for grinding corn. The megalithic tomb on a nearby hill is known locally, and more graphically, as the Banshee Stone. Having photographed the rock art, I thanked Peter and continued on my way.

As I approached Borris, an imposing viaduct came into view. It is a noble structure of 16 solid but gracious arches. It carried the Bagenalstown to New Ross railway across the valley of the Mountain River, which flows down from the western side of Mount Leinster. The embankment north of the viaduct has been cut away, and a school built on the land. I climbed up the bank to the viaduct, from which an excellent vista of the Blackstairs opens up. The viaduct was completed in 1862 at a cost of £20,000. The old railway line is now a grassy track, clear across the viaduct and to the next bridge, but it looked impassable beyond. The section from Borris south to Glynn is described in Kevin Cronin's book *Off the Beaten Track*, but he admits the way is blocked in places. I decided not to attempt this section, as the Barrow tow-path was a far more appealing alternative.

Borris is a quiet Georgian town, clean and pleasant, with some curious old-world shop fronts. The town is dominated by Borris House, ancestral home of the McMurrough-Kavanaghs, and its high boundary walls lining the west side of the main street give the town a stately if slightly sombre air. The house is private, but is now available as a venue for wedding celebrations. My evening meal, in The Green Drake, was ample in quantity, reasonable in cost and delicious after a day's trekking. I stayed with Mrs Susan Breen, whose house is opposite the church, right in the centre of the town. Mrs Breen loaned me a book about an extraordinary character,

Arthur Kavanagh of the McMurrough-Kavanagh family. Born in 1831 with only stumps for limbs, he overcame his acute disabilities, becoming an accomplished horseman, a world traveller, a Member of Parliament and a Privy Councillor. She told me that her father remembered 'the Major' riding through Borris or, as she pronounced it, Burris.

The Borris Kavanaghs can trace their ancestry back to Dermot Mc-Murrough, who sought help from the Normans in his dispute with the High King, Rory O'Connor. My knowledge of Irish history is patchy, but I recall the infamous Dermot McMurrough, aka Diarmaid na nGall or 'Diarmaid of the Foreigners', as the biggest villain in the schoolbook, the treacherous tyrant who betrayed his country. He ran off with the wife of Tiernan O'Rourke, King of Breifne. In the ensuing mêlée, he asked King Henry II for help and, as a result, Strongbow came over from Wales in 1170. Strongbow dispatched some of Dermot's enemies and, as promised, was given the hand of his daughter Aoife. They were married in Waterford in 1171 and, as Dermot had no legitimate male heir, his extensive lands passed to Strongbow through Aoife shortly afterwards. Strongbow was so effective against the unprepared and disorganised Irish that Henry, fearing he would become too powerful, came over himself to keep a lid on things. Thus, Dermot was the direct cause of the Anglo-Norman invasion of Ireland, and '800 years of Saxon oppression'. If I had ancestors like that, I would keep quiet about it!

Stage 13: Borris to St. Mullin's

I was awoken by the rooks nesting in the tall trees of Borris House. After breakfast with Mrs Breen, I started up the main street. To get to the Barrow River I had to follow the road for a mile north, and then branch off left to Ballyteigelea Bridge. This cannot honestly be described as a waymarked trail. The road was busy, with many heavy goods vehicles. Direct access from Borris down the Mountain River to the Barrow would have been convenient but I found no path marked on the map and the land seemed to be private and inaccessible to the public. Thus, a two mile detour along the highway was unavoidable. Near the bridge I startled a pair of pheasants, who rose noisily. These fat, ungainly birds, which were introduced to Ireland from Asia during the sixteenth century, move slowly and must be easy to hit. It seems unsporting to 'bag' such easy targets, yet perhaps they would long since have gone the way of the Dodo were it not for the 'sportsmen' who breed them for the pleasure of shooting them.

The Barrow is Ireland's second largest river, yet it was almost completely deserted during my April visit. Not a single vessel passed me during the day. The river rises in Sliabh Bloom, flows east to Monasterevin, then south through a fertile and prosperous region, joining the Nore above New Ross and the Suir, the third of the Three Sisters, at Waterford Harbour. It is linked to the Grand Canal at Athy, providing a waterway to Dublin and the Shannon. The navigation from Athy to St. Mullin's was built in the period 1759-1780, with 23 locks and some extensive canal cuts. The navigation tow-path is known locally as the Line. For over forty miles from Athy to St. Mullin's it affords a clear walking way with no fences or ditches to climb, no swamps or marches to wade through and no obstructions to surmount.

At Ballyteigelea Bridge, where I joined the Line, I met two men on a barge, enjoying a morning cup of tea before heading upstream to Goresbridge. They were the only boatmen I was to meet the whole day. There are four locks between here and Graiguenamanagh and four more to the tidal estuary at St. Mullin's. These locks have the most musical names. After Borris Lock come Ballingrane, Clashganny, Ballykeenan, Graignamanagh, Tinnahinch Lower, Carriglead and the Sea Lock at St. Mullin's. The walk along the Line is a great delight. The tow path provides an easy but interesting and varied day's journey. A symphony of birdsong enlivened the sunny morning, complementing the glorious waterscapes, ever-changing as I drifted along. The keeper's lodge at Borris Lock was derelict, but provided a dry shelter for fishermen. Reaching Bunnahown Bridge below Borris Lock I saw that there was a path, which may have led down from the town of Borris. Bunnahown (Bun na hAmhainn, the foot of the river) is where the Mountain River joins the Barrow.

Brandon Hill loomed into view as I approached Clashganny Lock. The beautiful weir here is one of the most photogenic spots on the Barrow. It is said that Thomas Moore wrote 'Oft in the Stilly Night', one of his most plaintive melodies, at this spot. Below the lock the river, always gorgeous, becomes more *gorge-ous*, with steep wooded banks rising high on both sides. A long navigation channel leads to Ballykeenan, a double lock with a swinging bridge over the lower chamber. I photographed an iridescent oil patch in the lock. Oil was bubbling up from an unknown source below, making patterns which were pretty but devastating for wildlife. Below the lock I came to a rocky promontory where the river bends sharply to the left. This is the Devil's Eyebrow, perhaps taking its name from the overhanging trees. Below it, the river opens into a broad valley and the entrancing panorama of Graiguenamanagh comes into view. Here I met the first people since Borris, a few anglers and some locals from Graigue out for a lunch-time stroll. Just above the bridge, on the opposite bank, stood the renovated and refurbished corn mill, now the Waterside Restaurant and Guest House. The tall roof of Duiske Abbey rose behind it.

Graiguenamanagh, the Village of the Monks, is a delightful town. It is full of character, with many interesting buildings and shops. The Abbey was founded by Cistercian monks who came from Stanley Abbey in Wiltshire. It takes its name from the Duiske (Dubh Uisce, Black Water), the little river that rushes down from Brandon Hill and flows behind the main street under numerous little bridges. The Abbey architecture is in the style called 'Early English'. It is the largest of the thirty-four Cistercian monasteries built in Ireland. Building commenced around 1207 and, for 300 years, the Abbey was an important focus for the region. All came to an end in 1536, with the Dissolution of the Monasteries by Henry VIII, and the Abbey fell into disrepair. It was carefully renovated in the 1980s and, although only a shadow of what was once such a major monastic centre, it is well worth a visit. The Abbey Centre, further up the town, has an interesting collection of exhibits and a shop selling original art works and books. Here I bought Michael Fewer's book *By Cliff and Shore*, an account of his walk along the Waterford coast.

The seven-arched bridge spanning the Barrow between Graigue in Kilkenny and Tinnahinch on the Carlow side was designed by George Semple. It was built in 1767, during the canalisation of the river. It is one of the most aesthetically pleasing bridges in the country, its beauty enhanced by the gracious crescent weir below it. The eastern arch was blown up by the forces of the Crown in 1798 to prevent the rebels from crossing into Kilkenny.

I lunched on burger and chips at The Duiske Diner, a small chipper in the narrow main street. The cuisine was perhaps not of the Cordon Bleu standard that might be available at The Waterside, but was adequate for my simple tastes. For a siesta, I sat on the quay below the bridge. A dozen boats were tied up here, but there was no sign of activity. I had acquired a mobile phone, a great novelty at that time, and I telephoned Cabrini to describe the scene, and to let her hear the water cascading over the weir. Behind the lock at Graigue stands the ruin of Tinnahinch Castle, a fortified house built around 1615 to control the river crossing. Mount Leinster provides an appealing backdrop to the town viewed from here.

Heading onward, I came after a short time to a reed-filled backwater. Here I spied a bittern, a relatively rare bird in this country, and the first I have seen. The bittern (*Botaurus stellaris*) is a mottled brown cousin of the heron. He has a stubbier neck and a heavy dagger-like yellow beak. These birds once bred widely in Ireland, but are now rare visitors. He stood with his beak pointing upwards, swaying with the reeds, a characteristic behaviour when alarmed. I photographed him, but there was little to see on the print, so well did he blend with the vegetation. He is described in my bird-book as skulking, solitary and usually crepuscular (active around twilight). The bittern was popular with Irish poets. Ledwidge's 'Lament for Thomas MacDonagh' opens 'He shall not hear the bittern cry'. The reference is to MacDonagh's poem 'The Yellow Bittern', a translation of 'An Bunnán Buí', written by Cathal Buidhe MacGiolla Gunna (d. 1750) at a time when these birds were much more commonly heard. Legend has it that Cathal Buidhe spied a bittern lying dead on an icy lake and believed the bird had died because he could not drink the frozen lake water. He took pity on the bittern because of his own 'terror of the thirst'. The poem speaks of how '... the bird of the long smooth neck / Could get his death from the thirst at last', and urges the listener to drink up, ' ... for you'll get no sup when your life is past...'

Whitethorn blossoms were abundant along the path's edge. Here the Barrow is sandwiched between the Blackstairs Mountains to the left and Brandon Hill to the right. A cross stands upon Brandon Hill, probably put there in the Holy Year of 1954, like that on Bray Head and in many other places throughout Ireland. After avoiding a shower of hail by hiding under a large thorn-bush, I came to a long navigation channel leading to Lower Tinnahinch Lock. The drop in water level at this lock seemed inordinately large; I wondered what is the practical limit to the change of level of a single lock. When there is a large difference in height, double locks or even flights of several locks are found. The keeper's lodge at Lower Tinnahinch was occupied, whitewashed and in good nick.

Just before the next lock, at Carriglead, stood a small construction like a sentry box. I guessed it was one of the many water-metering stations operated by the Office of Public Works. OPW, widely known as the Board of Works, has a mixed image in the public psyche. Often criticised for inefficiency, the Board does work of very high quality. On an earlier boat trip along the Shannon, I had seen some impressive harbour constructions carried out by this body. OPW is responsible for the upkeep of the canals and navigations. They have an excellent waterways museum in the Grand Canal Basin in Dublin with working models of locks and a range of other interesting exhibits.

The house at Carriglead Lock is a granite building that has been nicely renovated. After resting for a while, sitting on the lock gate, I continued along the soft turfy path which was such a pleasure to walk upon. Coming to a carved rock seat, I relaxed again for a spell. The river was flowing more rapidly here. I threw a branch in and followed it for a few minutes, having to step lively to keep pace. The flow must have been four or five knots near the bank and probably a good deal faster in mid-stream. You would need a powerful engine for this navigation channel.

Suddenly I saw a large bird rise from the river a hundred yards ahead and fly directly towards me. It was a mute swan who landed on the water and climbed up the bank in front of me. I was surprised, but took out my camera to 'snap' him. As I approached, he became more agitated and I saw that he was guarding his mate who was sitting on a nest right beside the tow-path. I was unsure of the best course of action: *The Beano*, so garrulous on goats, was mute on swans. But I was aware that these birds can attack, especially in these circumstances. He stood on guard, nobly protecting his pen. Having taken a photo, I made a fierce dash past the cob, being careful not to pass between him and his mate. He reared up until his head was above mine, his wings flapping wildly, and emitted a desperate hiss. But I was out of reach before he had turned. The pen sat through the adventure, apparently serene and quite unperturbed, but I suspect her heartbeat quickened a little, just as mine did. After another photo-call, I left the pair in peace.

Passing a lifting bridge, I came at last to the Sea Lock at St. Mullin's. The path here can flood at high water but, fortunately, the tide was very low at this time, so I strolled along, still dry-footed, to the grassy quay below the village. A handful of houses border the river at this serene spot, remote from worldly fuss, in the beautiful river valley embraced by high sylvan banks. The tidal range is surprisingly large, and the river can be turbulent at times. The tow-path ends at St. Mullin's, as the river gorge becomes narrow, steep and fast-flowing below.

St. Mullin's, or Tigh Moling, the house of Moling, has a long history as an important ecclesiastical centre and place of pilgrimage. St. Moling, who presided here in the seventh century, was Bishop of Ferns and of Glendalough. The remains of this early Christian monastic site are rewarding to visit. A variety of ruins remains, including the stump of a round tower. *The Book of Mulling*, a Gospel manuscript perhaps written by St. Moling himself and now in Trinity College, Dublin, contains a ground-plan of the monastery. The burial place of the kings of South Leinster, among them Art McMurrough, is here.

A large mound, a Norman motte, stands in front of the monastic ruins. These mottes were made during the first century of the Anglo-Norman conquest. They were topped by wooden castles or towers, providing defence from the wild Irish, and were situated within an enclosed courtyard or bailey, which was surrounded by a wooden fence and overlooked by the motte. This motte by the Barrow would have given the invaders complete control of all traffic on the river. I climbed it to enjoy the view of the old ruins, and of Brandon Hill in the setting sun. Then I repaired to Blanchfield's, the little pub in the village, for refreshment. Helen, the lady of the house, gave me a drink and I was made welcome by the locals, who chatted merrily. A snippet of the conversation sticks in my mind:

Mick: 'Have you seen Paddy lately?'

Jack: 'Noh, sure he's mindin' his mother.'

Mick: 'Mindin' his mother, me bollocks! Sorry Helen!'

Jack: 'What are yeh talkin' about?'

Mick: 'He's mindin' yer wan above on the hill.'

Jack: 'How do yeh know that?'

Mick: 'Sure, he have a track wore out through the field.'

Lucky Paddy, I thought, as I sat outside later at a picnic table writing notes. I stayed with Mrs Dwyer in Teach Moling, a little guest house beside the river.

Stage 14: St. Mullin's to New Ross

The forecast was for fresh north-westerly winds, with showers of rain, hail or snow. I was heading for New Ross, not by the busy main road, but on minor roads via Ballywilliam. I set out up the stiff hill from St. Mullin's. Mrs Dwyer had offered me a lift, but acceptance would have broken the continuity of my walk, and that was taboo for the Commodius Vicus. Brandon Hill was behind me now, and Blackstairs Mountain to my left was just covered by a layer of stratocumulus cloud. Knowledge of the mountain height, 735 metres on the map, permitted the elementary deduction that the cloud base was at about 2,400 feet.

At Drummin Bridge I came to a nice neat church, recently renovated, standing by a lapping brook. Continuing straight on, I soon came to an old railway bridge. Climbing up, I saw an old carved stone milepost: 84 miles from somewhere. I followed the derelict line for a mile or so towards Ballywilliam. But the going became more difficult, so overgrown was the way. Gorse-gashed and thorn-thwacked, I backtracked to Drummin, and took the road down a gorge where the brook cascades into the Pollymounty River on the Carlow–Wexford border. Pollymounty is traditionally the home of Eibhlin Kavanagh, who inspired the love-song, 'Eileen Aroon', written around 1600. I followed the bank of the river to the east for a while. At present the woods here are a popular dumping ground where redundant washing machines and suchlike are left to rot. There is an opportunity to make a most pleasant walking trail along this section of the river.

Taking to the road again, I soon saw the old railway embankment on the left. This railway once provided an inland route from Dublin to the south-east, branching off the Kilkenny line at Bagenalstown. The Bagenalstown and Wexford Railway (B&WR) was incorporated in 1854, and work started the following year. The line opened to Borris in 1858, it reached Ballywilliam in 1862 and the link to the coastal Dublin-Wexford line at Macmine Junction operated from 1873. Another branch from Palace East gave access to New Ross and Waterford. Several railway companies were involved, there were many financial hiccups, and the venture was never a commercial success. Passenger traffic ceased in 1931 and the line was completely closed in 1963.

Crossing a field, I tried again to follow the track, but this section was so waterlogged that again the attempt had to be abandoned. Soon I came to the tiny village of Ballywilliam, first spotting the solid elegance of the old granite Station House, somewhat diminished in splendour by the electricity sub-station plonked in front of it. I stopped for refreshment at The Ash Tree, a public house of some charm. The lady in charge, another Helen, upon hearing I was from Dun Laoghaire, told me she had trained as a nurse in St. Michael's Hospital there 'long ago, when I was young'. 'You're still young,' I said, but this attempted gallantry was too transparent to fool her.

A gentleman coming in was introduced to me as 'The Professor', and was evidently the local expert on just about everything. We chatted or, rather, he spoke at length on a wide variety of subjects while I listened, nodding as appropriate. He warned of impending terrible earthquakes and landslides, and bad weather too. I asked the cause and he said, 'It is written, the Art of Man shall destroy Man'. Upon seeking further clarification, I was told that we have disturbed a heavenly body, called Deedo or something like that, and that a great nemesis will be the result. Perhaps Deedo was an elevation of El Niño to the celestial sphere. The particularly vigorous manifestation of this phenomenon recently, with widespread anomalies in the weather, could just possibly have resulted from 'the Art of Man'. But I shall never know the secret of Deedo, as the Professor was loath to amplify this theme, switching instead to the Atlantic Alliance and Stalin's role as a peacemaker.

After buying supplies, I took the Rathgaroge road and then branched onto a quiet country lane that led straight towards my destination. At Ballyanne Old Bridge a muddy path led under the N30 to a track marked on the map as The Battery, apparently a direct route into New Ross. It looked as though I was home and dry but somehow either the map was wrong or I missed the way and was lost. Heading vaguely southward by compass, I followed the edge of several fields, carefully crossing some fences. One of these was electrified, as I discovered uncomfortably, with one leg on each side. Perhaps this was 'The Battery'. I found the track again at Bishop's Mill Bridge, and headed uphill past a football ground, O'Kennedy Park, to the main road a mile north of New Ross.

The Bunclody bus was not due for several hours, so I caught the Number 5 bus to a junction beyond Enniscorthy, and set up to hitch the rest of the way. A kind farmer from Kilmuckridge came along within five minutes and gave me a lift in his Volvo. Thank God for the generosity of the Irish. At Bunclody I enjoyed a quarter-pounder and chips at The American Diner, followed by coffee and cheesecake at The Cabbage Patch across the road. I had not realised that Bunclody was such a noted gastronomic Mecca. Almost anything tastes good after a day's walk. I moseyed around this pleasant town and down to the bridge, where the Clody joins the Slaney. Finally, I returned to where I had parked my car two days earlier, changed out of my boots and drove home.

Chapter 5

THROUGH NORMAN TERRITORY

Young Man: *You speak of Diarmuid and Dervorgilla*
               Who brought the Norman in?
Young Girl: *Yes, yes, I spoke*
               Of that most miserable, most accursed pair
               Who sold their country into slavery; and yet
               They were not wholly miserable and accursed
               If somebody of their race at last would say,
               'I have forgiven them.'
Young Man: *O, never, never*
               Shall Diarmuid and Dervorgilla be forgiven.

'The Dreaming of Bones' – W.B. Yeats

THE NEXT SEGMENT OF MY JOURNEY was from the Norman town of
New Ross, via the region of the Norman landings in 1170 to the city
of Waterford, where Strongbow married Aoife after capturing the town. I
drove to New Ross by way of Ferns, where I stopped for lunch. The notorious Dermot MacMurrough, directly responsible for the Norman invasion, founded an abbey here and is buried in the graveyard. The remains
of a cathedral and a large Norman castle can be seen. Also in the village
is the little church of St. Aidan, behind which are a group of small cells
or hermitages, where people retreat from the hurly-burly of daily life for
a spell.

The MacMurrough Farm Hostel, close to New Ross, is one of many
independent holiday hostels that have sprung up in recent years. They
provide basic accomodation, usually at rock-bottom prices. They attract

a young international clientele who are generally content to put up with conditions that can be quite spartan. The hostel is about two miles north of the town, up a long muddy track. I was warmly welcomed by the owners, Brian and Jenny Nuttall. Jenny was on her way to a choral recital in New Ross, and I went along with her. The Morris Beachy Choir, from Texas, was performing in St. Mary's Church. On the way I asked about the path called The Battery. She confirmed that it had been closed off years ago.

Returning to the hostel after the concert I enjoyed an evening of light-hearted conversation, mainly about music. A young Australian traveller expounded on the intricacies of manufacturing didgeridoos: apparently, they are made from tree trunks that have been hollowed out by termites. I shared a dormitory with ten other 'happy campers'. The night was filled with droning sounds reminiscent of the outback, a symphony of slumbers more snorious than sonorous.

Stage 15: *New Ross to Arthurstown*

I woke early, after a restive night, and headed into New Ross for breakfast. Someone told me the Mariner's Bar opened at 8.00 am. I arrived there to find two prospective customers, gasping for an early morning pint. One said, 'Yes, they serve breakfast, but he won't cook if he have no wimmen'. He told me of another place, up by the Tholsel, though I'd swear he said Tonsil. Tholsels, or Toll Stalls, are to be found in most Norman towns. They were buildings where revenue payments were collected. The New Ross Tholsel was originally a covered market with open arches on the ground floor. I decided to try my luck at the Hotel New Ross. 'Yes, we have breakfast, but the cook isn't here yet,' the receptionist said. Just then the cook came in. I ordered scrambled eggs. I got scrambled eggs; I got sausages; I got rashers and black and white pudding and tomatoes and mushrooms and fried bread. 'Eat what you can,' said the waitress; I ate the lot.

New Ross is a bustling, lively place, a hilly town with lots of steps and alleyways to explore. The town was still decked out in colourful bunting, as the Tour de France had raced through just one week before me. New Ross is the last river crossing on the Barrow. Isabella de Clare, daughter of Strongbow, and her husband William Marshall built the first bridge here in 1211. Above the town is the confluence of the Barrow and the Nore. Downstream, the river widens and joins the Suir, opening into Waterford Harbour. There was a monastic settlement here as early as the sixth century. New Ross has been an important sea port since the Middle Ages. The town was built shortly after the Norman invasion, and walled by the citizens in 1265. It was severely damaged by fire during the 1798 rebellion, when the rebels attacked the town but failed to take it.

Across the river a large wooden ship was under construction in the dry dock of the old Ross Co. The Dunbrody is a replica of a nineteenth century barque used to transport famine emigrants to the New World. At 450 tons with an overall length of 176 feet and masts towering to 130 feet, it is the largest wooden ship ever built in the Republic.

I headed south from New Ross on a minor road. There was a light drizzle, but the sky held hope of a clearance. At Kelly's Wood I faced Frost's Dilemma again. I chose left, through Upper Creakan, which sounded in sympathy with my bones. Soon, Slieve Coillte (888 feet) came into view. It is said that six counties can be seen from the peak. A puzzle occurred to me: what is the maximum number of counties visible from a single point in Ireland, and where is the point? Slieve Coillte overlooks Kennedy Park and Arboretum to the south. This park of 250 hectares, with 4,500 species of trees, commemorates President John F. Kennedy, whose ancestral home is at Dunganstown on the river-bank to the west. Kennedy's great-grandfather Patrick left Ireland around the time of the famine and journeyed to America on a ship like the Dunbrody.

Should I try to climb the mountain? I took a path to a farm and asked about the best way up. A woman told me it was all right to go up through her fields, but warned that I might have difficulties. I tried to climb up the north side. It might as well have been the north face of the Eiger: the woods were completely impenetrable. I skirted around to the west. Soon, dense bracken reached to chest height. Finally, I had to abandon the attempt and descended to the road, which had then to be climbed across the west flank of the hill. It had been much trouble for nothing, but at least I could enjoy the view to Cheekpoint in Waterford, and the confluence of the Suir with its Siamese sisters.

Soon I came to the JFK Arboretum. Its beautiful grounds are exquisitely maintained, and there is a visitor centre, café and recreation area. A serene lake with a flock of mallards lies in the park. I walked through avenues of trees, so dense that the darkness was broken only by pinpricks of light, like a starry night. I rambled on through the grounds, past the picturesque lake, to the southern limit where, behind a miniature railway, I found an unofficial way out over a fence and wall. Down the road a bit I spied a scarecrow. Seeking to take a snap, I discovered that my camera was missing. I guessed I had dropped it while climbing the fence. Uttering a prayer to St. Anthony, who is renowned for helping to find lost things, I returned to the point of my illicit exit, and reconnoitred for a few minutes until I found the camera lying on a tuft of grass.

I took a short detour to where a bawn, an enclosure for animals, was marked on the map. I found nothing there but an old farmyard. Perhaps there was some antiquity, but my untrained eye was unable to discern it. Continuing to Campile, I bought and ate some lunch. The next goal was Dunbrody Abbey, just west of Campile. The abbey is the finest medieval ruin in Wexford. There is a large cruciform church, mainly from the early thirteenth century, built by the Cistercians of St. Mary's Abbey in Dublin. Dunbrody was founded by Hervey de Monte Marisco, uncle of Strongbow, and he is buried in the abbey. It flourished until the Dissolution of the Monasteries by Henry VIII in 1539. Across the road stand the remains of a castellated house, with a mini-golf course and a full-sized yew-hedge maze. In the small café there is a doll's house in the pattern of the castle. I bought a pot of tea for the princely sum of fifty pence.

Richard Roche's well-written book *The Norman Invasion of Ireland* is an eminently readable account of the events surrounding the conquest. The invasion utterly changed the ensuing history of Ireland. South Wexford still retains a certain Norman character with its many castles and small well-tilled farms and family names. The Yola dialect, widely spoken in the baronies of Forth and Bargy until the nineteenth century, came with the early Norman settlers. The last known Yola speaker, Jack Devereux, died in 1998. The popular singer and songwriter Eleanor McEvoy recently issued an album with the title 'Yola'.

Joyce's Tower in Sandycove, the Alpha and Omega of the Commodius Vicus

Dalkey Island (photo by Owen Lynch)

Scotsman's Bay from Joyce's Tower

Bullock Castle

Sorrento Point with Dalkey Island in the background

Tunnels on the old and new railway lines, Bray Head

A bridge of the old mining railway in Avoca

*Conflicting messages at
Newcastle Flying Club*

*A lock on the Barrow below
Graiguenamanagh*

The elegant bridge and weir on the Barrow at Graiguenamanagh

Mr. Swan protecting his wife, by the tow-path near St. Mullin's

Water glistening on the Barrow near St. Mullin's

Unravelling the maze at Dunbrody

A delicate Celtic Cross at Ahenny

The beautiful and mysterious Slievenamon

Peter in front of the 'Hindu Gate' at Dromana Bridge near Villierstown

Round gateposts in County Cork

*Mark as understudy to Christy Ring,
the Cuchulainn of Cloyne*

*Ightermurragh Castle near
Ladysbridge, County Cork*

I covered the last leg of the walk along lanes purple with thistle and foxglove and loosestrife and the delightfully named great hairy willow-herb. Tired and stiff and subdued in mood, my spirits were lifted by the vista of Arthurstown Pier framed by the banks of Waterford Harbour, with the unmistakable black and white striped Hook Head Lighthouse vaguely visible on the horizon. Hook is reputedly the oldest lighthouse in Europe. I arrived at Arthur's Rest, a clean and comfortable B&B in the town, run by Peggy Murphy. After a rest I ended the day with a short walk on the pier, to watch the sun setting and the curlews working the tide along King's Bay.

Stage 16: Arthurstown to Waterford

I took the coast road around to Ballyhack. There stands by the harbour a fine castle or tower-house, allegedly built around 1450 by the Knights Hospitallers of St. John, though it may well be a Norman castle built on the site of an earlier structure. The Hospitallers and the Templars were the two great chivalrous Orders of Knights founded during the Crusades. I was shown around by Mary Murphy, who explained the history and architecture of the castle. It is of five storeys, built of old red sandstone. High over the door is a machicolation, a projecting structure with a slot for dropping missiles on unwelcome visitors. Inside the door a 'murder hole', with similar purpose, protected the entrance lobby. A secret chamber, or oubliette, whose only access was a trap-door in its ceiling, served as a dungeon. In 1649, Cromwell had the castle 'slighted', or blown up with gunpowder, to render it ineffective. But what remains today is still of great interest, and further renovation is afoot.

I thanked Mary and her colleague Caitriona for their courtesy, and headed down to the pier to catch the ferry. This is the oldest ferry crossing in Ireland, and there has been a service here on and off for about a thousand years. It brought me from Ballyhack to Passage East, from Wexford to Waterford, from the Model County to the Crystal County, from Purple-and-Gold to Blue-and-White, from Leinster to Munster. Passage East has been a royal gateway for a thousand years. Strongbow landed here in 1170 and marched on Waterford. Henry II followed a year later with a small army, landing at nearby Crooke, and Richard II came in 1394 with a huge army of 35,000 troops. James II embarked for France from here a few days after the Battle of the Boyne. And finally, Old Queen Vic spent a night at anchor in the Royal Yacht Britannia off Passage. I stepped off the ferry and into the village to find Derek Davis, with an RTÉ film crew, shooting for the marine programme *Out of the Blue*.

As a light drizzle began to fall, I followed the coast south to Crooke. A small church appealing in its symmetric simplicity stands in the village. A ruined castle nearby is said to have been built by the Knights Templar; perhaps they were keeping an eye on their opposite numbers across the bay. The phrase 'by Hook or by Crook' originates, allegedly, from the determination of the Normans to invade either here on the west bank of Waterford Harbour, or on the east at Hook Head. Another version ascribes the phrase to Cromwell. A third theory is that steamers leaving Cobh went eastward to Europe 'by Hook Head' or westward to America, 'by Crookhaven'. Take your pick!

A few miles on I came to Geneva Barracks. Michael Fewer has walked the entire Waterford coast and in his book *By Cliff and Shore* he tells the story of New Geneva. Here lie the remnants of an unsuccessful attempt to found a settlement for emigrant merchants from Geneva in 1782–84. There was to have been a university here, attracting scholars from all over Europe. During an insurrection in Geneva in 1781, the town was beseiged by French and Swiss troops and, after negotiation, the rebellious Protestant citizens were allowed to leave with their property. They scattered around Europe seeking sanctuary. One group of wealthy goldsmiths made arrangements to set up a 'New Geneva' here in Waterford and James Gandon was commissioned to design the town. Building began in 1783 but, for reasons unclear, the whole project collapsed.

The buildings were converted to a military barracks and, during the 1798 rebellion, held over a thousand prisoners, many of whom were hanged here. Geneva Barracks is featured in the traditional ballad 'The Croppy Boy':

> *At Geneva Barracks that young man died,*
> *And at Passage they have his body laid.*
> *Good people who live in peace and joy,*
> *Breathe a prayer, shed a tear for the Croppy Boy.*

Croppies were Irish countrymen who joined in the Rebellion of 1798, cutting their hair very short in the style of the French revolutionaries. Little of the barracks survives today, but a corner bastion of the outer wall remains. Most of the buildings have been adapted for farm use and are in a state of dereliction.

At Dromina Strand I headed inland, over low rolling hills towards the city of Waterford. Apart from a brief stretch on the R684, the route was on minor, unfrequented roads. But this was a fairly dull region. It is the ancient Barony of Gaultier, and most places of interest lie along the coast, with many fishing villages and beaches and coves. It is an excellent area for cycling. Strongbow marched this way from Passage to Waterford in 1170; I was more or less following his trail, but with less aggressive intent. Swallows flew low across the road and a low-flying turbo-prop aircraft crossed on approach to Waterford Airport. I approached the city through a district of large expensive houses, the Foxrock of Waterford.

I came to the western end of the city, along the Mall to Reginald's Tower. This tower is by legend that of Reginald the Dane, built in 1003, but is more likely a thirteenth century Norman tower. For a time used as a mint and later as a prison, it now houses the Waterford Civic Museum. The city of Waterford is steeped in history. It was founded by the Vikings in 914 as Vethrafjorthr, the Ford of Father (Odin). The city walls have been restored by the corporation. Following Derry, they are claimed to be the best examples of ancient city walls in the country.

Strongbow married Dermot MacMurrough's daughter Aoife in Waterford in 1170, after he had taken the town with much bloodshed. That was a crafty move: when Dermot died less than a year later, the kingdom of Leinster came into Strongbow's possession! In fact, this was in breach of Irish law, since no property rights came down through the female line. But Strongbow was unconcerned with such subtleties, taking whatever he wanted. The wedding set a precedent for intermarriage between the invaders and the indigenous Irish, which soon became common practice, as did the interchange of language, laws and customs, until the Normans ultimately became *Hiberniores quam Hibernos ipsos* – more Irish than the Irish themselves. There is a remarkable nineteenth-century painting of the marriage, by Daniel Maclise, replete with allegorical imagery.

It was originally commissioned to hang in the Houses of Parliament in London, but is now in the National Gallery in Dublin.

The city quays are a mile long, with a single crossing, Rice Bridge, at the eastern end. Edmund Ignatius Rice, founder of the Christian Brothers, was a wealthy merchant of Waterford who devoted his life to the education of the poor. From the quays there is an interesting panorama: the opposite bank is heavily industrialised, providing a vibrant vista of cranes, warehouses and shipping. Many people object to industrial landscapes. Personally, I find views such as this fascinating: they are – as my friend Mark Draper says of Woodbine cigarettes – scorned by the many, but relished by the discerning few.

After arriving in Waterford, I caught the 16:20 bus to New Ross to collect my car and meet my son Owen. We drove back to Waterford and reconnoitred the route for the next day's walk. Then we had a tasty meal in Sizzlers, followed by a drink in Katty Barry's. We stayed in the Viking Hostel, a cut above McMurrough's but twice the price.

The Crosses of Ahenny

The following day we bought supplies and headed for the railway bridge, but it was clear that no reasonable person would willingly set out on a walk in such torrential rain. We had planned to walk to Carrick-on-Suir, but the weather was such a wash-out that this was hopeless. We drove to Portlaw and around the boundary of the Curraghmore estate, then on to Carrick-on-Suir where we visited Ormonde Castle. Next, we headed a few miles north from Carrick to Ahenny to see the ancient High Crosses. These two crosses are among the earliest examples known. Their 'sun-rings' are relatively slender, giving them a delicacy not so evident in the later styles, and they are decorated with carved spirals and other abstract Celtic designs. The base of a third cross stands bare. This cross, reputedly the most beautiful of the three, was stolen around 1800 and lost in a shipwreck near Passage East. It occurred to me that the recovery of the third cross would be an excellent challenge for some intrepid adventurer or Indiana Jones wannabe.

Heading towards Clonmel, where we planned to stay overnight, we passed by Kilcash. There was an ancient monastic foundation on the

slopes of Slievenamon. The ruins of a Butler Castle hereabouts are recalled in an anonymous eighteenth century poem:

What shall we do for timber?
The last of the woods is down,
Kilcash and the house of its glory
And the bell of the house are gone;
The spot where that lady waited
Who shamed all women for grace,
When earls came sailing to greet her
And Mass was said in the place.

The lady mourned here was Margaret Butler, Viscountess Iveagh,
who lies buried in the churchyard nearby. The poem, translated by Frank
O'Connor, evokes an image so common in Ireland of forests destroyed
and castles despoiled.

The next day we decided to walk from Carrick to Clonmel, but first I
will describe the journey from Waterford to Carrick which comes before
it geographically if not chronologically.

Stage 17: Waterford to Carrick

Rising at 6.00 o'clock on 1 August 1998, I set out to catch the 07:40
train from Heuston to Waterford. The weather was overcast, with a
weak ridge of high pressure over the country. At Kilkenny the engine has
to be changed to the other end of the train. This curious arrangement
arises from the historical development of the railway. The line from Kilkenny to Waterford was completed before the Dublin and Carlow link,
which was then made to approach the station along the same route from
the south-east. Indeed, there was another line to Kilkenny via Port Laoise
and Abbeyleix and, for a time, trains from Dublin to Waterford split at
Kildare, one half travelling via Carlow and the other via Port Laoise, and
joined up again at Kilkenny. There was a short delay to the train, due to
a failure of the points at Lavistown Junction, which had to be changed
manually. The guard announced helpfully: 'We'll be here for 20 minutes.
There's a shop on the platform, so you can have a cup of tea while you're
waiting.' Soon we were off southward and Brandon Hill appeared to the

east. Just beyond the bridge over the Nore south of Thomastown stand the ruins of Jerpoint Abbey. It is reckoned to be the finest example of a Cistercian Abbey in Ireland. From the train, the ruins bore a resemblance to those of Dunbrody.

Arriving in Waterford about half past ten, I crossed Rice Bridge to begin the day's walk, and headed west along the south bank of the Suir. A number of travellers' caravans were parked on this road, and there were several old rust-buckets tied up along the river bank. The sound of shunting engines drifted across the river in the still air. My first goal was the river bridge of a disused railway. This line was opened in 1878 by the Waterford, Dungarvan and Lismore Railway Company (WD&L) and for a time was part of the link between the Rosslare ferry terminal and Cork city. The line closed in 1967 and rail passengers between Waterford and Cork now have to take the circuitous route via Limerick Junction. A section of line reopened in 1970 for goods traffic from Waterford to a magnesite plant in Ballinacourty near Dungarvan but this freight link closed again in 1982.

I climbed up the bank to the railway at a road bridge about two miles west of the city, near the southern end of the old rail bridge over the Suir. This bridge is 1,205 feet long with nine spans, one a lifting section. Built by Sir William Arroll of Glasgow, it opened for the boat train from Rosslare in August, 1906. The bridge is now impassable even to walkers, as the lifting section has been removed, presumably for reasons of safety, by the Corporation. I had spotted the missing span by the track near Waterford Station.

For the first mile or so the rails and sleepers remain in place, but after that they have been lifted. After twenty minutes I came to a chain-link and barbed wire fence across the track, with a ditch on each side. Someone had thoughtfully broken a hole in the fence. However, over the next few miles I had to climb over about ten such fences. Kevin Cronin described the railway walk from Waterford to Dungarvan in his book, but made no mention of the obstructing fences, which had been put there within the past few years. No doubt, the farmers have to have access across the line, but they do not have to block the route for ramblers. A simple stile or small gate would remove the temptation to breach the fences; as it was, I wished for a pair of wire-cutters, having torn my shirt-sleeve on the barbed wire.

The line runs alongside the river for several miles and, apart from the fence obstructions, is a delight to walk. An abundance of wildflowers grow along the track. The way passes the garden centre of Mount Congreve Estate and, further on, rhododendrons line the left bank. At two places bridges over streams have been blocked by security fences with spiked poles, erected by Iarnrod Éireann. These I overcame by climbing out to the end of the fence and squirming round while hanging over a long drop to the water. At the second of these bridges, over the Whelanbridge River, the line swings westward away from the Suir where a ruined castle stands on the bank. The line enters a cutting and soon arrives at Kilmeadan Station, the first station after Waterford. Little remains here but the ruined platforms.

Climbing up the bank to the village, I had a drink at The Cosy Thatch. Here I asked for advice on the best way to walk to Portlaw. A local 'expert' was consulted. 'Oh, there are no paths from here to Portlaw,' he pontificated. 'You'll have to go by the main road.' He gave me much more misinformation and dubious advice about places that could not be reached from Kilmeadan. I decided to ignore everything that he said, and headed onwards using my map as guide. Crossing the Dawn River at a house called Sleepy Hollow, I took a small path northward. Soon I had a view back to a tiny lake with a large country house on the shore. This is Pouldrew House, a luxurious Georgian mansion, built in 1841, with its own private lake and waterfall. From the hillside, the house and its reflection in the lake looked superb. It had recently come on the market with a guide price of £2 million. Rumours that the Hollywood actor Brad Pitt was interested allowed a property correspondent to quip that it might soon be accurately described as The Pitts.

From here I followed a series of intricate branching paths. Nifty map and compass work was called for, and I consulted both at frequent intervals. Passing through a farmyard gated at both ends, I turned left to reach an old rustic road along the hillside. It afforded magnificent views to the north, with the Suir meandering below, and Kilbunny Church in the hollow of the hills with Portlaw behind it. I stood for several minutes admiring the scene and enjoying a refreshing drink. I followed the mountain trail west for a few miles, until it veered left, when I turned right across a small stream to another trail. From here a forest track led me due north through Kilbunny Wood. At an opening in the wood there was a colourful carpet of pink flowers, Rosebay Willow Herb. This flower spreads rapidly through woodland clearings where large areas of trees have been burned or blown down by gales. It is also known as Fireweed, and can be identified by the multitude of reddish spines emerging like flames from the stem. The track brought me to a church on a minor road just south of Portlaw. Despite the gloomy advice in Kilmeadan, I had managed to get this far without going near any roads!

Portlaw, on the Clodiagh River, is a model village built by the Quaker family Malcolmson. It is architecturally dismal but geometrically interesting. The streets have a pattern very untypical of Irish villages, splaying out from a point like the fingers of the left hand (the Port lámh!). The wrist leads to the ruins of an old cotton mill and a much later leather factory. The Malcolmsons' cotton mill was one of the earliest industrial developments in the country. However, it soon went into decline. A resident of the village told me that the Malcolmsons had put their money on the Confederate side in the American Civil War, and had lost the lot. However, he didn't explain what Quakers were doing gambling on a war, in support of those favouring slavery.

Feeling tired now, I looked for accommodation in Portlaw. Someone directed me to a house which she called 'Directory'. I soon discovered that she meant De Rect'ry, or The Rectory. This involved a detour of a mile, but the journey was in vain as the owner was away. I enquired at the butcher's shop but they didn't know anywhere else where I might get a shakedown. It was now five o'clock and I decided that the best bet was to press on to Carrick-on-Suir, about eight miles away. I should do that in around two hours; in fact, I did not arrive there until half past eight.

As I walked up the crooked thumb of the village, a man called after me, a tall, wild and disreputable-looking fellow with dark, grimy skin, teeth at every angle and the mien of a cut-throat. 'Come here. Will you not talk to an Irishman?' He asked me to have a drink with him and pointed to a small green shop with neither nameboard nor notice, which he referred to as The Pig and Whistle. 'Come on, have a drink, just one. Have a glass of cider.' I explained that I was walking to Carrick. He was very insistent: 'Come on, you're Irish. Have one drink, just one and I'll drive you to Carrick.' I declined. He asked who I was going to see in Carrick. I made up a name. 'Vincent O'Sullivan? Sure, I know him. Come and have a drink and then I'll drive you to Carrick.' Loud raucous laughs issued from The Pig and Whistle. I felt that to accept his invitation would be to risk a more difficult parting later, and finally managed to convince him that I was going to Carrick, going by foot and going now!

West of the village is Curraghmore House, the seat of the Marquess of Waterford. My intention was to walk through the grounds of the demense. Knowing that it was private, I rehearsed what I would say if and when confronted. I would, grudgingly, recognise the legal right of the owner to limit the access of others to his property, but would strenuously challenge his moral right 'to stop an Irishman from walking through Ireland'. I might even question the legitimacy of the Norman Conquest. Yes, this would be an excellent ploy! However, I never got an opportunity to argue the case: when I arrived at the estate, the gate was closed and locked. So, I followed the road around the eastern boundary, a much more hilly route. This caused me to change tack, and I headed north on a forest trail to Clonagam Hill (232 metres) where an eighteenth century round tower stands at the summit. The tower is about 75 feet high, in the style of the ancient round towers but without a conical cap. Inside, a spiral staircase of 92 steps brought me to the top, from where a splendid all-round view could be enjoyed.

From here the trail led down to a featureless minor road heading west. Some relief from the tedium was afforded by the glorious mountainscape of the Comeraghs, with Knockanaffrin to the north and Fauscoum, the highest peak in the range, to the south, separated by a pass known as The Gap. The Comeraghs are noted for their many glacial lakes. I had learned at school of these 'coums, corries or cirques' from a brutal Presentation Brother, who dug a few of them in the side of my head. These features, originally formed by the ice, are horseshoe-shaped depressions in the mountainside, with steep walls surrounding a flooded hollow. Coumshingaun, the largest lake in the Comeraghs, is said to be one of the finest examples of an ice age corrie formation in Europe.

I reached a road junction marked on the map as Piquet's Cross Roads. Could this French name have a Norman origin? I doubted it, suspecting that it is named after a local inhabitant, Peadar Kearney or Paddy Kavanagh or some other PK. I was on a major road now, long and straight and busy. At the top of the ridge across the river from Carrick, I planned to take a path marked on the map but no such path was there. It appears to have been 'privatised' and a house-owner nearby told me it had long since gone. So, I had to descend by the hairpin road and trudge the last few miles into the town. I was now exhausted, after ten hours walking with few breaks, having covered about 25 miles counting some detours. I was also dehydrated. For the last few miles I had noticed a dryness in the mouth and a worsening headache. All my water had long since been exhausted. This was another warning: I must be careful not to run out of water in future.

I stayed at a large B&B called The Gables, right in the centre of the town. The next morning I caught the 09:20 bus to Kilkenny, via Grange-mockler and Callan. Callan looked like an interesting town, with a ruined abbey right in the centre, and I resolved to take a closer look later. On the train journey from Kilkenny to Dublin, there was a delay at Athy. 'We're awaiting line clearance. The football special from Athy departed late and we're waiting for it to pass Cherryville Junction.' This is a very common style of anouncement: 'Train X is delayed because train Y was late.' Travellers on Irish Rail must have a sense of humour as well as boundless patience.

Stage 18: Carrick to Clonmel

I enjoyed the company of my son Owen for the next stage, which we walked two days after the section from Arthurstown to Waterford, as the intervening day, when we had hoped to walk from Waterford to Carrick, had been a complete wash-out. It was a bright day, with fresh north-westerly winds. We took the bus from Clonmel to Carrick-on-Suir at 10:30. A heavy shower fell as we boarded, but this was the last rain we had all day. A square in the town of Carrick bears the name of Sean Kelly, the great cyclist. A week before we were there, the Tour de France had raced through the town on its second stage, before crossing to Brittany to follow a more conventional route, and the town was still decorated with bright banners in a blaze of bunting.

The most notewothy old building in Carrick-on-Suir is Ormonde Castle. Part of the castle dates from the thirteenth century, but the most striking part is the Elizabethan manor house, built around 1560 by 'Black Tom' Butler, 10th Earl of Ormonde. He was a cousin of Queen Elizabeth I, through Ann Boleyn who was born in Carrick, and he built the house to please the Queen, expecting that she would visit; she never did! The castle has a commanding view over the River Suir, and over the lands of the Powers on the opposite side. The building is the best example of a Tudor manor house in the country. The Long Gallery extends for almost one hundred feet and must have been most impressive in its day. The Carrick Bend, which occurs frequently as a decorative motif in the castle, is a much older pattern, and is also found on the beautiful eighth century High Crosses at Ahenny, a few miles north of the town.

Our young guide told us about a tragic barge accident in Carrick about 150 years ago. More than one hundred people were drowned and the Carrick people turned their backs on the river afterwards, refusing to work on the water. This brought about the commercial decline of the town. An ill wind for Carrick was a fair one for Clonmel, which flourished as a result of the opportunity afforded by the need to provide services for river commerce. Clonmel is today far bigger and wealthier than Carrick.

The River Suir, the third of the Three Sisters, follows a winding course from its source in the Devilsbit near Templemore, south through Thurles and Cahir and then eastward through Clonmel and Carrick to join its two sisters at Waterford harbour. The Old Bridge in Carrick was built in 1447. For centuries, there was no crossing point downstream of Carrick, so the bridge was strategically important. Access to the city of Waterford was through the town, and much wealth was derived from tolls charged to cross here.

After buying light provisions in the town, we started the walk westward along the Suir, back to Clonmel. Walking conditions were excellent. There is a riverside park for some distance from Carrick, then a grassy track, originally used as a tow-path. A few townsfolk out for a stroll greeted us. Here and there small fishing cots were tied up at the bank. The tidal limit is at a weir about a mile above the town. Little fishermen's huts along the route provide shelter, though we had no need of them this day.

After the first mile we met only a single fisherman. This path is part of the way-marked East Munster trail, which stretches from Carrick to the Vee Gap in the Knockmealdown Mountains. Judging from the vegetation, it is not heavily used. An abundance of wild flowers added beauty to the walk, with myriad black dragonflies and orange butterflies. The river was swift after the heavy rain of the previous day. Soon we saw the first of what turned out to be a series of tower houses. A chain of watchtowers, each within sight of the next, stretches for miles along the Suir. Many of these were built by the Butlers of Ormond to oversee activities on the river and to provide early warning of any unwelcome visitors.

About five miles from Carrick we met an angler and chatted for a while. He had caught nothing, the river being too agitated, but recent fishing had been very good, he said. We asked if the path could be followed all the way to Clonmel. 'It can indeed. You have a right to walk it, and if anyone tries to stop you, tell them to fuck off.' He emphasised the last two words, smiling in delight at his own eloquence. He told us about the Merck factory upstream, 'the one that polluted all the land', and about how we could get lunch and a pint in Ike's and Mike's just a mile further on. 'There's a dance there on Sunday night, if you can wait.' However, we decided to carry on to Kilsheelan. At one point, the path degenerated into an impenetrable mass of vegetation, and we had to skirt a large field of sugar beet for about a mile before returning to the river bank.

The setting of the walk is quite beautiful. The northern hills of the Comeragh range flank the river valley to the south, while the graceful isolated Slievenamon provides an attractive vista to the north. Slievenamon (721 metres) – the Mountain of the Women, one of the enchanted mountains of Ireland – is immersed in folklore. When Finn McCool was still the most eligible bachelor in the land, all the women wanting to marry him raced up the mountain in a contest. However, Finn fancied Grainne, daughter of King Cormac, and told her the best way to win the race. Grainne, first to the top, married the mighty warrior, but later left him to elope with his nephew Diarmuit.

At a sharp bend of the river, just below Kilsheelan, stood one of the series of towers, a large one with glazed windows that appeared to be occupied. On the opposite side the Glasha River, flowing down from the Comeraghs, joins the Suir. We crossed through an old graveyard and passed a ruined church to come to the award-winning village of Kilsheelan. Here we had lunch in a small café. There were three options for continuing the walk: to follow the river, uncertain if the path would be overgrown; to climb the slope to the south, following the East Munster Way; or to take a route in between, through the estate of Gurteen le Paor. The café owner told us that Count de la Paor had died a few years before, and that the estate was being sold. 'They thought they'd live for ever, and now there's none of them left.' She said we were not supposed to cross their land, but that we might chance it if we liked. We asked about the Count. 'He mellowed a bit in his later years,' she said. I wondered aloud if this meant he had not been too popular in earlier times; she did not disagree. *De mortuis nihil nisi bonum.* A small motte built by William de Burgo in the twelfth century stands in the village. It would have had a protective palisade fence and a wooden tower at one time. Now it is a Marian shrine, funds for its construction having been provided by the Count.

We crossed the bridge and entered the estate of Gurteen le Paor. A sign read Private, but we were unsure what this meant. The estate castle stands in a pleasant sylvan setting. We skirted the castle and carried on through a large meadow. A bull, moving among the cattle, eyed us but, fortunately, was more interested in his female companions. Fields of barley were ripening in the sun. No one stopped us as we continued along the trail to a small lake. There was an eruption of ducks as we approached. Presumably, the shooting is good here. At the western limit of the track stands an elaborate gate-lodge. It appeared deserted, and the gate was locked, so we climbed the wall and followed a minor road to Twomilebridge. Here stood yet another large ruin, beside a beautiful bridge. Nearby was a large apple grove. This must provide some of the raw material for Showerings of Clonmel, who produce cider and Cidona.

The Anner River, rising near Mullinahone, the home of Charles J. Kickham, flows around the west side of Slievenamon to join the Suir near here. Slievenamon is much celebrated in story and verse. Kickham's lines were often quoted in earlier days:

> *Oh! sweet Slievenamon, you're my darling and pride,*
> *With your soft swelling bosom and mien like a bride,*
> *How oft have I wandered in sunshine and shower,*
> *From dark Kyleavalla to lonely Glenbower.*

Kickham (1828–1882), the poet and patriot, novelist and nationalist, grew up in Mullinahone. He was disfigured in a gunpowder accident at the age of fourteen and had poor health all his life. He was a founder of the Irish Republican Brotherhood, or Fenians, and was President of the IRB in the 1870s. In 1865 he was arrested and sentenced to fourteen years for treason, serving three years in Woking gaol. A fine bronze statue of Kickham, by John Hughes, stands in Tipperary town. His best known literary work is the novel *Knocknagow*, a tale of Irish rural life in the mid-nineteenth century. Subtitled 'The Homes of Tipperary', it was something of a national epic and remained the most popular book in Ireland for over half a century after Kickham's death.

There is a good river path from Twomilebridge to the town, with herons and swans providing entertainment. On the opposite bank, before the town, is the Minella Hotel, a gracious yellow building, formerly the home of the Malcolmson family, whom we met already in Portlaw. When we reached Clonmel, we had walked about 15 miles in around seven hours, a thoroughly enjoyable riverside ramble.

Clonmel, the chief town of South Tipperary, is a thriving town of about 20,000 souls, bustling with activity. There is a variety of industries – computers, pharmaceuticals and cider-making among them. Like Bunclody, the name Clonmel has a gentle musical sound – Clúain Meala, the Meadow of Honey. The town is of Anglo-Norman origin, and has several interesting buildings, the Town Hall, the Main Guard and West Gate amongst them. It was once known as the Quaker City of the South as it was the centre of a large community of the Society of Friends, who were involved in the milling industry in the eighteenth and nineteenth centuries. The Suir was a vital transport channel and barges of up to 200 tons could dock at Clonmel which, at its peak, was the largest inland trading town in the country. When a new Court House was to be built here around 1800, a resolution was issued by the Civic Authorities stating that:

1. A new Court House must be erected
2. Materials of the old building must be used for the new one
3. The old building must not be removed until the new one is completed.

This must have posed quite a conundrum for the builders.

Charles Bianconi (1786-1875) – 'the man who put Ireland on wheels' – took up residence in Clonmel in 1809. He was born at Tregolo near Lake Como, but was sent away from Italy to avoid a scandal after he became too friendly with a local girl betrothed since childhood to a nobleman. When he arrived in Ireland in 1802, public transport was almost nonexistent. After the defeat of Napoleon, horses bred for the army were going cheap. Availing of this, Bianconi set up a coach service between Clonmel and Cahir in 1815. Within thirty years a communication network with Clonmel at its hub covered most of the country. Some coaches could carry twenty passengers. Coach building became a major enterprise in Clonmel. In recognition of his efforts, Bianconi was made Mayor of the town. He was a friend of Dan O'Connell and contributed generously to funding the struggle for Catholic Emancipation. In 1834, the first Irish railway opened between Dublin and Dun Laoghaire. Bianconi saw the implications of this: he handed his headquarters over to his friend Daniel Hearn, who converted it into a hotel, and invested in various railway lines as they were built. The great coaching days were soon at an end, but long afterwards people still continued to call the coaches on Irish roads 'Bians'.

Chapter 6

WHERE THE STARS ARE BIG AND BRIGHT

I see His face in every flower;
The thunder and the singing of the birds
Are but His voice – and carven by His power
Rocks are His written words.

'I See His Blood upon the Rose' – Joseph Mary Plunkett

I WAS ACCOMPANIED ON THIS SECTION by Mark Draper, old school chum, boozing buddy, fellow bird-fancier and long-standing friend. On the way to Clonmel we stopped at Callan for lunch. This town is the birthplace of Edmund Ignatius Rice, founder of the Christian and Presentation brothers. A nice statue of Rice with a young boy stands in the main street, opposite the church. He did great good for the country, sacrificing his own comfort and wealth to provide education for the poor of Ireland at a time when it was not otherwise available. Unfortunately, huge controversy in recent times concerning the inordinate fondness of some of his followers for young boys has sullied irreparably the image of the entire movement founded by him.

Stage 19: Clonmel to Glasha

In Clonmel, we parked the car at a shop just beyond the Memorial Park dedicated to Edel Quinn, an Irish missionary who worked in East Africa until her death in 1944. Before setting off, we notified the shopkeeper that we would be walking in the region for a few days. This was to have significant repercussions later on.

Passing the Emigrant's Rest pub, we headed up Roaring Spring Road, a stiff climb. This section of the walk is on the East Munster Way, but it is poorly signposted and we didn't manage to keep to the way. As the trail evaporated in the hillside moorland, we followed a route over the pass between the hilltop and Long Hill to the east. Thus, we missed the Holy Year Cross that stands on the hilltop. We rested for a while, admiring the view over Clonmel. There is a glorious panorama from here, with the rich Golden Vale to northward, flanked by the Galtees and Slievenamon.

On the descent, we found a wonderful tunnel through rhododendron bushes. Motorcycle tracks showed that it had recently been used for scrambling. Coming to the bottom of the valley, we rested and had a snack by the Glenary River. Then, hopping over a stile, we followed the river downstream, diverting to jump another stream, and finding a small trail westward. When this veered uphill, we took a side path down to the river, a treacherously slippery slope, hoping we would not have to retrace our steps. We managed to cross the river again on stepping stones which were just visible below the rushing water. This brought us to another path with foot-deep mud. A yellow flash-sign showed we were again on the East Munster Way, but heading in the wrong direction! Anyway, we reached a tarred road as the light began to fail. With several miles still to go to Glasha, we were relieved to be out of the woods before dark. I phoned Olive O'Gorman, the landlady of the B&B, to let her know we would be late. 'And will you have dinner? There's steak, duckling or fish.' We opted for duck: it was fun to order dinner by mobile phone when we were still in the wilds. Mobile phones, so ubiquitous today, were still a novelty at this time.

I had a small torch, good enough to read a map or road sign, but not much use for anything else. As the sky blackened, a thin crescent moon appeared, accompanied by a bright 'star' which we took to be Jupiter. The lights of 'The Homes of Tipperary' twinkled to the north. We continued along minor roads, glad of the pale moonlight, and making intermittent quacking noises to spur each other towards our duck dinner. At last a sign showed our destination to be '1 km' away. I had seen such signs before, and was not surprised that we walked for about three kilometres, through the tiny village of Fourmilewater, before arriving at O'Gorman's, where a warm welcome awaited us. The en suite jacuzzi was most welcome too, and we made great use of it – sequentially, not simultaneously.

The Nire Valley extends eastward from Fourmilewater, by Ballymacarbry, up between the Comeragh and Monavullagh Mountains, the river flowing out from Coumalocha, one of the many spectacular glacial lakes in these ranges. The area is famous for rambling: the local residents have cooperated effectively to promote it as a popular holiday area, organising a walking festival each autumn, and many visitors come to walk, ride, golf and fish.

Stage 20: *Glasha to Cappoquin*

Leaving O'Gorman's at around 10.00 o'clock, we came immediately to the Nire River, small but swollen, and just over the bridge was Lonergan's Public House. It was near here in 1637 that, as a youth of ten, Robert Boyle was swept away by the raging river and almost drowned when the coach of his father Richard, First Earl of Cork, was overturned at a ford. Perhaps you recall Boyle's Law of 'the spring of air' from school physics: pressure and volume are inversely proportional for a fixed mass of gas. Boyle did not specify that the temperature must be held constant for the law to hold; presumably, he took this for granted. The law was discovered independently by a French scientist, Edme Mariott, who did state explicitly the requirement for constant temperature. Had Boyle not been snatched from the Nire we should probably have learned Mariott's Law instead, as French schoolchildren do.

As we climbed the hill we could see the Nire meandering north-westward in the open valley to the point where it joins the Suir. We left the East Munster Way here, heading south along a series of small lanes, bordered with emberried bushes. There were rosehip and blackberry – *le rouge et le noir* – sloes and wild plums. We nibbled some sorrel leaves, lemony flavoured, to pass the time. At a house by the road, a curious concrete head inserted in a gatepost was indicated on a notice to be that of J.S. Doyne, K.N.C. I have yet to find out what K.N.C. means.

We followed the road across an open heath to a coniferous forest. Coillte (I presume it was they) had craftily planted a shield of broadleaf trees around the edges of the evergreens so that, from a distance, the forest had all the gold and copper hues of autumn. We lunched in the beechwood on brown bread, corned beef and cambazola, the last a curious hybrid of camembert and gorganzola, and quaffed a bottle of Australian Shiraz.

After lunch there was a steady climb through open moorland to about 1,200 feet. Close together lay a dead fox and badger, both killed by cars and in advanced stages of decay. The fox's ribs were exposed like a ghoulish cage, his bared teeth grinning garishly in a sinister grimace. Looking up, we beheld more edifying views: the Comeraghs and Monavullaghs stood noble to the east and the peaks of the Knockmealdowns were bathed in the morning sunlight to our west. Knockmealdown means the Mountain of the Honey Fort, a name as beautiful as the hills themselves.

On the eastern slope of the Knockmealdowns stands Mount Melleray Abbey, founded in 1832 by a group of Irish monks who had been expelled from France ten years earlier. These Trappist monks, Cistercians following the strict rule of St. Benedict, lead a life of considerable austerity, one of the most penitential regimes in the Church. Near the abbey is a grotto with a marvellous Marian miracle, one of the many moving statues that were at their most dynamic in the 1970s, but that appear to have run out of steam in more recent times. The Lord moves in mysterious ways, and his Mother even more mysteriously.

We left the main road to Cappoquin and followed a minor route downhill, planning to enter the narrow valley of the Glenshelane River. After resting at a curious circular well protected by a small walled enclosure, we reached a little stream that joined the river. Crossing a field and then a small wood, we scrambled down a steep incline through dense thistle and bramble to reach the river valley, thorn-torn but triumphant. The Glenshelane flows southward through a narrow gorge. The maps showed paths on each side. If we followed the river, we should come out near Cappoquin, our target for the day. The path was in good condition except for a few muddy patches. It rose and fell like a rollercoaster, sometimes close to the river, sometimes high above it. Finding a wooden footbridge, we crossed to the west side where a good track brought us to the road near the town of Cappoquin. This walk down the Glenshelane, about 10 kilometres in length, was a truly enjoyable ramble through a mixed oak and spruce wood. In Cappoquin we hunted around for a place to stay. The first two B&Bs were full but then we found a room with Michael Doherty at Glenside, in the middle of the town. We had been walking for about six hours and covered roughly 15 miles.

After a snack in a greasy chip-shop we went into the Central Bar for refreshment. We fell into conversation with some amiable locals who were discussing the plight of the farmers. A Limerick butcher had offered £1,000 to a local farmer for 250 mountain sheep. 'I'll just take the ones I want. You can shoot the rest,' the buyer had said. We asked about Mount Melleray Abbey. There are just 40 monks there, mostly of advanced age. The school is gone now, but the tradition of hospitality continues. Travellers can stay at the hostel for just £10 per night. But for how much longer will the monks be there? There is another religious centre nearby at Glencairn Abbey with 40 nuns whose age profile is similar to that of the monks. Even if vows of celibacy did not prohibit them from combining forces, it's a bit late now to attempt survival by such natural means.

I asked one of our companions what was remarkable about Cappoquin. 'Well, there's the Blackwater, the finest salmon river in the country. And there's the chicken factory. You must have heard of Cappoquin Chickens?' I may have eaten them, but I've never heard of them, I thought silently, nodding affirmatively. There are 250 jobs in the chicken factory but a once-thriving bacon factory is now greatly 'down-scaled'. My interlocutor, Lar Loobey, turned out to be distantly related to Mark, by a complex sequence of cousins and marriages which they disentangled in a joint genealogical tour de force.

The fishing rights of the Blackwater are owned by the Duke of Devonshire, who owns Lismore Castle, just four miles upstream from Cappoquin. In 1753 the castle, together with the Boyle estates, passed to the Fourth Duke upon his marriage to Lady Charlotte Boyle. It had been bought in 1602 by the notorious land-grabber Richard Boyle, First Earl of Cork, from Walter Raleigh, who had acquired it in 1589 from another notorious rogue, the 'Vicar of Bray', Miler McGrath. The First Earl's son, Robert, the chemist and formulator of 'Boyles Law', was born in Lismore in 1627. The present castle was built by the sixth Duke of Devonshire in the early 1800s. The 'Bachelor Duke' was the richest man in England at that time, richer even than the King.

Stage 21: *Cappoquin to Clashmore*

We left Cappoquin next morning after the usual substantial breakfast, heading down the east bank of the Blackwater. We soon passed the chicken factory. From now on we would be able to answer with clear conscience, hand on heart, 'Yes, of course, not only heard of it but seen it!' if ever anyone said, 'You must have heard of Cappoquin Chickens?' What a relief! (Sadly, Cappoquin Chickens has since gone bust, so we are unlikely to be asked.)

For a short time our route was on St. Declan's Way, a marked trail between the ancient ecclesiastical centres of Ardmore and Cashel. By the middle of the fourth century the Roman Empire was generally Christian. Although Ireland was never part of the Empire, it had trade links with Britain and France, and a number of missionaries brought the Christian message to Ireland. Of course, Patrick was foremost among them and is credited with christianising the country, but he was not the first missionary. Ardmore is the oldest Christian settlement in Ireland. St. Declan lived here around 400 AD and christianised the region of Decies before the coming of Patrick. Reputedly, the two Saints met a number of times in Cashel. The Rock of Cashel was the seat of the Kings of Munster for over a thousand years, and a major ecclesiastical centre for nearly as long. The path between Declan's base at Ardmore and the Rock of Cashel became known as St. Declan's Way. Part of the path is also known as the Path of St. Patrick's Cow. The full way is about 60 miles in length.

Leaving St. Declan's Way, we turned right and soon came to the Finisk River. Here at Dromana Bridge a curious oriental gate with an onion dome straddles the road. It is known as the Hindu Gate but is more Moorish in style with a Gothic arch. Apparently, it was inspired by Brighton Pavilion and dates from 1851. Henry Villiers-Stuart was a rarity in Ireland, a popular landlord and, when he married, his tenants erected an elaborate gate of wood and papier maché over the bridge to welcome his new bride. It so thrilled her that Villiers-Stuart arranged for a permanent erection, which delighted her even more!

Nearby is Affane, where the Butlers of Ormond and the Desmond Fitzgeralds joined battle in 1565. Crossing the river we entered the former Villiers-Stuart estate of Dromana Wood. We took a digression down a lane towards the broad river. A meadow pipit twittered on a wire and a small Charolais bull eyed us suspiciously as we passed. Forced by a torrential shower to shelter in an old cow-shed, we munched sandwiches and studied the map. Coming back to the road, we passed through an avenue of laurel trees. Dromana Wood is fungus-fancier's delight. The hot and humid autumn weather seemed ideal for fungi to flourish. Puff-balls and oyster mushrooms and a whole variety of other fungi were to be seen. I photographed a relatively rare hedgehog fungus by the side of the road. We would have to look in the book to identify many of the others.

About noon we reached the village of Villierstown, established in 1740 by John Villiers, First Earl of Gradison, for the foundation of a linen industry. It was populated by linen weavers from Lurgan, but the industry did not survive the Famine. The village church, a Queen Anne building of cruciform style, with an interesting range of stained glass windows, is now a community centre. Henry Villiers-Stuart was victorious in the 1826 election, winning the parliamentary seat for Waterford when he stood for Catholic Emancipation. Villierstown is also the birthplace of John Treacy, the renowned cross-country runner who won two golds and a silver in the Olympics in 1984. John used to run from here to school in Cappoquin each day and back again, according to Lar Loobey.

The unrelenting drizzle served to accentuate the dismal air of the place. There was not a soul to be seen. The one pub, An Crúiscín Lán, was *folamh agus dúnta*. The only shop in the village, a general store cum Post Office, was closed too. We visited the church and photographed the stained glass. A recent Celtic cross outside the church and a tree, planted by Mary Robinson and standing forlorn on the village green, did little to lift the gloom. With no prospect of refreshment, we headed onward, past fields of sugar beet and cut maize, to the next village, Aglish, which has two churches and two pubs. Both the pubs were closed, so we bought some hot sausage rolls in a filling station, and guzzled them avariciously while sitting on a wall.

The remainder of the walk was in a constant heavy drizzle, a five mile hike over a low ridge with nothing much to see and not much to break the monotony. The biggest excitement was meeting a farmer and his son bringing the cattle in for milking. We plodded on until we reached Clashmore, where we planned to stay for the night. As we reached the village, we came to the old church ruin, which was to be converted to a heritage centre. Here workmen were cutting down a giant ash tree, some 80 feet high, lest it fall through the yet-to-be-built roof of the church. Clashmore is a pretty village, with the Holy Well of St. Mocha, a shop and four pubs: The Decies, The Rising Sun, The Coopers and The Old Still.

An unusual square chimney stands in the village, by the little river Creagagh. It belonged to the old still, which produced 20,000 gallons of whiskey annually. Once, when excise officers raided the still and dumped a large quantity of whiskey into the river the cows downstream – you've guessed it – all got drunk. One of the earliest abbeys in South Munster, after Ardmore and Lismore, was established in Clashmore, on the site where the present church stands. Following the Dissolution of the Monasteries, the Abbey and lands passed to Sir Walter Raleigh.

We stepped into The Rising Sun for a drink, and then headed the '1 km' to Marlia, the farm bungalow of Mary and Liam Curran, who have a B&B service for travellers such as ourselves. I had phoned ahead from Aglish to book a room here. The 'one kilometre' took half an hour, in failing light and pouring rain. Our hosts were most hospitable and, after a wash and a meal, we had an enjoyable evening of conversation. Liam was planning to take part in a protest march in Dublin the next day. The farmers were looking for compensation for the low beef prices and for the effects of the dreadful summer weather. The protest was the main item on the news. Another TV programme dealt with the surprisingly low level of income tax paid by farmers when compared with 'city folk'. Clearly, while many farmers were in trouble, some were doing pretty well.

Stage 22: Clashmore to Youghal

After a slap-up breakfast, including lamb's liver from Curran's own farm, we set out for Youghal. But first we digressed to explore the Kilmaloo Walk. We left the town by the grotto built in 1971 and dedicated to Our Lady of the Wayside, and climbed a steep hill past the GAA grounds. At the crest of the hill we came to the remains of an old lime-kiln. Limestone quarried locally was burned with charcoal to produce quicklime, used to reduce the acidity of the soil. Descending to Bally-heeny Bridge we crossed the Lickey River, dedicated, according to Mark, to Sappho, the poetess of Lesbos. As we climbed the road, the ruins of Heeney Castle were visible across the river. We continued up the hill and then crossed a stile up a steep path, bordered by hawthorn and ash trees heavy with berries.

We came then to one of the three ice houses in this area. The struc-ture was about twenty feet high, completely overgrown with bracken and brambles. Ice cut from a lake nearby during the winter was stored in this large igloo-like structure, which had cavity walls to protect it from the summer heat. The door would be sealed with clay and reeds. The ice was used by salmon exporters in Clashmore and Youghal to preserve fish dur-ing transport. Blackwater Salmon, shipped in ice, was a prized speciality of high society restaurants in London and farther afield. I reckoned that the ice house would have held about 500 tons of ice when full. We carried on in a circular loop to Kilmaloo Lake, once the source of the ice but now drained dry. It must have been tough and risky work cutting ice in the harsh winter weather and hauling it to the ice houses for storage.

The path just west of Kilmaloo Lake is not marked on Sheet 82. The lake itself is marked on the map, despite its having been drained years ago. Luckily, I had picked up a leaflet in Curran's that gave details of the walk, so we managed to follow the route. However, we were not quite so lucky later. After the diversion to the ice houses, we headed westward towards the Blackwater and Youghal. We planned to get to Youghal Bridge by back lanes but somehow, falling between Sheet 82 and Sheet 81, we took a wrong turn at Tiknock and, descending a steep hill by a rushing stream, came out onto the N25 a mile east of the bridge. We followed the main road round the river, past the old bridgehead. Then, crossing the new bridge, built in 1963, we jumped up and down shouting in celebration at our arrival in County Cork. Another look at the map indicated that we were prancing prematurely, being still in Waterford. Rincrew Bridge across the River Tou-rig had to be crossed before we were in 'The Texas of Ireland'.

The tall chimney of the Youghal Brick Factory still stands near the bank of the Tourig just upstream. Here we left the road again to follow a dike around the river's edge at a place called Foxhole. Snipe rose in bursts, and a variety of waterfowl that feed here took wing as we advanced. The old bridge, now pier-like and disappointed, juts out into the river. We followed a path south along the river, on an embankment cutting off a large salt-marsh. A number of large waders were busy there, which we first took to be curlews but then recognised as black-tailed godwits. Suddenly, Mark spotted a large white bird perching in the marsh. We stood for a while peering and saw that he had a long black beak. As we approached, he rose and winged away with slow and gracious flight. It was a little egret, once unknown in Ireland but now becoming more common, breeding in a few places along the south coast.[5] These are beautiful birds, like herons in shape but smaller, completely white, and more gregarious in nature. They have the most magnificent Latin designation, *Egretta Garzetta*. What a wonderful name for a stripper. With this thought, we proceeded into Youghal to see what delights were on offer there.

Youghal is a pleasant tourist centre and a town with interesting historical connections. The name means Yew Wood, though most of the forest hereabouts was cut down by Walter Raleigh & Co. and exported for ship planks. The town spreads along the steep west bank of the Blackwater estuary. A long sand spit juts out from the opposite bank, reaching like a finger for the town. The distance across to Ferry Point is only about 400 yards, or should I say two cables. A Viking settlement here was destroyed by the Deisi clan in 864. The town really got going when the Normans arrived in 1173 and the Fitzgeralds, the Earls of Desmond, were Head Honchos on and off for the next 400 years. Stout town walls were built and trade links established with ports all over western Europe: wine, salt and spices inward and wool, timber, meat and fish outward. A beacon light to guide vessels into port has shone from the high river bank since the twelfth century. The current lighthouse, built in 1852, still serves this vital role.

---

[5] They have since spread widely throughout the country.

In the 1580s the English drove out the Desmonds and 'awarded' the lands here, including Youghal and Lismore, to Walter Raleigh. Raleigh, an explorer, courtier and man of letters was, depending on your point of view, one of the most colourful characters or one of the most scurrilous adventurers of Elizabethan times. He was Mayor of Youghal for a few years, and lived in Myrtle Grove, where he allegedly planted the first potatoes in Europe. He had of course introduced both spuds and smokes from the New World. The potato was to have a major impact in Ireland. It enabled subsistence on a tiny holding and contributed to a population explosion over the next 150 years. But the complete dependence on the crop had disastrous consequences when it failed repeatedly during the Famine. Thus, the potato was a mixed blessing for Ireland. Tobacco, on the other hand, was an unmitigated curse.

Raleigh was chummy with the poet Edmund Spenser, who had also grabbed some land nearby. Spenser wrote much of *The Faerie Queen* during the time he lived in Cork. In 1602, Raleigh sold his 40,000 acres to Richard Boyle, later First Earl of Cork, for £1,500. In the course of the Plantation of Munster, Boyle acquired a vast acreage when the Irish landowners were expropriated, and he brought over settlers from England to populate his ill-gotten lands.

A tall clock tower straddles the Main Street, at the site of the old Trinity Gate. Built in 1777 it served for a time as a prison, and several United Irishmen were hanged from its windows in 1798. Later, in 1846, there were serious riots in the town when grain exports were interrupted. The export of food from Ireland at this time was an abominable atrocity. Emigration during and after the Famine halved the population of Youghal to 6,000 by 1900. With the development of deep water facilities at Cork and Waterford, the importance of Youghal as a port declined. Lace-making, pottery and brick-making grew in importance and, later, a carpet factory which was busy until 1984 when market forces caused it to close.

Although the Golden Age of Youghal is gone, it is still a delightful place. There is an excellent visitor centre on the waterfront near the Clock Tower, with many interesting exhibits and a good scale model of the town. It is there that I acquired the historical information related above. I also picked up a glossy brochure about birdwatching in East Cork, depicting our friend *Egretta Garzetta*, the Stripper of Youghal. We entered Moby Dick's Pub nearby for a drink. Youghal was the setting when Gregory Peck starred as Captain Ahab in John Huston's epic film of Herman Melville's 'cracking sea-tale' in 1954. The pub walls are plastered with memorabilia of the film. We chatted with a local, who confided candidly "'Twasn't much of a film anyway; sure, 'twas a flop'. Having seen the film many years ago, I was inclined to agree that it was not one of Huston's best.

We stayed in the Walter Raleigh Hotel, which had recently been re-furbished and was very comfortable and excellent value (£25 per person sharing). The room overlooked Youghal Harbour and the Memorial Park dedicated to the memory of Fr. O'Neill who was 'cruelly flogged by British soldiers' during the '98 Rebellion. Is there another way to flog someone?

Stage 23: *Youghal to Ladysbridge*

On a glorious bright morning we set off up the hill from the Walter Raleigh Hotel. An attractive lighthouse stands by the road at the south end of the town. From here there was a magnificent vista over Youghal Harbour, with the sunlight glinting on the waters of the bay, and Capel Island just off Knockadoon Head to the south. Rounding the corner we could see the old railway station, now sadly derelict, and the golden sands of Youghal strand, a Blue Flag beach stretching for miles to westward. Nearby is Perk's Amusement Arcade. Here you can 'Meet Perky Bear, the Fun of the Fair', at least during the summer months.

From the ruined red-brick Station House we started out along the disused railway. The 20 mile line from Cork to Youghal was opened in 1860. Original plans to extend it to Waterford were never realised. A branch line to Cobh is still operating, but the Youghal line closed to passenger traffic in 1963. Until then, Youghal was a popular seaside re-sort for Corkonians. As the terminus is situated somewhat south of the town, day-trippers probably brought their picnic lunches with them and may not have brought much benefit to local commerce. Still, it is sad to see a line with such potential lying derelict. For long stretches the rails have been pulled up. The line has not been officially abandoned by Irish Rail so perhaps there is some faint hope of development in the future.

There was talk at the time of re-opening the section between Cork and Midleton.[6]

For the initial stretch, the line was overgrown and waterlogged but soon the way became clear. The track ran through the extensive Ballyvergan reed-beds. Ballyvergan is one of the largest continuous reed-beds in Ireland. The glossy bird brochure that we had picked up in Youghal told us to watch out here for reed warblers, sedge warblers and water rails. We saw none of these, but several goldfinches and two reed buntings (another first for me) who brazenly ignored our approach, sitting boldly on a bush even as we passed very close to them.

After the first few miles there are no rails or sleepers, but the way was firm and clear and a joy to ramble on. At the end of the reed-bed the track entered a low cutting and became hellishly overgrown. Mark was in bush-whacking mood and slashed wildly at the dense thorn bushes. But progress was slow and painful and we soon decided to abandon the track. We climbed up at a bridge but found that it led nowhere. Checking later we saw it was marked on the old half-inch Sheet 22 but not on Sheet 81. More bush-whacking through bramble and thorn was unavoidable. In this inaccessible stretch the rails had not been lifted. The line was badly waterlogged and progress involved a delicate dance from sleeper to slippery sleeper, avoiding deep pools of water between. It requires great agility to remain vertical while hacking through hawthorn, balancing on greasy logs, and we were not entirely successful. At last we came to another bridge and climbed up to the road.

Rambling along the quiet country road was a joy after the dense undergrowth of the railway. Meadowsteet and purple vetch and scabius and woodbine adorned the roadside. We came to a little stream and sat on the bridge to rest and enjoy a snack. The Womanagh river flowed eastward to our south and we came to a tributary, the Finisk, near where two small pill boxes guarded the road. We wondered when they were built: probably during the Black and Tan era. A small lake, Ballyhonock Lough, could be seen to the south. Then we came to the River Dower, which seemed both from the map and in reality to spring from nowhere. Perhaps it is an underground river, or perhaps just a backwater of the Womanagh. A

---

[6] And, happily, trains are now running again to Midleton.

large building was visible across the valley, which we later identified as Ightermurragh Castle. In a farmyard we spotted some shaggy inkcaps. As the name suggests, these mushrooms were once used for making ink. Apparently, they are edible but react with alcohol like a primitive form of antabuse or anti-booze.

We came next to a sign reading Bridgefield Buggies. At Bridgefield Farm you could rent an ATV – an All Terrain Vehicle – and drive around a rough, hilly and challenging track, 'the ultimate cross-country driving experience'. Since we were already enjoying 'the ultimate cross-country walking experience', we passed on towards Ladysbridge. There was great activity in the fields. The sugar beet crop was being harvested and trailers laden with beet passed us on the road regularly. After a while we came to Carewswood Garden Centre, set in a sixteenth century walled garden. We enquired about accommodation but could not get any useful information, so we headed on into Ladysbridge and hove up to The Bridge Inn. We fell into conversation there with John (New) Holland and Paddy Murray, local Fountains of Knowledge. They explained the origin of the Irish name of the village, Driochead na Scuab, the Bridge of Brooms. They told us that the villagers beat the Black and Tans off the bridge into the river with brooms. 'And why is it Ladysbridge?' we asked. 'Sure, 'twas the wimmen was holdin' de brushes!'

We were heading for Cobh, which meant either going round by Midleton or finding a way across the harbour to Great Island. We asked about the chances of a boat-ride across. This generated an animated debate the result of which was that we had little chance. One man said we should make for Lower Aghada. Someone else ludicrously suggested Ballycotton. The best bet seemed to be to head for East Ferry and try to pick up a lift across, but the likelihood of success was small. Leaving the pub, we promised to send a postcard from Cobh if we ever made it. Walking out the '1 km' to Mary Murphy's B&B we fell into conversation with a farmer on his way home from the village. We asked him to confirm the origin of the name Ladysbridge. 'I don't know. Dere's no ladies here anyway, only a few oul' biddies.' What lady would stand a chance against such irresistible charm? Mary Murphy's house is called Allabri. I guessed that she had children called, maybe, Alice, Laura and Brian. But no, the name is for

Allan, Larkin and O'Brien, the Manchester Martyrs, who were executed in 1867. One of them, Michael O'Brien, was born in Ladysbridge and a small Celtic cross in the village commemorates them.

Stage 24: *Ladysbridge to Ballinacurra*

Before setting out for Cobh, we detoured to see Ightermurragh Castle, a fortified house near Mary Murphy's B&B. In the early seventeenth century the Seneschal, or Stewart of Imokilly, a man called Fitzgerald, having no male heirs, divided his lands between his three daughters. The two eldest having chosen, by seniority, the better higher lands, the youngest, Margaret, said '*Agus an t-iochtar mo rogha*', the lower is my choice. Hence the name Iochtar mo Rogha or Ightermurragh. Margaret married Edmund Supple, a local landowner, and they built a large castle. But in the very year of its completion, 1641, they were forced to flee for their lives during the Great Rebellion.

The castle was large, of cruciform shape, about sixty feet high, with five floors. Over a fireplace on the first floor is a Latin inscription which reads 'Edmund Supple and Margaret Gerald, whom love binds in one, built this house in 1641'. It was one of the last castles to be built in Ireland. It is a very fine edifice and appears structurally sound. Perhaps renovation would not be an impossibility but for the time being only the rooks and pigeons have their home here.

In Ladysbridge we stocked up at the village store and then set out over a low sandstone ridge towards Cloyne. This is one of several ridges in south Munster that separate the river valleys. Originally a flat layer of limestone overlaid older sandstone. At some time in the distant past, seismic convulsions crumpled the land into a series of huge corrugations, oriented more or less east–west. The limestone tops of the ridges weathered away over the aeons, exposing the lower rocks, so that now old red sandstone on the ridges alternates with limestone in the valleys. Large rivers flow eastward along the valleys – the Blackwater, the Lee and the Bandon. A casual glance at a relief map of the region would suggest that the Blackwater should reach the sea at Dungarvan, the Lee below Youghal and the Bandon at Crosshaven. But, for reasons unclear, each of these rivers has a change of heart, and they turn suddenly southward towards the sea through narrow gorges in relatively higher ground. The bend in the Blackwater at Cappoquin is particularly striking. Geologists do not appear to have a convincing explanation of this behaviour, though there are several theories.

Cloyne, or Clúain Úamha (Meadow of Caves, from the limestone caves nearby) was granted to St. Colman by the King of Cashel in 580 as a site for a monastery, and has been an important ecclesiastical centre ever since. St. Colman's was the Cathedral of the Church of Ireland diocese of Cloyne, later amalgamated into Cork, Cloyne and Ross. The present building, dating from the thirteenth century, was extensively renovated in the eighteenth. The famous Cross of Cloyne, a gilt bronze cross from about 1100 AD was found in the Cathedral precincts in 1885 and is now in the National Museum in Dublin.

George Berkeley (1684-1753) was Bishop of Cloyne for eighteen years from 1734. A renowned philanthropist and man of culture, he was Ireland's foremost philosopher. His courtesy and upright character made him a universal favourite, and he did much to better the lot of the residents of Cloyne. Berkeley wrote on the efficacy of tar-water as a treatment for smallpox, and was critical of the infinitesimals of Newton's calculus, calling them 'the ghosts of departed quantities'. More solidly, he formulated the concept of mind as the centre and spring of the universe. His philosophy may be summarised in the aphorism 'It's all in the mind', for he postulated that material objects have no existence apart from mind. In 1752 he left Cloyne to live with his son in Oxford, and he died there the following year. There is a memorial to Berkeley in the Cathedral in Cloyne. A plaque on the Cathedral wall reads:

As a Philosopher he loved the Truth
As an Irishman he loved his Native Land
As a Bishop he loved his Flock
As a Man of God he loved Cloyne.

A round tower opposite the Cathedral dates from the tenth century. Such towers, peculiar to Ireland, served as belfrys, lookouts and refuges in times of attack. Cloyne's tower is built of sandstone and is about ninety feet high. The conical cap is no longer on the tower. It is possible to climb

up inside, but we did not have the energy for this vertical digression. Instead, we headed west past the statue of Christy Ring, the eminent hurler,
born in Cloyne. Heading towards Cork Harbour, we missed a shortcut
through Castlemary and so came to the R630, the Midleton-Whitegate
road, turning north on this busy road to Saleen. The sight of a goldcrest
compensated for the detour. We also spotted evidence of eco-activity in a
sign reading Ni Maith Linn PYLONS. Skirting through a wood we emerged
at Saleen to be greeted by some children playing. 'Are ye eeeco-warriors?'
they asked. Mark's affirmative nod elicited the response, 'I don't believe
yeh. Yer not durty enough!' We took some comfort from this, and headed
out the south bank of the peninsula towards East Ferry.

Cork Harbour is a twitcher's paradise, with several mud-flats, estu-
arine channels and brackish lagoons which are excellent birding sites.
Saleen Creek is the haunt of a large variety of waders and waterfowl. It
is a good place to sit quietly, sweeping the shore with binoculars. As we
rambled out along the creek we saw no fewer than four little egrets out
on the mud. The air was resonant with the calls of curlews, oystercatchers
and numerous other water birds.

As the evening was darkening, we pressed on to the end of the peninsula, where the Ballinacurra River separated us from Great Island and
Cobh. We had hoped to hitch a ride across from some kind-hearted angler or yachtsman, but there was nothing moving. Just 250 metres separated us from our goal, but it looked as if the Fountains of Knowledge
in Ladysbridge were right: we would not find anyone to bring us across.
We came to Murph's Pub and went in for rest and recreation. Here the
landlady confirmed that our plan was hopeless. She said we would have
to head back towards Midleton, told us where we could get a bed and
kindly phoned to arrange it for us.

Thus we arrived at Loughcarrick House in Ballinacurra, the home of
Brian and Cheryl Byrne, after a long slog back the north side of the Saleen
Peninsula on a dark road. They welcomed us and provided much-needed
refreshments. Brian owns a boat, the Lagosta II, available for charter, and
specialises in wreck, reef and shark fishing. Since trawlers avoid wrecks
like the plague, the sea-bed around them is like an oasis, with many large
and exotic fish, and anglers have a good chance of catching record-break-

ing specimens. Brian has won the 'Skipper of the Year' award repeatedly for his angling skills. But that is nothing: Mark could boast that he had recently been awarded the 'Salmon Rusty Cup' for the lowest catch in an exclusive fishing competition in Dun Laoghaire.

Return to Clonmel

Over breakfast next morning, leafing through the guest book, I saw that Derek Davis was among the first visitors when Brian and Cheryl began taking guests. He had left the modest comment, 'At last, a Master in the master bedroom!' As the weather was miserable, with pouring rain, we accepted the offer of a lift from Brian to Midleton. There we caught a bus to Cork and, after a three-hour wait, which gave us a chance to mosey around the town, another bus – the 007 – brought us, via Fermoy, Michelstown, Ballyporeen, Clogheen and Ardfinnan, back to Clonmel. There we had sustenance in Sean Tierney's Pub in O'Connell Street. Tierney's is the consistent winner of the Tipperary Pub of the Year award. Inside, the pub was like a miniature museum, with an interesting collection of artefacts. The atmosphere was warm and welcoming and the food tasty.

After the heavy rain, the River Suir was in spate and was pounding the upstream side of the bridge. We returned to the car to find a note on the windscreen. Carefully unfolding the sodden paper, we discovered that the Gardaí wished us to call into the station 'to collect some property'. The shopkeeper, whom we had notified earlier in the week of our plans, had been worried when we had not returned sooner, and had notified the Guards. They had examined the car and taken some papers for identification. So, our families had been contacted, causing some concern and not a little confusion.

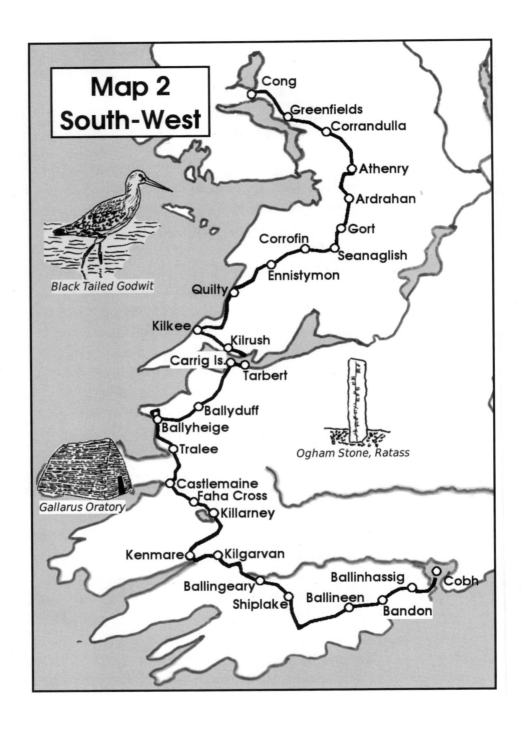

Map 2
South-West

Black Tailed Godwit

Ogham Stone, Ratass

Gallarus Oratory

Cong
Greenfields
Corrandulla
Athenry
Ardrahan
Gort
Corrofin
Seanaglish
Ennistymon
Quilty
Kilkee
Kilrush
Carrig Is.
Tarbert
Ballyduff
Ballyheige
Tralee
Castlemaine
Faha Cross
Killarney
Kenmare
Kilgarvan
Ballingeary
Shiplake
Ballinhassig
Ballineen
Bandon
Cobh

15 May 2011 Eileen and I are having an easy day after Eleanor s wedding at Finstown House.

Mon.16 may 2011 To-day I assisted Tony Donnelly, Joe O'Toole, Morgan Sharpe, & Eddie Creevy, in painting the entrance wall to the Grove, I also cut back the hedge in the front garden after frost & Snow damage last winter. Tuesday 17 May 2011 Brought hedge cuttings for re-cycling to Bally mount. Wed. Went walking saw Queen Elizabeth 11. leaving Memorial Park during her state visit at Island Bridge. Thursday went to Henry St. with Eileen and to the Old Stand for a drink. Friday I went to see Jacinta and Barry, then I went walking in the Phoenix Park and I had a pint in the Villager. Sat.21 I Planted bedding plants in the borders at the Grove entrance for the tidy towns competition. Went to evening Mass with Eileen. Sunday I went walking with Anoige . Ballinastoe wood to Knockree Hostel via Maulin, J.B. Malone memorial walk. Garrett Fitzgerrald was laid to rest in Shanganagh Cemeterery , Shankill R.I.P. Monday U. S. President Barak Obama arrived in the Poenix Park for a one day visit, Eileen & I watched the visit on TV.

Chapter 7

THE REBEL HEARTLAND

The Cliona, the Meabh and the Macha,
The pride of the Irish Navy.
When the captain he blows on his whistle
All the sailors go home for their tea.

'The Irish Navy' – The Dubliners

WE DROVE TO CORK, IN OVERCAST AND misty weather, with intermittent heavy drizzle. Having parked the car at the railway station,
we took the 15:00 train to Cobh. This is a delightful rail journey, along the
north shore of Lough Mahon, then crossing a long viaduct to Fota Island
and Fota Wildlife Park, a 70 acre park with giraffe, zebra, antelope and
monkeys. From the train we saw only a flock of flamingoes. Or is flock the
correct collective? A pinkitude, perhaps? No, a flamboyance of flamingoes seems just right. Crossing to Great Island, the train passed the IFI
fertiliser factory at Marino Point, and then followed the shore of the West
Passage past the ferry pier at Carrigaloe. The ferry to Glenbrook provides
a handy route between Cobh and Cork city. Passing the high cranes of the
old Verolme Shipyard, the train turned east to the terminus at Cobh.

We checked into Westbourne House, a small hotel that charged us
£12 each for bed and breakfast. Not bad! The lady of the house asked
where we had come from. 'Ah, from Kingstown to Queenstown,' said she
on hearing we were from Dun Laoghaire. 'There was a boat train between
them long ago,' she recalled. The hotel overlooks the harbour, with the
island of Haulbowline just across the water. Haulbowline has been the
headquarters of the Irish Navy since 1940 (the origin of the name is ob-

scure; it is marked on older maps as Holboling Island). Our plan was to take the Navy tender across to the island next morning. But how to get permission? The tender was tied up at the quay directly opposite the hotel. I spoke to the pilot, who told me to enquire further from the Duty Coxwain. He advised me to phone the Master-at-Arms Office and ask for the Warrant Officer. Phoning the Warrant Officer, Pat O'Sullivan, I mentioned that Mark and I were both formerly enlisted in An Slúa Maraí, the Irish Naval Reserve. During the sixties we had boldly defended the coasts of Ireland, so effectively that not a single hostile invasion had taken place. In apparent recognition of our services to the State, Pat O'Sullivan gave us clearance to travel over on the tender the next morning.

At the time we were in the Slúa Maraí, the Navy was chronically under-funded, the entire fleet comprising three Second World War corvettes – the Macha, the Maebh and the Cliona – seldom simultaneously seaworthy. The Navy was a regular butt of derision; Brendan Behan said it was the only Navy in the world in which you could cycle home for lunch. The story of the Navy around that time is told in Jim ('Masher') Brady's hilarious and irreverent book *The Irish Navy – What a Life*. Brady has brilliantly caught the language and atmosphere of life amongst the ratings. Beneath the ribaldry is a genuine affection and respect for the men who kept the service going in impossible circumstances. The book reminded me of the time we spent at Fort Camden near Crosshaven. Due to the lack of vessels, a huge deception was maintained in which the Fort was treated as a ship: the floor was the deck, the kitchen the galley, the toilets the heads. Sleeping billets were occupied by 'First Starboard Watch', etc. I recall a Petty Officer entering the billet and roaring at one of our 'shipmates' who was gazing longingly through the window at the girls outside: 'Get your head out of that port-hole.' During my brief service, Fort Camden was 'the only ship I ever did see'. Things are much better now and the Navy has a respectable fleet, though I suspect that it is still under-resourced.

Stage 25: *Marlogue to Cobh (in reverse)*

On our previous excursion we had walked out to the end of the Saleen Peninsula, hoping for a lift across the Ballinacurra Channel. Failing to find any movement on the water, we had had recourse to a pint in

Murph's, and the landlady had found us a B&B with Brian and Cheryl Byrne. The only unbreakable rule of the Commodius Vicus was that the journey be continuous in space if not in time. So, there remained the segment of the journey from Marlogue, at the eastern end of Great Island, to Cobh to be completed. Being now in Cobh, we decided to make this journey in reverse.

We climbed the hill above the town and found a minor road to the north of the island. The hedgerows were lush spring green, with an abundance of whitethorn blossom, brightened by stitchwort, violets and primroses. The island land looked rich and fertile. By the road a large makeshift sign read 'What Goes Up Must Come Down', another indication of the resistance to power pylons in this neighbourhood. Coming to the north shore, we followed the road by the water's edge. Shelducks were feeding in the reeds, and a lone egret flew lazily along the horizon. We soon saw a Martello tower standing on a hillock. This is one of about six in this region, built around the same time as those near Dublin, but different in style. We passed a small castle with an incongruous satellite dish on the roof. Beyond stood a lime kiln in good condition. As we neared the end of the island, the light began to fail. Considering it unattractive to walk back in darkness, we headed for the Marlogue Inn at East Ferry Marina, a restaurant by the water's edge. At the marina there were about twenty yachts moored, but little activity. Standing at the pier, we looked across the channel, a few tens of metres wide, to the Saleen Peninsula and the little church we had passed months earlier, and to Murph's pub. Allowing for this short aquatic gap, the journey was now complete to Cobh.

We enjoyed a delicious turkey and ham dinner in the Marlogue Inn, served up by Paddy from Ringsend. A five pound taxi ride brought us back to Cobh. We asked the driver to drop us at the east end of the town. As he gave me change of ten pounds for my twenty, he blew his chance of a tip. This area is known as the Holy Ground and was once a great place for naughty nautical fun and frolics. It was all but deserted this evening, but the walk along the waterfront was a delight, with the buildings stacked up in tiers, crested by the beautifully flood-lit cathedral with its tall spire. St. Coleman's Cathedral was designed by Pugin and Ashlin, in the French Gothic style. Made of Dalkey granite, it took 47 years to build, being completed in 1915 and has a famous carillon of 49 bells. It is dedicated to St. Colman (522–604), the Patron of the Diocese of Cloyne.

The town of Cobh has a spectacular setting, overlooking one of the world's finest natural harbours. Cobh has a long history as an important port. It was the main departure point for emigrants to America and convicts to Australia. The Cove of Cork was renamed Queenstown in 1849 when Queen Victoria came by, and renamed Cobh in 1921. The maritime history of the port is retold in the Queenstown Story, a 'stunning multimedia exhibition' at Cobh's restored Victorian railway station. Here we got some idea of conditions aboard the Famine coffin ships. Some three million emigrants departed from Ireland through Cobh since Famine times. We learned something of the life of the convicts, who were held aboard hulks in the harbour before transportation to Van Diemen's Land or Botany Bay. In all, 40,000 convicts were transported to Australia, many for mere misdemeanours. There is also an exhibit on the ill-starred Titanic, whose last port of call was at Cobh four days before it went down; and another on the Lusitania, sunk by a torpedo from the German submarine U20 in May 1915 with a loss of over 1,000 lives. Visitors to the exhibition also get a taste of the luxury of the great ocean liners that called at Cobh up to the 1960s.

There are several very interesting old military installations around the harbour. Carlisle and Camden Forts, now officially called Davis and Meagher, were built around 1798 to guard the harbour mouth. Fort Westmoreland, now renamed Fort Mitchel, is on Spike Island. The island was a penal station where many convicts, John Mitchel amongst them, were held en route to Australia. Under the Treaty Ports Agreement, Spike Island remained under British control until 1938, long after independence. Ireland's first yacht club, the Royal Cork Yacht Club, was established in Cobh in 1720. The original, Italianate clubhouse is now a tourist office. A monument to the Lusitania, by sculptor Jerome Connor, stands in the town square. Many of the victims of that disaster lie buried in Cobh cemetery.

As we returned to our lodgings, we passed the more upmarket Commodore Hotel. The propellor of the M.V. Samson, a huge bronze piece about nine feet in diameter, stands outside the hotel. This was taken from a crane barge wrecked on the Waterford coast. The wreckage of the Samson is still on the rocks near Ardmore and is an impressive sight.

Stage 26: Cobh to Ballinhassig

We crossed the road from Westbourne House to the quay and awaited the Navy tender to take us across to Haulbowline. A small craft pulled up to the pier at 10:30 on the dot. She was named Fuinnseoig (Ash), although Fuiseog (Lark), for the Navy Lark, might have been more apposite. At the end of the short crossing we were met by a leading seaman, who escorted us across the base. Another Martello tower stands high above the base. Half of Haulbowline was occupied by the Navy, the other half by ISPAT, Irish Steel. A bridge on the south side links it, via the tiny Rocky Island, to the mainland near Ringaskiddy. We nosed around Rocky Island, where the remains of a barracks and magazine still stand.

Yet another Martello tower stands on the hill above Ringaskiddy, and we decided to head for it. As we climbed the hill, larks sang in the morning sun, and a snipe rose suddenly from the grass in a white-striped flash. The deep-water terminal at Ringaskiddy was now below us. Reaching the hill-top we found that the Martello tower was surrounded by a deep moat, something I had not seen before for these towers. The towers around Cork Harbour are cylindrical, not tapered like those in Dublin, and have flat wall-tops, not the gracious bevelled finish of the latter. I have to say that, in aesthetic terms, the Dublin towers win hands-down. In terms of defensive efficacy, who can say? They were never put to the test.

We headed down the hill and followed a small road westward, passing through the Ringaskiddy Industrial Zone, where there are several pharmaceutical and chemical plants. The most noteworthy of these is Pfizer, the producer of Viagra, the Pfizer Riser. One experiences a certain uplift when breathing the exhilarating airs of this region. We soon passed a large ruin, Barnahely Castle, once home to the de Cogans. Further on we came to the gate of Coolmore House, where there stand about ten gracious little estate houses with tall Tudor chimneys. And as we approached the town of Carrigaline, we spied on a hill the birthplace of James Fitzmaurice, who in 1579 led the great Munster Revolt against Elizabeth I. This was the ruin of Carrigaline Castle. In the estuary of the

Owenboy river to the south is Drake's Pool where, according to the *Shell Guide to Ireland*, Francis Drake once hid from a Spanish fleet.

When we reached Carrigaline a heavy shower began, so we ran into the first hostelry, Collins' Bar, and had lunch. Soon the rain cleared and we continued out the Kinsale road, climbing a hill and branching off to the north in search of the Abbey. Finding nothing at the spot marked on the map, we continued to Ballea Bridge, where we could admire the vista up the valley to Ballea Castle, one of the few castles in the locality occupied as a private residence. We then followed a small road along the ridge that forms the south bank of the Owenboy River valley. Owenboy is Abhann Buí, or Yellow River; you might say, the Hwang Ho of County Cork. After a few miles, we sat by an old church for a rest. Opposite was a standing stone, one of hundreds in this area. An aircraft flew low over us on final approach to Cork Airport, not far to the North.

Chiff-chaffs made their presence known by their characteristic if monotonous calls. Willow-warblers were also in abundance hereabouts, with their more melodious songs. We saw neither of these birds, who have lurking ways and are difficult to distinguish when they do appear. At an unnamed crossroads we noted a complex shrine. The Saviour appeared in various manifestations, from infant in arms through child of Prague to grown man, then on the Cross and finally in glory. We dubbed the spot 'The Cross of the Five Saviours'. The road soon veered away and we kept straight on along a dirt track and through a farm complex, climbing four or five gates, to come to the road near Ballinhassig. Here we found Kirby's Korner, a pub painted bright pink.

We went into the pub and felt instantly welcome. A fire blazed in the hearth and the warmth was also evident from the lady of the house and from the handful of locals who chatted with us in a friendly manner. They were amazed when Mark told them I was walking around Ireland. 'You must be a shkilled walker, are you?' asked Mrs Kirby. 'Well, I learned when I was very young,' I answered. After refreshments in Kirby's, we bought some food in the shop next door and headed for our accommodation in a downpour. We stayed at Ardfield a comfortable B&B on a farm at Gogginshill, where horses are bred and trained for show-jumping. Bernadette Murphy made us welcome and loaned me a copy of Daphne Pochin Mould's book on County Cork, a mine of interesting local information.

Stage 27: Ballinhassig to Bandon

We left Bernadette Murphy's about 9.00 o'clock, equipped with Hillpigs and torch. The Hillpigs I will describe anon; the torch we had bought in Cobh, to enable us to pass through a long railway tunnel. It was a nifty little torch, made in China. On the box it was described as a heavy-duty anodized aluminium torch of sleek, high-tech design. The enclosed leaflet commended the lucky purchaser: 'Congratulations. You now own a top-quality product – thoroughly tested to meet our exacting quality control standards.' Not bad for a fiver.

Climbing Gogginshill we spotted a broad, squat chimney-like structure in a field. This is one of the three ventilation shafts of the railway tunnel. We passed a road unmarked on the map and found a farm track that led down to the valley near the northern end of the tunnel. Gogginshill Tunnel is about 900 yards long and, since it curves, is completely dark within. The vent shafts, about three metres across, shed a diffuse light at three points. The way was mainly dry, though water from the heavy rain poured down the ventilation shafts. We reached the end of the tunnel, which was made wide enough for a double track, and came to Ballinhassig Station. The old station house remains, and the platforms, but that is about all. Kevin Cronin described it as a contender for the title 'most inaccessible station in Ireland', as it stands on a slope too steep for wheeled access.

An aerial ropeway from the brickworks at Ballinphelic, three miles east, to the railway at Ballinhassig once carried bricks westward and coal eastward. The brickworks closed in 1912, but the aerial ropeway is marked on my half-inch Sheet 25, dated 1968. However, we found no trace of this industrial curiosity, which is not marked on the modern 1:50,000 map (sheet 86 or 87).

We were planning to follow the old course of the railway to Crossbarry. According to Rowledge in A Regional History of Railways, the Cork and Bandon Railway was 'a miserable concern with a parsimonious director-ship which tolerated frequent breakdowns of ancient engines until the reality had to be faced that railway equipment does wear out and needs renewal'. The line between Ballinhassig and Bandon opened in 1849. The connection to Cork was due to open in June, 1851 but, as the contractors had not been paid, men were sent out to make the line unusable. Rails were ripped up and the line covered with rubble. In the ensuing court case, Isaac Butt represented the defendants, who were found not guilty. The line finally opened in December, 1851. The railway was later extended from Bandon to cover much of the south coast, to Kinsale, Courtmac-sherry, Clonakilty, Skibbereen and Bantry. The line to Bandon has several interesting features. As well as Gogginshill Tunnel, there is a large viaduct at Chetwynd, four miles from Cork, and another tunnel, 170 yards long, at Kilpatrick, which we would pass through later in the day.

We followed the route of the old railway for a mile or two. It is completely ploughed over in places. Near the village of Halfway, there stands an impressive viaduct of three broad and gracious arches that carried the track across a gorge. As the old line looked overgrown and hard to follow, we made our way down to the road at Halfway. The village takes its name from its position half way between Cork and Bandon. There was a station here once but we found no trace of it. At the Ramble Inn in the village there is an Agricultural Museum. Unfortunately, it was not open at the time we passed. However, in the back yard of the inn stood a few old tractors and miscellaneous obsolete farm machines. From here we took a small road to Crossbarry, expecting it to be unfrequented. But, due to the quarry at Killean, the road was busy with heavy lorries. So, we followed a grass path back up to the railway, and tried to follow the 'permanent way', but it was either overgrown or ploughed over.

Eventually we came to the village of Crossbarry, known to all true Republicans as the scene of the largest action during the War of Independence, and a noted Rebel success. We entered the Crossbarry Inn, and found the patrons huddled in groups, eying us suspiciously. The owner, Jerry Delaney, was friendly. We asked him about the ambush. He produced a hardback copy of Tom Barry's book *Guerrilla Days in Ireland*. This is said to have been a classic, used by both security forces and freedom fighters in many parts of the world. A photo of Barry's wedding (1921) hung in the bar. Strangely, de Valera sat mid-stage, between Barry and his bride. Michael Collins was skulking in the back row with head lowered, as if he suspected the photographer to be a spy for the British. Many other protagonists from both sides of the subsequent Civil War were in the photo.

Jerry offered to show us a recently erected memorial to another rebel, Charlie Hurley. He was treating us with kindness but also with some caution. I suspect that he thought that we might have some attachment to the Republican cause. He drove us north for two miles to the memorial, a limestone Celtic cross on a minor road. There are quite a few such monuments in this neighbourhood. We showed a polite interest in it, accepting his offer to 'snap' us with Mark's camera. Back in the pub we had another drink for form's sake and then visited the main memorial near the village before heading south. It is a limestone monstrosity in neo-Stalinist style, erected in 1966, the fiftieth anniversary of the Easter Rising, and commemorating the ambush in 1921.

General Tom Barry was the legend of the West Cork Flying Column. With just 100 men, he ambushed a convoy of 19 military lorries. As British reinforcements arrived, he overcame a much larger force of some 1,200 Auxiliaries and Black and Tans. Barry's men evaded all attempts to surround and capture them. The action was hugely popular, as the Tans had been atrociously terrorising innocent citizens, stripping and beating them. Sadly, the shortly-to-follow Civil War showed that the Irish were only too good at terrorising each other. The inscription on the monument ended with the prayer '... that Ireland in her hour of need may always have sons like these to fight and die for her'. We were truly in the heartland of the Rebel County.

We now headed south to Upton. We intended to pass by a reservoir marked on the new map, but found St. Patrick's, a home for the bewildered, run by the Rosminians. We looked into the chapel where we spoke briefly to a girl cleaning, who told us a little about the place. Antonio Rosmini (1797–1855) was the founder of the Institute of Charity (Rosminians) and the Sisters of Providence. The grounds of St. Patrick's are large and beautifully kept. In a small graveyard, many headstones marked the graves of young children. Presumably, they died young as a result of serious handicap. But so much has been revealed of late about abuse of power by churchmen that it was difficult for me not to consider more sinister and horrific alternatives. I shuddered at the thought and dismissed it, reflecting on the beauty of the surroundings.

At Upton, the railway platform remains and the Station House is now a private residence. Another stone cross commemorating the Troubles stands nearby. The track was again completely obliterated by farming activity. We followed the road west to Dardan Bridge and then south to pick it up later, behind a farmyard, just before it entered a sheer rock cutting. The vegetation on the rock walls was lush, almost tropical, being well sheltered with an abundance of water. After the cutting the way was on a good grassy track which soon passed over the Brinny River. It led us to Kilpatrick Tunnel, which is 170 yards long and the earliest railway tunnel in Ireland.

Exiting the tunnel, we soon came to the Bandon River, where further progress is impossible as the metal viaduct no longer remains. After resting at the bridgehead and enjoying the river views, we climbed down to the river bank and made our way upstream. This was a difficult process, involving much clambering over fallen trees and slashing of dense vegetation. At one point we had to crawl along the trunk of a fallen tree over the water. After about a half mile the going became easier, as we reached a wide grassy flood plane. Soon we came to a footbridge and crossed to the south bank. The old railway track which runs beside the N71 has been converted to a dedicated walking trail. We followed it towards Bandon to come to a notice-board giving interesting information about the history of the railway. It seems the line was constructed largely by mining workers from Allihies, far to the west at the tip of the Beara Peninsula. Unfortunately, the walkway expires about two miles before Bandon, so the last section was the now-familiar slog on the hard shoulder of a busy road. At the edge of the town we came to the old Station House, now converted to council offices.

Bandon has little to attract the visitor. We checked into The Munster Arms and, after a soak, went in search of excitement. The zenith of gastronomic ecstasy in the town was the Ho Kee Chinese restaurant. In fact, this was the only eatery we found apart from the hotel itself. I am afraid that, of all the places I had visited so far, Bandon seemed the dullest. The town was founded by our old chum Richard Boyle during the Elizabethan Plantation. It is popularly said of the town that 'even the pigs are Protestant'. Perhaps that was once the case: the *Shell Guide* has a little ditty, said to have been inscribed on one of the town gates: 'Turk, Jew or Atheist / May enter here but not Papist'; to which a local wit had appended, 'Whoever wrote this, wrote it well / For such is written on the Gates of Hell'.

Though reputedly steeped in history, there was little of evident interest apart from the river itself. Even the Heritage Centre, a converted church, would not open till May, and we were not prepared to wait a month. I visited the local library to enquire about the town. The helpful librarian gave me some useful information about the twin villages of Ballineen and Enniskeen, which we expected to pass through later, and about other places on our route; but she was apologetic about having nothing to offer on Bandon itself. I suspect that the Bandon people are failing to make the most of their history.

Stage 28: *Bandon to Ballineen*

The next leg of the journey began with a climb up the hill westward from the town of Bandon. A stout stick is a boon for a hill-climb. For our adventure, my wife had thoughtfully bought us two Burmese Army trekking sticks. The documentation accompanying them deserves the most assiduous attention. According to the notes, these bamboo sticks were originally designed by Sir Jeffrey Hillpig-Smyth for British Special Forces stationed at Mandalay in 1941. Hillpig-Smyth was born in London in 1910. An overweight schoolboy with few friends, he was nicknamed 'Hillpiggy' by pupils and staff. Sent down from Oxford in 1930 for indecency, he published a spirited, vitriolic collection of essays called *Sticks and Stones*. Upon joining Military Intelligence, he was assigned to Burma in 1940, where he designed the Military Trekking Stick. He disappeared without trace while on an exercise within the military compound in 1944. A search party was organised, but they abandoned the search after having combed the compound minutely for over an hour to no avail. Sightings of Hillpig in the Burmese jungle have been reported periodically but are unconfirmed. The search goes on: there is a 'Find Hillpig Society', and a £25 reward for information about

Hillpiggy's status remains on offer. We decided to keep a sharp lookout for traces of this inimitable character.

At the top of the hill we passed some estate houses on Castle Road and then came to Castle Bernard, the family pile of Lord Bandon. Disregarding the 'Estates Private' sign, we walked into the grounds and came to the extensive ruins of the castle. It is an elaborate edifice, apparently built in several stages. The frontage is impressive, with elegant decorative windows and excellent stone carvings. Castle Bernard was built in one turbulent year and burned in another. It was constructed in 1798 for Francis Bernard, First Viscount Bandon, beside a much earlier towerhouse. On mid-summer's night, 1921, the Fourth Earl and Countess were roused by intruders. They were forced to watch as Republicans put the great house to the torch. The Countess, game to the last, stood on the lawn singing 'God Save the King' as her beloved home went up in flames. The title is now extinct, since the death of the Fifth Earl in 1979. Castle Bernard was one of sixteen great houses burned in the troubled month of June, 1921.

Passing on through the grounds, we met a young man exercising two drag-hounds. We asked him if it was possible to walk along the Bandon River bank. He told us to double back along the road for a few hundred yards to a gate and take a path down to the river. At the gate there was yet another memorial to rebels who died in the Troubles. We found a long woodland trail along the ridge south of the Bandon River, and followed it for about three miles. It was pure delight to walk this trail, away from the rush of traffic, with the river flowing serenely below and a variety of wild flowers about us. The woodland floor was carpeted with wood anemones and celandine. We met an old couple with several dogs. For reasons unclear, our friendly greeting was answered by a frosty glare. They say people come to resemble their pets: some of the curs looked decidedly curmudgeonly.

The trail brought us eventually to the road at Gurteen Cross. We had lunch by a small stream and then continued on a by-road, coming eventually to a bridge over the course of the old railway. Again, the track was either overgrown or ploughed away and, thus, effectively impassable. Stopping at a house by the bridge, we spoke to a woman and her two young children. She told us that her husband remembered the days when the railway was still running, and that his father had worked as a railway-man on this line.

Shortly afterwards, we came to Desert Serges Post Office. It must qualify as one of the most isolated post offices in the country. It is sad that so many of these are closing down, but difficult to see how they can be maintained. We bought some buttermilk at the shop here, to refresh ourselves and for the novelty; it is not so often found nowadays. The name Desert Serges has nothing to do with the Sahara, but was the Hermitage of St. Sergius, a monk who had his home in this region.

After passing a house called Kilcoman Park, we came to St. Mary's Church. In the churchyard there is an ancient graveyard. It is said that some of the graves date back to the ninth or tenth century. The entry slab of one of the tombs had sunken down, leaving a gap. Peering in we saw scattered skulls and bones. I photographed this *memento mori*, a sombre reminder of the mortality of man, and we continued on our way. We took to the fields again after a while, through grassland with cuckoo flowers or lady's smock and eyebright. Soon the river meandered away and we returned to the road. After Hatter's Cross we came to a Church of Ireland church, beside a much earlier ruin. It is interesting how often a new church is built beside an older one, rather than as a renovation of the latter. From the church, we took a little path northwards to the river, and over a ten-arched bridge to the village of Ballineen. Here we went into Dessy's Pub, but the whiff from the toilets was enough to repel us, so we bought food in the supermarket and sat on a bench by the bridge over the Bandon, munching our makeshift sandwiches.

We were booked into The Red Fort, which I had found in the *Bord Failte Guide to Accommodation*. We had visions of the elaborate architecture of the British Raj. It turned out to be a road-house, about a mile west of Ballineen on the busy Dunmanway road. So, once again, our walking day ended with a slog along a hard shoulder. On the hillside just to the south, Fort Robert is marked on the old half-inch map, though not on the newer Discovery Series map. Fort Robert was the home of Fergus O'Connor, leader of the Chartist Movement, a revolutionary democratic agitation in Britain in the 1840s. He was a follower of Daniel O'Connell, but the Liberator had him unseated in 1835 for indiscipline. Although the reforms sought by the Chartists have long since been achieved, the movement itself collapsed ignominiously, driving O'Connor, who was already extremely eccentric, over the brink. He was, belatedly, declared insane in 1852 and died three years later. We were unable to find out if The Red Fort had taken its name from Fort Roberts or had some other origin.

Stage 29: *Ballineen to Shiplake*

Initially, we had planned to continue along the Dunmanway road to a bridge further west but from the window in The Red Fort we spotted a metal footbridge directly opposite where we were staying. So we set out across a field, finding on the way two girders spanning a little stream, an echo of the old railway. We crossed the footbridge over the Bandon and climbed a ridge to the south. We looked back to see if we could identify Fort Robert, but we couldn't locate it with any certainty. We came soon to a farmyard, and waded ankle-deep in cow-dung past the farmhouse. The farmer emerged and we explained our reason for being there. He was not perturbed, and just told us the best way to reach the road. Now we followed a small backroad to Ballinacarriga Castle. As we rounded a bend, the castle loomed ahead, standing majestically on a rocky hillock, framed by the hedgerows.

Ballinacarriga Castle is a fortified, four-storey tower house standing on a high rock overlooking the small Ballinacarriga Lough. The castle is very well preserved and is in the care of the Board of Works. The metal gate had been vandalised, so entry was easy. There is a good vaulted roof and spiral staircase giving access to the uppermost levels and ramparts. The upper level was used as a church for some time, and there are some beautiful carvings on the architraves of the windows at this level. We could make out a crucifix and angels, and the letters RHCC under the date 1585. These were the initials of Randal Hurley, one-time master here, and Catherine Cullinane, whom he married. But the castle itself may well be older than this date. Also evident were several masonic-looking motifs and symbols. However, of most interest to our lascivious tastes was a Sheela-na-gig carved in a stone high up on the outside wall. We sat on the remains of a round tower, which once formed part of the bawn or enclosure around the castle, under the gaze of Sheela, and enjoyed some refreshments.

This particular Sheela-na-gig is in good nick, considering her age. She is carved in relief, with a large grotesque head, knees spread wide and feet together, her hands grasping the lips of her open vulva. As she is somewhat the worse for the weather, I could not discern if her pose was one of invitation or intimidation. These extraordinary figures date back as far as the twelfth century. Tradition and folklore are vague as to their origin and function. The earlier examples are found on churches and may have served as warnings against the sin of lust. Later Sheelas were built into castle walls, perhaps as protective icons or fertility symbols. Contemporary interpretation takes a feminist slant, stressing the power of female sexuality and reproduction. Whatever their origins, it is always a delight to come upon one of these uniquely Irish ladies, with her legs asplay. And Sheelas are a diverting topic of conversation, if the mood ever flags at a cocktail party.

Continuing westwards past Ballinacarriga Lough, we spotted two yellowhammers, getting a good view of these birds. At Clubhouse Bridge we came to Cotter's Bar. It had been my intention to stop here for a celebratory quaff, as this was the southernmost point of the Commodius Vicus. But Cotter's was closed, so we followed a small road round by Mahona Lough to avoid the busier road into Dunmanway. The town of Dunmanway, with two triangular 'squares', is where the Brewery River and the Dirty River come together and then join the Bandon. It was Market Day, so the town was bustling with activity. We looked around for a while and, after buying some food, continued onwards out the Collkellure road to our destination for the day, the Shiplake Hostel. En route we passed a number of standing stones. The land changed from the verdant green of the Bandon valley to rougher, rocky scrubland and snipe-grass. We were also entering more hilly terrain and the scenery was becoming more interesting.

The Shiplake Hostel is an independent hostel at Carrigaphuca, a few miles north of Dunmanway. Reaching the hostel, we were offered a choice: dormitory accommodation, or a 'private' room in a gypsy caravan. As the latter had only a double bed, we opted for the communal solution.

In fact, there was only one other person in our dormitory, though the adjoining dorm was packed with a group of German visitors on some sort of acting course. Mark cooked up some pasta concoction which wasn't too bad, and our German fellow-guests shared an apple strudel with us. The hostel has been run for several years by a German girl, Uli, who provides various vegetarian meals including apple pie.

Stage 30: *Shiplake to Ballingeary*

A glorious rainbow behind the hostel signalled a showery day. Uli gave us a delicious breakfast of homemade muesli and brown bread, a change from the cholesterol specials we had had on previous days. She also gave us some information about things to see on our walk to Ballingeary. We headed north, enjoying bright weather, but were forced to shelter from the showers now and then.

At Derrynacaheragh we passed another remote post office. Further on, we searched at a spot marked on the map for an ogham stone, but found nothing. Then, seeing Togher Castle across the fields, we decided to make a bee-line for it. This was a mistake, as we were soon in marshy ground, with forward progress blocked by a wide drainage ditch. It took us some time to work back to the road, so we decided to skip Togher Castle and continue northwards. We spotted a donkey in a yard beside a house and Mark cut up a apple to feed him. The photo I took could be from the original John Hinde series, so typically Irish! We were near Coolmountain now, home of a hippie colony. Indeed, we passed a bald lady who looked as if she might be one of this group. Further on we spied colourful caravans and brightly painted Ford Transit vans. Near Farrinahineeny we found a stone circle, but it was small and unspectacular.

A stiff climb brought us to a pass through the eastern flanks of the Shehy Mountains. As we neared the top a beautiful view west to a tall peak opened up. This we took to be Shehy More, one of the the highest peaks in the range, at 564 metres (it is unnamed on half-inch sheet 25, and on Sheet 85 the name appears displaced a square NE). Arriving at the top of the pass, near the appropriately named Mount Prospect, a view to the Boggeragh Mountains opened up, with the TV mast on Musheramore clearly visible. Two twin peaks to the west we took to be The Paps, but a look at the map later suggested that they could be Caherbearnagh and Mullaghanish. In any event, this was our first sighting of the Kingdom of Kerry. Lough Allua, on the Lee, appeared as a silver stripe below. The way was now downhill; it should be easier. Climbing is hard on the lungs, but descent is tough on the calves. The road brought us to a point where a Cillin, or children's graveyard, was marked, but we found nothing. Passing a small stone farm house, we saw swallows darting about, the first of the year. Birdlife was plentiful hereabouts. Among other species, we spotted some willow warblers and several reed buntings.

Soon we were down by the lakeside and followed it around to westward until we found a small stone bridge across the Lee. Crossing the bridge in bright sunlight we noticed those strange insects known as pond-skaters or waterboatmen. They are X-shaped, and dart across the water surface, suspended by surface tension. We noticed that the shadow of each insect had large dark patches around the tips of its four legs. This is due to the distortion of the flat water surface by the legs, which reduces the transmitted light. I tried to photograph this effect, but the results were indistinct. However, the phenomenon itself is unmistakeable.

A path from the bridge led us into the village of Ballingeary. In a bright craftshop, I bought a colourful candle for Cabrini. We strolled through the village and came to Seartan's Pub. As we went in, the Grand National had just begun. For a pound, I took even numbers and Mark took odd. Number 21, Bobbyjo, won so I lost a quid. Paul Carberry was the rider and it was the first Irish winner for 24 years, since Paul's father Tommy had won on L'Escargot. After the race, we caught a bus back to Cork and drove home, stopping in Abbeyleix for a snack.

Chapter 8

INTO THE KINGDOM

Ar mo ghabáil dom siar chun Droichead Uí Mhórdha,
Píce i m' dhóid is mé ag dul i meitheal,
Cé chasfaí orm i gcumar ceoidh
Ach pocán crón is é ar buile,
Alliliú puilliliú, alliliú tá an poc ar buile.

'An Poc ar Buile' – Traditional Song

SUMMER 1999 PASSED WITHOUT PROGRESS on the Commodius Vicus, due to many outside pressures. But now, at the beginning of October, we set out on the great traverse of the Derrynasaggart Mountains, from West Cork into the Kingdom of Kerry. Starting at Ballingeary, the idea was to cross Lackabaun to Kilgarvan on the first day, and climb the mighty Mangerton mountain (2,756 feet) to reach Killarney on the second. We had studied An tAthair Peadar O'Laoghaire's book *Mo Scéil Féin* in school. Although as teenagers we had little interest in the historical significance of the book, O'Laoghaire's boyhood adventures were much to our taste, where he had described exciting mountain climbs in the Cork and Kerry mountains. In particular I recalled vividly his trip up Mangerton and his description of the Devil's Punchbowl, a corrie gouged out of the mountain by the ice or, according to legend, scooped up by the Devil and hurled elsewhere to form a mountain. I was eager to reach the top of Mangerton and look down on this diabolical cirque. However, the weather was not too friendly, so the plan to climb Mangerton had to be altered.

Into the Kingdom

We stayed at the Victoria Hotel in Macroom and, before heading across the road for a suite of nightcaps, we watched the news and weather forecast. NASA had admitted that their Mars Orbiter had become an unplanned Mars Lander due to a mix-up between metric and imperial units. In Japan, a major nuclear accident had been narrowly avoided. We were reassured that the most technologically advanced nations were watching over us. At home, the scandal of the Ansbacher accounts raged on. Then Evelyn Cusack appeared and told us of showery, blustery weather to come, with occasional gale gusts and heavy rain, far from ideal for walking. She ended her presentation with a fond farewell. This was to be the last night on which the Met Éireann weather presenters would appear; they were to be replaced by non-meteorologists, a decision made by RTÉ to the satisfaction of no one but themselves. A decision, too, that was reversed some weeks later in response to strong popular demand.

There were three of us on this segment of the Commodius Vicus. Together with Mark and myself was Frank (Redser) McKenna, another old 'school chum'. We met up in Andrew Golden's pub in the square of Macroom. Mark and I had driven down from Dublin and Frank later from Enfield. Golden's is an amazing menagerie. As you enter the gloom, the bar is on the right, and a shop counter on the left. An unbelievable variety of goods are on display. Buckets and brooms hung from the ceiling, together with flashing rotating mirrored dance-hall crystal balls. A small nook is set out like a shrine with a poster of Che Guevara. Jimi Hendrix's death certificate was on display. I was assured it was the original, but this was Cork. The cause of his demise: inhalation of vomit after barbiturate intoxication. We spent the evening in Golden's with another old friend, Tom O'Leary, the local vet, and his brother Tim. Much porter was quaffed, and many stories swapped, becoming more unprintable as the night advanced. Techniques useful in assisting relationships with sheep and other amorous animals were analysed in detail. We learned that failure to pack our wellies and Velcro gloves would severely cramp our style.

Before leaving Golden's, Frank bought three bowls, 28 oz steel balls used for the local and popular game of road bowls. This game is played along quiet country roads; quiet, that is, apart from the roars of onlookers, who often have large financial interests in the outcome. The winner is the one who covers the course in the fewest throws. An underhanded hurl of the bowl is used, the player's arm flailing like a windmill before letting the bowl fly, often for several hundred yards. 'Shkilled bowlers' know how to use the camber of the road to negotiate corners. The game is also played in parts of the North and, curiously, in Holland.

Stage 31: *Ballingeary to Kilgarvan*

Macroom Castle was the boyhood home of William Penn, who founded the state of Pennsylvania. The grounds are now a public park belonging to the people of Macroom, thanks to a generous gesture of Lady Ardilaun of the Guinness family. Before we set out, Frank decided to polish his bowling technique. Heading through the castle gates to the sports field, he let fly the bowl with a mighty hurl. It has yet to be located. We drove to Ballingeary with only eight balls remaining (two of steel) and parked the car opposite the Irish School, Coláiste na Mumhan. Ballingeary – Beal Átha an Ghaorthaidh, or the Mouth of the Ford of the Berries – is a noted centre for students learning Irish. We took the road northwards in damp and misty weather. Another bowl was produced, and after Mark and I had hurled it up the hill with modest pace, Frank gathered his strength for another try. This time he launched it on a quasi-vertical trajectory. Its future was now mapped out immutably by the principles of Newtonian mechanics. High and far it travelled, like the slither struck by Cuchulainn, in a mighty parabolic orbit over the roadside ditch to land in a rushy, mushy field.

Further up the road, we met a dapper little man with slicked black hair, who spoke with a sharp, high-pitched voice. It turned out that he kept bees. He told us that this had been a bad summer for honey. He had three hives and the bees fed mostly on brambles and clover. He would not feed them this winter as he reckoned that this would result in a better yield next season. We chatted for a while to this friendly man, who warned us about the dangers of a hidden lake when we told him our route. It was impossible not to see the similarity between the bee-man and the denizens of his apiary. Like the grumpy pair by the Bandon, who had come to resemble their pugnacious pugs, he had taken on some of the outward characteristics of the bees in his care.

Onward we went up the hill to a left turn over a little stream and took a westward road past Cois na Coille, where a large carved wooden pig stood like a totem in a garden. We saluted him, 'presenting Hillpigs'. A dark ridge loomed ahead as the road became a track and steepened sharply. An entrepreneurial farmer had placed a tupperware container with a hole in the lid by the track. Beside it was a roughly scribbled sign reading 'All Walkers £5 fee'. We admired his imagination but not his neck, trying to cash in on a mountain track which, we speculated, had probably been build by subsistence labourers struggling to survive after the Famine. I suppose the odd sucker puts money in the bucket.

There was now a stiff climb up to the crest of Lackabaun. The name means White Slabs, supposedly from the white quartzite layers in the old red sandstone making up this mountain range. We saw a cluster of mistle thrushes high on the hillside. The grassy track zig-zagged to ease the gradient but the wind was strong and we were breathless when we reached the top. This was the Kerry border; we had crossed the mighty Rebel County and our next step would take us into the Kingdom. The map had given me hopes of a glorious view of the Derrynasaggart mountains to the north and Macgillycuddy's Reeks to the west. I had anticipated ogling the cairn-capped Paps of Danu, and admiring Carrauntoohil, but all we saw was the local mist-shrouded hillside.

We headed down a path through open heath. A red squirrel bounded along the track ahead of us before disappearing into the undergrowth. Passing a farmyard we were harried by six dogs but our Hillpigs kept them at a safe distance. We sat on a grassy wall shaded by high hedgerows, with a view of a small cascade on the Roughty River (named for a local family, O Rúachtan). After enjoying a lunch of ham and cheese rolls, we turned northward down the river valley. We were to follow the river all the way to Kenmare, thought we did not know it yet. At Sillaherdane, we searched for a hunting lodge that Tom had told us about. We slogged up a driveway lined with rhododendrons and hydrangeas. Apparently, hydrangeas are red or blue depending on the acidity or alkalinity of the soil. They thus act like large litmus plants, indicating the pH of the underlying ground. We gave up on this detour after about a kilometre, having failed to see any trace of the hunting lodge.

We marched on down by the river, which was now thundering through a deep canyon bored in the red rock. Ahead we spied a striking feature, a deep groove in the hillside. The map identified it as Esknacappul or Horses' Glen, but as the bare red rocky landscape hereabouts reminded us of a cowboy film, we devised a more apposite appellation, Mustang Gulch. Soon we came to Morley's Bridge or Droichid Ui Mhordha. This is where the adventure of 'An Poc ar Buile' begins:

As I set out with me pike in hand
To old Dromore to join a meithil
Who should I meet but a tan puck goat
An' he roarin' mad, in ferocious fettle.

(Translated by James N. Healy)

The singer follows the mad goat from here, in the story set to music by Séan O'Ríada and made popular by Séan O'Sé. It is claimed that the man who wrote the lyrics got half a plug of tobacco for his pains.

Morley's Bridge, now no more than a minor road junction, has seen busier times. The ruin of an old schoolhouse stands on a high embankment above the road. The railway from Kenmare was routed via Kilgarvan to a station here, and onward down the Loo Valley to Headford, where it joined the main line to Killarney. The line was closed in 1960 and little evidence of it now remains. The railway traversed tortuous terrain, making progress difficult. Writing in 1937, Praeger remarked that the railway company helped to keep the holiday crowds away from Kenmare 'by making you spend an hour and a quarter over the last twenty miles'. We had hoped to find a pub or even a shop here, but were disappointed, so we went back across the bridge to avoid the main road, and headed west towards Kenmare. We followed a minor, wood-lined road, spying a variety of puff-balls and other fungi by the verge. No goat, angry or otherwise, appeared, but a monster ram with huge curled horns scurried along the road before us for half a mile before heading into a field. As the rain was now becoming very heavy, we crossed the Roughty River again at the next opportunity, to shorten the journey at the expense of a slog along the main road.

We came soon to Kilgarvan and stopped at O'Reilly's pub. After liquid refreshment we popped next door to The Village Grill, where we devoured three huge T-bone steaks plus trimmings. On the wall of the restaurant was a poster of Kilgarvan's most recent 'Famous Son', Jackie Healy Rae, a 'colourful' local politician, straight out of *The Colleen Bawn*, who had won an independent seat after he was passed over by the Fianna Fáil party. Because of the delicate balance of power, he had disproportionate influence in the Dáil. That he was aware of this was confirmed by a newspaper headline, displayed beside the poster, quoting him:

'If Bertie Ahern doesn't listen to me, he can whistle for ducks.'

After our meal, we crossed the road to Healy Rae's pub. It was a drab, unattractive bar with indigent atmosphere and indolent service, and we did not tarry long.

We stayed at Gortnaboul House, a pleasant B&B run by Danny and Kathleen O'Sullivan. Gourtnaboul, the Garden of Holes, is named for the holes left when many large rocks were removed for production of lime in a local kiln. After a wash, we had tea with Danny and Kathleen, and enjoyed an evening's conversation. They told us of the plight of the farmers, the worries of running a B&B, the state of the tourism industry, and the great changes in lifestyle over recent times. I asked them about the old railway. Danny remembered travelling to football matches in Tralee on special Sunday trains. We heard too about the local poet, Johnny Nora Aodha O Tuama, commemorated on a plaque on the Community Centre wall in the town. When I asked if Danny was related to another O'Sullivan whom I knew, he laughed, saying there were so many O'Sullivans in south Kerry that they often acquired an addendum to their name. His family had been called O'Sullivan Caum, or stooped. Such names are inflicted rather than selected.

Stage 32: Kilgarvan to Kenmare

The weather next morning was damp and overcast. An attempt to climb Mangerton would have been reckless, so we reviewed our options. The course of the old railway to Kenmare was a theoretical possibility, but from what little evidence was available, the prospect of a trouble-free

journey by this route looked slim. So, when we left O'Sullivan's we headed over Cahergal Bridge to follow the small road along the south bank of
the river, thus avoiding the busier main road to Kenmare. We crossed the
Slaheney River. A mile upstream is the site of the Battle of Callan, fought
in 1261, between the McCarthys and the FitzGeralds. At Letter Upper we
came to another old schoolhouse. Then a large telephone mast loomed
ahead on a hill. We looked back to admire the view of Mangerton, gradually appearing from an evaporating overcast. After stopping to exchange
pleasantries with a local farmer, we fed apples to some donkeys in a field.
Reaching the top of a ridge, we could enjoy the vista of the Caha Mountains, the beginning of a rocky spine that stretches out to the end of the
Beara Peninsula. Kenmare Bay now spread out before us, and the many-
peaked Carrauntoohil complex loomed darkly to the north.

At Roughty Bridge we took a short-cut, marked on the map, which
appeared to be a right-of-way. There were signs indicating it as private
land, which we decided to ignore. As we proceeded, a man came out of
his house, approaching aggressively to challenge us. 'Can 'ou not read the
sign? Who do you tink 'ou are?' 'We're Irish,' I replied, implicitly claiming
the right to ramble through my own country. This belligerent man was
unimpressed and ranted on, so we quietly withdrew to the road and took
a marginally longer route. But I was convinced that, once again, public
access had been illegally blocked.

From a small hedge a wren sprang out and darted across the road in
front of us. These small birds have the latin name *Troglodytes troglodytes*,
or cave-dwellers, from their habit of building cave-like nests. They are
found all year round in Ireland. Looking where the wren had flown, Mark
spied an interesting fungus with flattish red top, which he identified as
Flyagaric. Apparently once used in the manufacture of fly-killer, it has a
much more interesting and exotic use: it has hallucinogenic qualities, but
is also an emetic. However, if it is ingested, the psychoactive ingredient
can be gathered from the urine, whereas the vomit-inducing constituent
takes another route. Thus, the lucky imbiber of the 'processed beverage'
gets the buzz without the biliousness. The use of animals as filters in-
volves tricky logistics in inducing them to partake of the fungus and then
collecting the output, so a man of power and influence might employ his

underlings for the task. We imagined the plight of the unfortunate lack-
eys – 'Oh no, it's Flyagaric night again!' – and speculated on the relative
merits of male and female filters. It may have been this fungus that was
taken by the wild Norse warriors known as Berserkers before they went
into battle.

At Sheen Bridge we joined yet another way-marked trail, known as
the Beara Way. The Sheen Falls Lodge stands by the bank here where
the river rushes over a splendid series of rapids down to the Roughty.
The screw-joint of my Hillpig had gradually been working loose and,
at this point, the two halves of the stick parted company. After another
mile, we crossed the head of Kenmare Bay on a two-arched suspension
bridge, an old-style reinforced concrete construction. In a small park by
the bridge stood a sculpture of three large, rough-cut granite figures of
Irish musicians. A curlew rose from the shore and flew gracefully downstream towards a pier where a few small boats were tied up. One was the
Seafari, which brings visitors on 'Eco-Nature Cruises' of the bay, to see
seals, sharks and so on. But Kenmare Bay does not have a dolphin to rival
Fungi in Dingle.

Arriving at the town, we passed the entrance to the Park Hotel. Since
rooms here were well in excess of £100, we took another few paces, to the
Failte Hostel, where a room for the three of us came at £8 per skull. At a
bike shop opposite, I asked if my broken Hillpig could be repaired, and
received only the unhelpful advice that it should be thrown away. What
an insult to the memory of the great Sir Jeffrey! (Frank took the broken
stick and returned it in working order some time later).

Kenmare is a cheerful, brightly coloured town with a lively, cosmopoli-
tan atmosphere. It was founded in 1670 by Sir William Petty, Surveyor-
General to the dreaded Cromwell. Petty managed to acquire vast estates
in the land confiscations that followed the Cromwellian wars. He had a
varied career, being professor at Oxford of both anatomy and music, and
a founder member of the Royal Society in 1662. He carried out the first
extensive survey of Ireland, known as the Down Survey, covering about
two-thirds of the country. An atlas of Ireland based on his work was published in 1685.

The name of Kenmare derives from Ceann Mara, Head of the Sea, although the name used in Irish is Neidín, the Little Nest. Both are geographically appropriate, as the town has a spectacular location, at the top of Kenmare Bay, a ria or submerged river valley, nestled between the high mountains. The town was laid out in an 'X-plan' comprising Henry Street and Main Street. Shelbourne Street, added later, completed a triangle, and the smaller triangle to the north is a park called, in defiance of Euclid, The Square. A heritage centre is located at the tourist office in the old courthouse in the square. Kenmare is attractive, with many good bars and restaurants, and is described in the tourist literature as a gourmet's haven. Not being fanatical foodies, we decided to rustle up some spuds and lamb chops in the hostel.

After our dinner we surveyed the town. With three main streets, it was an easier task than the survey undertaken by Sir William Petty, but a few detours added some spice. A couple of hundred yards to the west of the Square we found a stone circle, the Druids Circle, comprising fifteen standing stones, with a small dolmen in the centre. The circle, which stands on a hillock over the River Finnihy, is about 17 metres in diameter, and is believed to date from the early Bronze Age, about 3,000 years ago. Possibly the burial place of a megalithic mega-star, it may also have had some ritual or astronomical significance, or functioned as a primitive calendar. But it's easy to find three stones in a row, and easy too to imagine a link with some solar or lunar phenomenon. On the return journey, we stopped off at the Lansdowne Arms Hotel in Shelbourne Street.

Stage 33: *Kenmare to Killarney*

We marched north from the Square of Kenmare, up a stiff hill past the local hospital. As we climbed higher we stopped occasionally and looked back to enjoy the view of Kenmare Bay. We reached the first crest at the gap between Strickeen and Inchimore and saw that, after a deep plunge into a valley, the path reached ever higher to the pass known as the Windy Gap, between Peakeen Mountain (1,825 feet/555 metres) and Knockanaguish (1,645 feet/509 metres). We headed down to the river valley and, before attacking the great ascent, sat on the bridge, reverentially, while Mark delivered 'the first reading from the Book of Barry'.

He had bought Barry's *Guerrilla Days in Ireland* in a Kenmare book-shop. The reading told of a thrilling deed of derring-do, in which 'The Lads' ambushed an armoured troop-carrier and dispatched its occupants to Kingdom-come.

Filled with zeal to slay the Saxon foe, we strode up the mountainside with determined gait. Meadow pipits and stonechats were in abundance here, flitting from bush to branch before us. Soon the tarred road became a stony path, muddy in spots. As we crested the Windy Gap we were blasted by a cold force-seven wind, but it eased off as we began our descent. The view now was spectacular. Purple Mountain loomed before us, a dark and sombre mass. The Upper Lake of Killarney appeared, and the massive spirit of Mangerton watched over our progress from the east. A lone raven, perched on a windswept branch, observed us closely. After continued heavy rains, the path was waterlogged in places. Huge stepping-stones eased our crossing of a broad stream. We passed a number of other hikers, heading south to the Gap. At an old oak grove we stopped in the shade to have a lunch of bread and cheese and fruit juice. After our meal, Mark delivered 'the second reading from the Book of Barry' but, as I dozed off, its content cannot be reported.

The path we were travelling is part of the Kerry Way, which encircles the entire Iveragh Peninsula. We could have followed the main trail, but it would bring us to the remote and desolate Black Valley, so we branched off to the right near Galway's Bridge, to follow the route east of Cromaglan Mountain. Crossing a wooden bridge, we climbed a steep path through an ancient oak forest. The atmosphere here was mystical; one had the impression of being totally alone in a forest that seemed to have been untouched by human hand for centuries. At the top of Esknamucky Glen we stopped again for spiritual renewal and temporal revival (another 'reading' and a feast of Jammie Dodgers). Then we made our way down the glen, a sometimes difficult scramble over steep and rocky terrain. Even the higher ground was sodden. We were on what was once the main route from Killarney to Kenmare. For long stretches our passage was on a boardwalk made from old railway sleepers. Laid longwise in pairs and covered in chicken-wire to provide purchase, the sleepers must have stretched for over a mile.

As we rounded Torc Mountain (from Torc, a boar), with the Owen-garriff River to our right, we spied a herd of about twenty Kerry Cows, a sturdy, all-black breed, probably owned by the State, as we were now in the Killarney National Park. Reputedly, there are red deer in the park, but we saw no signs of them. Many showers required us to shelter frequently, but eventually we reached a series of steps that led us down to the spectacular Torc Waterfall, a cascade about sixty metres high. Here a kind Scottish tourist photographed us with the waterfall as a backdrop.

The path then brought us to the main Kenmare–Killarney road, where a clutch of young ravens scurried about the car park. We were tired and hoped to catch a bus, but as it was now late, the chances of any bus coming looked slight. So, we crossed the road into the grounds of Muckross House and walked up through the beautiful gardens, bedecked with a wide variety of exotic plants. We followed the path around the shore of Muckross Lake. The banning of motorised traffic helps to preserve an atmosphere of serenity in the park.

Soon we came to Muckross House, a neo-Elizabethan mansion, which houses a museum of furniture, history and folk-life, open to the public. However, it was closed at the late hour of our arrival. A group of jarveys were waiting by the house and one approached us with an offer to bring us to the town for £20. We laughed out loud, but he persisted with another offer, to take us to the Abbey for £5. Since this was only a stone's-throw away, we carried on on foot; though tired out, we were not so desperate as to be ripped off on such a cosmic scale.

Muckross Abbey was founded in 1448 for the Franciscans by Donal MacCarthy Mor, whose remains are buried in the chancel. The famed Kerry poets Aodhagen O Rathaille and Eoghan Rua O Suilleabhain are also buried here. A huge yew tree grows in the cloister of the Abbey. We took a few photos and then trudged onward. The view across Lough Leane was refreshing, with the ever-changing patterns of light and shade on the water, as the sun sank slowly behind the mountains. But, as so often happens, the last stretch of the walk was on a busy road, this time past several modern hotels. Crossing the Flesk River, we came to the Holiday Inn, and decided we had had enough. After a sandwich and drink, we called a taxi, which brought us back to Ballingeary for a fare that I forget but recall as reasonable. We drove back to Macroom, booked into the same room at the Victoria Hotel, and headed next door for a Chinese meal.

Stage 34: *Killarney to Faha Cross*

The next stage is on Monday 3 January 2000. A new millennium has dawned: the excitement of the celebrations has waned, the party buzz is gone, and the last millennium candle has sputtered and died. The Y2K bug has failed to bite, and we live in hope that this new age will bring peace and harmony. The holiday weather has been atrocious, with one gale after another, but Ireland has been spared the worst extremes of violent storms that have wreaked terrible havoc in continental Europe. They would appear to have been the worst weather conditions since records began, causing serious damage and loss of life. At home, a cold front has passed rapidly over the country during the night, leaving a brief spell of clear weather. Another rain-band is forecast to pass through tonight. With luck, we might get bright weather for this bank holiday Monday, with little more than a few showers to worry us.

For company on this section I had a friend, Tom Murphy, whose family hail from this neck of the woods. We drove down from Dublin to Killarney and parked at the Holiday Inn, our stopping place at the end of the previous stage. We planned to aim for Castlemaine, where we would stay overnight and then head over the eastern flanks of the Slieve Mish Mountains to Tralee the next day. We set forth at about 2.00 p.m. walking the short distance to the town centre.

The town of Killarney is not of any great antiquity. Indeed, no town or village of this name was identified in William Petty's survey of 1654. The name means 'Church of the Sloes'. The town is pleasant enough but its beauty is completely overshadowed by the surrounding lakes and mountainscapes. Killarney is perhaps the most internationally famous place in Ireland. Poets such as Scott, Tennyson and Wordsworth, who have visited the area, have written in glowing terms about it. The beauty of its lake and mountain scenery fully justifies the superlatives lavished upon it. And local guides will tell you romantic tales of the Colleen Bawn – the Lily of Killarney – whose delight is undiminished by their dubious provenance. Since every guidebook deals extensively with Killarney and its environs, no more need be said here.

From the town we turned westward through a passage beside the Three Lakes Hotel, which was closed for the winter. We came soon to St. Mary's Cathedral, a large cruciform church with centrally located spire. It was designed by the renowned architect Augustus Pugin, in Gothic Revival style. As time was precious, we did not delay here, but pressed on over the little Deenagh River, which was in spate, and entered Kenmare House Estate. Kenmare House, the seat of the Browne family, Earls of Kenmare, was destroyed by fire in 1913. The demesne is now part of the Killarney National Park. It is a truly beautiful estate, with the most wonderful lakeside walks.

We passed a small cottage, probably a former gate lodge of the big house, and took a path marked as the Fossa Way, along the north shore of Lough Leane, enjoying the splendid prospect. Out on the lake we could see several islands, including the unique Innisfallen. On this island are the remains of a monastery founded in the seventh century, which was an important centre of learning for almost a thousand years. It is said that Brian Boru received his education here. The twelfth-century *Annals of Innisfallen*, amongst the earliest reliable Irish historical records, were written here. They contain extracts from the Old Testament and a history of the ancient world to the time of St Patrick's arrival in Ireland in 432. They also contain a detailed record of events in Ireland up to 1319. The *Annals*, now in the Bodleian Library in Oxford, provide a valuable source for historians.

We turned north past a golf course to cross the main Killorglin road and headed up-hill at a gallop to Aghadoe. Breathless, we came to an old ruined church. Aghadoe Monastery was originally founded by St. Finian the Leper in the seventh century. The ruins, with a door and two lancet windows in the Romanesque style, date to about the twelfth century. A huge tomb stands in the church nave. We spotted the stump of an old round tower, four or five metres high, in the graveyard nearby. Across the road was another tower, Parkavonear Castle, a round Norman keep built about 1300. Little is known about this castle, locally called the Bishop's Chair.

Lush vegetation in a railway cutting near the Brinny River

View of Cobh from the Navy tender en route to Haulbowline

A Sheela-na-gig on the outside wall of Ballinacarriga Castle

Stepping stones on the path from Kenmare to Killarney

Polychromatic houses in Kenmare

Frank peeling an apple as Mark delivers the First Reading from the Book of Barry

Two Hillpigs heading north from Kenmare to the Windy Gap

Tom standing by the door of the wonderful Gallarus Oratory

Mute swans on the water at Gougane Barra, County Cork

The Jeannie Johnston under construction in Blennerville, County Kerry in April 2000

Cannon commemorating 'The Men of Kerry who fell in the Service of their Country' during the Indian Mutiny

*A plaque in Ardfert, commemorating
St. Brendan's 1500th birthday*

*An ogham stone at Ratass
Church, Tralee*

Mark and Frank inspecting a carriage of the Lartigue Railway

If you can read the signs, you can probably see the water

The Colleen Bawn (Jim Connolly, 1987) at Killimer – she is is buried in the nearby cemetery

Clare County Council embraces the Euro with commendable precision

Surrounded by water in Coole Park

*The leaning tower of Kilmacduagh,
near Gort*

*Frank relaxes by a cottage at Killeeneen,
near where Anthony Raftery is buried*

From Aghadoe we followed a narrow road northward, heading for Castlemaine. The way was featureless, the hedgerows bare, and on this cold January day there was little in the way of bird or animal life, or even wildflowers, to be seen. Only the old reliable robin and a few crows kept us company. Soon the light began to fail and it became clear that we had no hope of reaching Castlemaine before darkness. Studying the map, we decided the best strategy was to head west to the Milltown road, where we might find a shop or pub, or even a B&B for the night. We pressed on-ward hastily, passing the Killarney Country Club, to come to Faha Cross. Enquiring at Doohan's shop, we were advised to try for accommodation at the Country Club, but a phone call informed us that there were no vacancies. So we called a hackney and returned to Killarney, where we found a comfortable room at the Fairview Guest House, right in the cen-tre of town. A shower, followed by a hearty meal in Cronin's Restaurant, restored our feeling of wellbeing.

Stage 35: Faha Cross to Castlemaine

Next morning, on my own again, I caught a taxi back to Faha Cross to resume the journey that had been so suddenly interrupted by fail-ing light the previous evening. I took the small path northwards opposite the gate of the Killarney Country Club. I was looking for an old burial place that was marked on the map. However, at a junction I decided to follow a new hard-core road rather than the overgrown path. This was a mistake as the road soon expired. I presume it was under construc-tion to provide access to a house yet to be built. Anyway, I now found myself facing a confusion of fields and fences. After crossing three of the former and climbing two of the latter, I came to a stable yard. There were a few horses in the stables but no human presence. An angry dog growled at me but, fortunately, he was chained up. I walked hurriedly down the drive and back to the public road. A glance at the map showed that, after almost an hour, I was just one mile from my starting point.

The snow-capped Reeks, with the deep defile of the Gap of Dunloe sharply delineated against the bright sky, towered majestically over the southern horizon. Leaving them behind, I crossed the little Gweestin River and climbed a stiff hill. Reaching the top I was rewarded by a magnificent view of the Slieve Mish Mountains. A long rising ridge reached westward to the noble peaks of Baurtregaum (2,796 feet) and Cahercon-ree (2,713 feet), looking resplendent with a light dusting of snow. Beneath them was Castlemaine Harbour, at the head of Dingle Bay.

Apart from the mountain views, the road was dull and featureless, the only relief of the monotony being a slight bump as I crossed the bound-ary from Discovery Sheet 78 to Sheet 71. I decided to seek out an ogham stone that was marked on the new map. Heading up a side lane, I was harried by three dogs until a woman appeared at a farmhouse door and hushed them. I asked if she could advise me where to find the stone. 'Tis gone,' she said. I thought that perhaps it had been taken to a university or to a museum, for study or display to the public. 'Where is it?' I asked. 'My husband buried it.' 'Whereabouts?' 'Under the dung-heap,' she said. 'Oh, that's a pity,' said I. 'Why? Sure, what use is it?' quoth she. I said it was probably over a thousand years old, and might have an interesting inscription that could be of historical significance and tell us something about our past. 'Well, 'tis gone now, anyway!' she concluded triumphant-ly. I consoled myself with the thought that, somewhere around here, an ogham stone is resting safely under a dung-heap, to be found in ten or a hundred years by more enlightened people.

I marched onward down the hill enjoying the mountain panorama. A bright double rainbow appeared ahead, soon followed by a heavy shower that forced me to shelter by the path to Poll an Afrinn, a wood in the care of Coillte. Using the opportunity to rest and have a snack, I carried on refreshed after the shower had passed. Coming close to Castlemaine, I kept an eye out for traces of the old railway that once passed here en route from Farranfore to Caherciveen. I was poking around in a field when the land-owner came along. I told him what I was about and he took me across to the site of the old line. The railway land has been sold to the farmers, minimising any prospect of re-opening the line.

A notice above the village placename declared Castlemaine to be the birthplace of Jack Duggan. Near the road junction just south of the Maine River, I found the old Station House. It was reputedly from here that Jack Duggan – the Wild Colonial Boy – ventured forth to find his fortune in Australia:

Into the Kingdom

There was a wild colonial boy, Jack Duggan was his name.
Of poor but honest parents, he was born in Castlemaine.

Crossing the river, I went into The Jack Duggan Pub, hoping to learn something of this adventurer. But the barmaid could tell me nothing about him. Her thoughts were clearly more on the immediate future than the distant past. As she supplied no information, I have only the words of the song to go on. Jack Duggan was born in Castlemaine sometime in the mid-nineteenth century. He left home at the early age of sixteen years to become a bushranger, a wandering brigand like Ned Kelly, and a 'terror to Australia'. He held up the Beechworth mail-coach, and robbed Judge MacEvoy. This was the last straw: three troopers – Kelly, Davis and FitzRoy – tracked him down and captured him after a gunfight. I looked up Castlemaine in my old *Encyclopædia Britannica*, the 1929 edition. The solitary entry described a gold-mining town in Talbot county, Victoria. So, it seems that Jack Duggan was not a Kerryman at all, but an Aussie of Irish extraction. Perhaps it was no surprise that the locals here in Castlemaine could tell me nothing about him.

I met up again with Tom in the village and we went into Griffin's bar, where we found a cosy fire. Making plans for the rest of the day, we briefly considered the possibility of continuing the walk to Tralee. But I was tired and the weather looked undependable, so we spent the afternoon touring the Dingle peninsula. We drove out by Inch, where we stopped to admire the rolling waves. The beach stretches out three miles across Dingle Bay, completely exposed to the south-west winds, and is a popular place for surfers, though there were none there on this cold January day. In Dingle, we spied a curious sign over a shop; it was in ogham script, so I photographed it for later decipherment. The ogham script is for Ireland what the runes are for Scandinavia. The letters are those of the Roman alphabet, and are comprised of strokes above, below or across a medial line. There is a key to the script in the *Book of Ballymote*, in the library of the Royal Irish Academy, but I found a more accessible reproduction on page 275 of Praeger's book, *The Way that I Went*. The sign turned out to read simply An Siopa Oghaim.

After a snack, we drove on towards Smerwick Harbour to visit Gallarus Oratory, a remarkable ancient monument. This is one of the finest examples of early dry-stone building in the country. The oratory, in the shape of an upturned boat, is most pleasing in its symmetry and simplicity. The design of Gallarus seems to be a transition between the earlier hemispheric bee-hive huts also found hereabouts, and the rectangular churches that became common later. A nearby plaque indicated that it was built in the seventh or eighth century. The origin of the name is uncertain, though it may be simply Gall Árus, House for Foreigners, in reference to pilgrims who came from afar to worship or meditate here. The method of building is that of corbelling: flat stones are used, and each layer projects slightly inward from the one below. They are capped off where they meet at the top. The stones slope slightly, lower on the outward side, allowing water to drain down. Apart from a slight sagging in the centre, Gallarus is in as fine condition now as when built over a thousand years ago. The end walls are vertical, with a lintelled door at one end and a small circular window at the other. There was not a sign of dampness in the tiny interior. The oratory commands a splendid view of Smerwick Harbour, with the Three Sisters beyond.

We returned via the Conair Pass, enjoying breath-taking views of Brandon Mountain and its glacial lakes. Continuing eastward, the massive bulk of Caherconree rose up ahead of us, where stands the promontory fort of Caherconree, a high dry-stone wall cutting off an enclosure protected on the remaining sides by high cliffs. It was, in legend, the fortress stronghold of Cú Raoi Mac Daire, a powerful tribal chieftain. Cúchulainn, who fancied Cú Raoi's wife, Blathnaid, plotted with her to overthrow him. She tricked Cú Raoi into sending his army away and, when the coast was clear, poured milk into the stream as a signal to Cúchulainn, who was waiting in Camp below. Cúchulainn stormed the fortress, killed Cú Raoi and returned to Ulster with Blathnaid. However, Cú Raoi's Druid, Feircheirtne, later avenged him by leaping off a cliff with Blathnaid in his arms. To prove beyond doubt that all this is the truth, the river flowing down from the flanks of Caherconree is the Finglas, from Fionn Glas (White Stream). Q.E.D.

Chapter 9

THE ROAD FROM RATASS TO RATTOO

He sat, in defiance of municipal orders, astride the gun Zam-Zammah on her brick platform opposite the old Ajaib-Gher – the Wonder House, as the natives call the Lahore Museum.

Kim – Rudyard Kipling

MARK AND I DROVE DOWN TO TRALEE for the next stage of the circumambulation. The weather prospects were not good: a complex area of low pressure covered the country, indicating winds described by the forecaster as 'cyclonic variable', and frequent heavy showers. We stopped at The Arches, a restaurant in Adare, for lunch and had a look at the White Abbey. In Tralee, we booked into the Lisnagree Hostel, and then spent a few hours exploring the town. Near the hostel stands Ratass Church. The ruins date from the twelfth century, though the church was much renovated in the seventeenth. The name is at first astounding: surely 'Rodent's Rump' is an improbable moniker for a place of worship. In fact, the name derives from Séipéal Ráth Theas, the Church of the Southern Rath. In the church we found an excellent ogham inscription on a block of old red sandstone about 1.5 metres high. I photographed this, and also copied down the 24-letter inscription, which was quite clear. The key in Praeger's book, and in Harbison's *Guide to the National Monuments of Ireland*, is reproduced here:

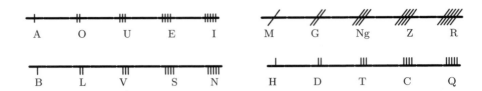

Using this, it is easy to transliterate the system of strokes into letters. I tried to decipher it on the spot; the inscription (with some spaces inserted in an effort to clarify) seemed to read:

GGODDIVV ATNA MAQQ ADDIC MAQ.

The meaning was immediately clear: Lady Godiva had eaten a Big Mac, and became addicted to them! Isn't that interesting! Checking later, I realised that the inscription must be read from bottom to top. The interpretation of some of the symbols also changes with this inversion, and the inscription then reads:

NAM SILLANNA MAQ VATTIL LOGG.

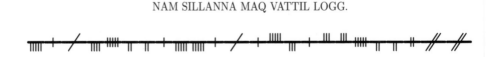

This may not look much better, but it indicates that the stone is dedicated to someone called Sillann. The string MAQ is not Big Mac, but an old form of the Irish word mac, or son. The initial NAM is short for anam or soul. The final string may be cognate with Lugh, the Celtic fertility God. So, the stone holds the message: The soul of Silán, son of Váttil Lugh. This interpretation comes not from me but from a publication of the Royal Irish Academy. It is fun to try to decode these inscriptions, many dating to the fifth or sixth century, and to puzzle over the meaning of these ancient stones.

Tralee, from Trá Lí, the strand of the Lee, stands on the river of that name at the head of Tralee Bay. The county town of Kerry, it has been an important focal point for centuries. The Earls of Desmond had their main castle here. Tralee was once a notable port, with a ship canal permitting passage for vessels up to 200 tons. Larger ships docked at Fenit, eight miles to the west, which had a rail link to Tralee. Once, grain, butter and livestock were exported from Tralee, and coal, iron and timber imported. Nowadays there is little or no sea trade.

We visited the Court House, designed by William Vitruvius Morrison, with its Ionic portico. More to my interest were the two large cannons mounted on plinths at each side of the steps. These were in memory of 'The Men of Kerry who fell in the Service of their Country, in the wars in Russia, India and China, 1854–1860'. The gun on the left was subscribed 'Crimea', that on the right 'India'. The period includes the time of the Crimean war (1854–56) and of the Indian Mutiny (1857–58). I was immediately reminded of Kipling's masterpiece *Kim*, one of my favourite books, which opens with the sentence quoted at the head of this chapter. The great bronze gun, now known as Kim's Gun, still stands in the city of Lahore. It is described by Peter Hopkirk in his book *Quest for Kim*, an account of a kind of pilgrimage to the locations where the action of Kipling's remarkable adventure took place.

We rambled on, past the 1798 memorial in Denny Street, a fine statue of a pikeman by Albert Power, to the Ashe Memorial Hall, which now houses the Kerry County Museum and Exhibition Centre. Onward we went, past Siamsa Tíre, the National Folk Theatre, to Ballyard Station, the old railway platform of the narrow gauge line to Dingle, which I shall describe below. Later that evening, we drove to Fenit Pier to see the Jeannie Johnston, a reconstruction of an old famine ship. It had been planned to transport this ship by barge from Blennerville to Fenit a few days earlier to step the masts and finish the fitting out, but technical hitches had delayed the operation. As time and tide wait for no man, the transport would be delayed for a further two weeks. At the onset of a thundery shower, we sheltered at the end of the pier, near a generously carved mermaid, admiring both her opulent curves and the new yachting marina. Returning, we stopped at a local restaurant for a meal where, for £18.00, I had a Dover sole which tasted like papier maché dipped in cod-liver oil. I could have bought a ream of blotting paper and a large jar of fish-paste, and been better off.

Stage 36: Castlemaine to Tralee (in reverse)

Our plan to catch a bus to Castlemaine to continue the Commodius Vicus was changed when we discovered that no bus ran at a suitable time. Driving to Castlemaine would require us to leave the car there, necessitating its later retrieval – bad logistics! We decided to walk this segment in reverse, which had the added advantage that the wind would be at our backs.

Leaving the hostel, we headed around the town by the Dan Spring Road – Bóthar Dónal Mich Earraigh. A huge flying saucer hovered before us, the Aqua Dome, a futuristic water sports facility – 'It's Wet, it's Wild, it's Wonderful'. We found the basin of the old ship canal and started out along the tow-path on its south side. Our way was blocked by an iron fence and an OPW sign prohibiting access. Ignoring the sign, we scrambled around the fence and continued along this beautiful path. House martins and a few sand martins zipped about us. Swans, herons and moorhens sported and played in the backwater beside the path. This area is a game sanctuary, so wildlife is protected from disturbance. As we neared Blennerville we beheld a sight which was any young boy's dream: in one field of vision were the large white windmill, the huge red hull of the Jeannie Johnston, and some rolling stock of the Tralee and Blennerville Railway.

We reached the end of the tow-path, circumventing another fence to come to the works where a canal lock is being renovated. Blennerville Windmill, a five storey grain mill, is the largest working mill in the country. It is the focal point of a visitor centre with an exhibition gallery, craft workshops and a restaurant. Just behind the mill, the full-size replica of the Jeannie Johnston stood on a barge, awaiting the return of the spring tides. This ship-building project is very similar to that in New Ross, where I had earlier visited the reconstruction of the Dunbrody. The Jeannie Johnston was a three-masted barque with four square sails on the fore and main masts, and fore-and-aft rigging on the mizen. Her overall length was 37.5 metres and she had a displacement of 510 tons. The original ship was built in Quebec in 1847 and owned by the Donovan family of Tralee. She plied the North Atlantic route, transporting timber and food to Ireland and returning with emigrants fleeing the famine. She could carry over 200 passengers, and it is said that in sixteen voyages to Quebec and Baltimore, not a single soul was lost to disease or to the sea.

The steam-train which runs between Tralee and Blennerville is the last remnant of what was Ireland's only mountain railway, the narrow gauge (3 foot) Tralee and Dingle Light Railway, running from the County Town of Kerry to the fishing port of Dingle. The line followed a difficult route over the spine of the peninsula, with gradients of one in thirty rising to a summit height of 680 feet. It opened in 1891 and, from the beginning, failed to make a profit, the 50 kilometre journey taking about two hours. By the time of its closure in 1953, the only traffic was a monthly 'cattle special' on market day in Dingle. The three kilometre section between Tralee and Blennerville is serviced by one of the original locomotives and the rolling stock is in the original T&DLR livery.

We continued southward, over the flanks of Slieve Mish, passing an army rifle range, where we could just make out a line of targets on the hillside. We climbed the mountain road to Glenaskagheen, where we spotted a signpost indicating Scotia's Grave. We followed the path down the glen, crossing two little bridges made of railway tracks. Near the confluence of two streams we found a large round stone with a recess carved in the centre. In front of this 'mill stone' were steps, apparently for kneeling, but no other indication of its significance was evident. Continuing, we crossed another bridge and came to a large boulder, surrounded by three smaller stones, with a second circle of larger stones further out. This we took to be the final resting place of Scotia or Scota, daughter of the Pharaoh and Queen of the Milesians. According to legend, the Milesians fought a great battle with the Túatha Dé Danann on the slopes of Slieve Mish, near this spot, in which Scotia perished.

Returning to the road, we met a local farmer who grazed his sheep in the glen. He was dressed in a style that is de rigeur for mountain farmers: a pre-war gabardine coat, shiny with age, held fast by a sisal cord, and head-gear like an airman's helmet, with loose flaps, not totally dissimilar to Mark's Biggles-like model. He complained about visitors to the glen, bringing horses and dogs that caused damage and difficulties for his sheep. He told us the history of how Scotia had come from Egypt, and how a British officer had excavated the site of her grave in 1914, 'before any of us was on the planet', but had found nothing. The great battle was said to have taken place in 1200 BC, 'and isn't it time we stopped worrying about her?' he concluded.

We continued to the crest of the pass, and detoured to the top of Knockmoyle, where there was an array of TV and communication masts. The wind here was strong from the north and we reflected on our good fortune in following a reverse trajectory. The road down to Castlemaine was a steep descent, overlooking rich pasture land with lush hedgerows. Violets and stitchwort and lady's smock decorated the verges. Approaching the village, we passed the ruin of an old grain store, burned down some years ago. The castle that gave the village its name is long since gone, we were told in Griffin's, where we relaxed while waiting for the bus back to Tralee. At the station we met Frank, who was planning to join us for the following few days while Anne and Donncha, his wife and son, toured in the locality.

Stage 37: *Tralee to Ballyheige*

The three of us left Tralee in a heavy drizzle, crossed a little rivulet called the Big River, and took a back road to Ardfert, turning north at Lisloose reservoir (capacity 6.75 million litres, according to the notice erected by Tralee UDC, who clearly wish to promulgate this vital information). The hedgerows were bright with May blossoms and a variety of other flowers. As we tried to discern which trees were in bloom, Mark reminded us of the old rhyme:

> *Oak before Ash: in for a splash*
> *Ash before Oak: in for a soak*

In response to which, motivated by the gloomy day, I muttered into my beard, 'Oak and Ash together: foul and stormy weather'. At the top of a steep hill, a tractor towing a four-wheeled trailer approached us. Though we heard no unusual sound, we noticed a wheel by the roadside after it had passed. Mark put his hand on the hub, detecting an elevated temperature and deducing by this scientific means that the wheel had come off the trailer. Complimenting him on this scintillating sleuth-work, we called after the driver, who stopped and returned to collect it. We crossed the dismantled railway from Limerick to Tralee, noticing an old platform nearby. This line did not close until 1978. Coming to the village of Ardfert, we headed straight for the cathedral, an imposing ruin just to the north.

Ardfert, in medieval times a major ecclesiastical centre with a university, was the site of the monastery founded in the sixth century by St. Brendan the Navigator. Brendan was born here in or around the year 484. He voyaged in a leather boat across the Atlantic to the Faroes and Iceland and may have reached North America, though scholarship is against emotion here. A carved plaque, erected to commemorate the fifteenth centenary of his birth, shows the Saint standing in the prow of a clinker-built boat. Indeed, if he did get to the New World, it must have been in a wooden vessel. The impressive cathedral ruins date mainly from the thirteenth century. There are three magnificent lancet windows in the east wall of the large rectangular cathedral, and an elegant row of nine smaller windows on the south side, partially obscured by an incongruous flying buttress. The cathedral is described in the *Shell Guide to Ireland* as 'scandalously neglected', so we were happy to find a major renovation in progress. The south transept has already been completely repaired and roofed, and serves now as an exhibition centre. The main body of the church will not be roofed, but the walls will be repaired and strengthened, allowing the removal of the buttress, which was added about a century ago to prevent collapse. Due to the renovation work, we could not enter the cathedral, but explored the small ruined chapel behind it, Temple-na-Hoe, with a fine Romanesque doorway and interesting carvings.

There is a ruined friary about a mile to the east, founded by Thomas Fitzmaurice in 1253 for the Franciscans. The friary was used as a barracks in Elizabethan times. As the rain was heavy, we did not detour to see it, but repaired instead to Flaherty's in the village for refreshments. The toilet door in the pub bore a cute notice – 4U2P.

A notice in Ardfert indicated 'The Akeragh Way'. We later noticed a lake of this name near Ballyheige, whither we were headed. We explored McKenna's Fort, now also called Casement's Fort, where Roger Casement was arrested by local police on the eve of the Easter Rising in April 1916, shortly after landing from a German submarine at Banna Strand. We also visited Rahoneen Castle, an old ruin on a hillock near Carrahane Strand and carried on around this land-locked beach. An obelisk commemorating Casement and his companions Robert Monteith and 'a Third Man' prompted us to march on towards Banna Strand humming the Harry Lime Theme. As we reached the shore, we saw the isolated rock of Muckalaghmore far out to sea, a little reminiscent of Ailsa Craig off the Scottish coast.

Roger Casement was born in 1864, in Sandycove, County Dublin. He served as British consul in Mozambique, Angola, the Congo and Brazil. His exposure of the appalling cruelty towards native labourers by white traders in the Congo led to great improvements and earned him a knighthood. In 1912 he returned to Ireland, where he helped form the Irish National Volunteers. During World War I, he travelled to Berlin seeking support, but the German government was unwilling to risk an expedition to Ireland. He was arrested almost immediately upon his return, and taken to the Tower of London. Roger Casement was convicted of treason at the Old Bailey, and sentenced to death. He was hanged at Pentonville Prison in August 1916, despite efforts by several influential people to obtain a reprieve in view of his earlier record of humanitarian work. In 1965 Casement's remains were returned to Ireland and buried in Glasnevin Cemetery. The notorious 'Black Diaries', allegedly written by Casement and giving graphical details of putative homosexual affairs, are still a source of controversy.

The beautiful Banna Strand stretches for over five miles up to Ballyheige, our destination for the day, so the remainder of the journey should have been simple. However, the wind was strong from the north, so our journey up Banna was a heavy beat to windward. At Black Rock, progress was barred by a broad stream, but we easily found a way round by a sluice gate and bridge. We revived ourselves by scoffing a large block of Marzipan Schwarzbrot, a delicious and energizing snack. Moving onward, I lifted the wire of a fence to crawl under it and discovered by painful means that it was electrified. Frank and I argued about the voltage, he maintaining it was 12 volts and I, with direct experience, insisting it was nearer to 100 volts (I suspect that he was right).

Birdlife on the beach was sparse, with most sensible birds probably sheltering further inland, but we saw lots of dunlins and turnstones and a few curlews and greenshanks. As we approached Ballyheige, the shell of the ruined castle, which was once a home of the Crosbie family of Ardfert, became prominent. The castle was burned down by Republicans in 1922. Ballyheige is a quiet little resort nestled in the crook of Kerry Head. By the time we reached the village we were exhausted from our battle against the wind. We were hungry enough to eat a horse so, struggling up the slipway, were delighted to see GiGi's Restaurant, where we enjoyed a delicious meal, the best we had ever eaten, or so it seemed at the time. We stayed at the Wave Crest B&B, a little to the west of the village and overlooking the bay, which was run by Michael and Anne Lean.

Stage 38: Ballyheige to Ballyduff

We left the Wave Crest and headed out the Cliff Road and then upwards towards Maulin, at 717 feet the highest point of Kerry Head. A farmer warned us that the track was very muddy and wellingtons would be essential. We carried on through the farmyard, ankle-deep in dung, but the way was clearer beyond. We noticed the orderly division of the farms on the south side of the head; Mark speculated that this area had been divided up systematically, probably by the Land Commission. Higher up, waist-deep gorse (*Ulex europaeus*, variety Bolokhai) made the going prickly but eventually we reached clearer boggy ground near the top. We could now enjoy a view northward across the estuary of the Shannon to Loop Head, our first glimpse of County Clare. After a rest during a shower, we headed eastwards, to the sound of skylarks, to a peak with a triangulation pillar, a truncated concrete pyramid about four feet high. From here we headed on to another lower peak, Cloghaun, where we found the remains of an old round hut of rough stones. We noticed a low ridge extending down the mountain, the remains of an ancient boundary marked on the map as An Claí Rua, the Red Fence. We followed it until we came to a dirt path, where a hare bounded along before us. Lower down we found a way-marked trail, leading through leafy lanes and primrose and violet bedecked paths, back down past Ballyheige Castle to the village.

At Kirby's Lounge we enjoyed refreshments and sandwiches, and studied the photos on the walls. Every Kerry sportsman since time immemorial is depicted here, and there are various mementos of the War of Independence. One might form the impression that the war had ended only last week. Also prominent in the lounge was an oversize picture of C.J. Haughey, who enjoyed a particular popularity in the Kingdom.

We took a minor road known as 'the Line', which ran eastward to Ballyduff like a Roman road in straight line segments. For long stretches it was on an embankment, which we thought had been constructed. Later, we learned that the road was not raised, but the surrounding land lowered by the harvesting of turf over many years, leaving the road high and dry. We got a close-up of a stoat, as he bobbed back and forth undecidedly across the road. Stonechats and larks provided amusement but, apart from this, the journey was quite boring: with little to distract us, it was becoming a tedious slog, and we were tired after the great ascent of Kerry Head. A rest and some glucose revived us for the remaining miles. Praegar, normally ebullient, comments, 'Of Kerry north of Killarney there is little to be said'. Reluctantly, on the evidence before us, we were inclined to agree.

Traffic was light, but soon a large tanker approached, shooting a wide brown parabola, a lethal slurry dung-bow, into the field beside the road. Frank made some mental computations and concluded that the concentration of nitrogen being spread was far above the recommended dose, and would cause severe damage to the vegetation. Moreover, with a series of drainage ditches criss-crossing the land, much of it would find its way into the river system, where further damage would result. We felt that there must be a less harmful way to dispose of this material, by spreading it more thinly but, no doubt, hard economics are against such a 'green' approach.

We came to Tobairín Domhnach, a Marian Shrine, where we rested. This well kept shrine, with a well of crystal-clear water, has been enhanced by the installation of a glass-fronted hut where the pious can pray undisturbed by rainy weather. Soon afterwards we saw a tall stone tower above the trees. It was the site of Rattoo Church and Round Tower. Little is known about this old monastic foundation. The Round Tower is well preserved. There is a Sheela-na-gig, but she is carved on the inside of a window, high up on the tower, out of harm's way and safe from our ogling eyes.

Rattoo is Rath Thúaidh, the North Rath or ring-fort. We had now come from the south fort to the north, from Rath Theas to Rath Thúaidh, which called for a celebration in verse:

> The talk of our ramshackle crew,
> Was puerile, shambolic and blue,
>   With anecdotes lewd,
>   And repartee rude
> On the road from Ratass to Rattoo.

The lewd anecdotes must remain unrecorded. As we neared Ballyduff we noticed a loud commotion above us: a flock of crows was mobbing a hawk, who quickly fled, leaving them clacking triumphantly. We asked someone how the town had got its name, and were told in all seriousness that Baile Dubh, the Black Town, was named as a result of an earlier village having been burned down by the Black and Tans. Perhaps there is some truth behind this, but we never got to the bottom of it.

We trudged up the long main street of the village to our B&B. There we were greeted by a snooty, overbearing woman with an unnaturally affected accent identifiable as 'posh Galway', if that is not an oxymoron. She lectured Mark and Frank on the evils of cigarettes when they politely enquired whether and where smoking was permitted. However, we overlooked the inhospitable and unbusinesslike reception when she served up a delicious meal of fresh salmon. I asked where it had been caught and she named the Cashen, as the Feale is called for its last few miles to the sea. She asked, disapprovingly, if we would be going for a drink that evening, warning us about a particular pub (let's call it Kelly's) in the town. She recommended Purcell's, saying they were 'mad about dawks'. What could this mean? Of course, Kelly's was the very place we headed for directly after dinner! Later, we moved on to Purcell's. On the wall of this pub is a plaque to a greyhound, Joan's Legacy, interred below the floor. Joan herself was our gracious hostess; we were warmly welcomed and enjoyed a pleasant evening of conversation. Indeed, they were 'mad about greyhounds' in Purcell's, and perhaps other 'dawks' too.

We were hoping to continue next day to Ballybunion, but only if we could arrange a lift across the mouth of the river, to avoid a long slog on the main road. We enquired in the pub and were told there were boats at Moneycashen, but there would be no one there until the opening of the salmon season on the Cashen in another two weeks. Interesting, considering the dinner we had earlier enjoyed!

Stage 39: Ballyduff to Carrig Island

As we departed our B&B the next morning, I wished the landlady 'the best of luck with the fishing', but the irony was completely lost on her. As we were not hopeful of a ferry across the mouth of the Cashen, we changed our plans and decided to head directly for Carrig Island. The first few miles were on a busy road, so we crossed the Cashen bridge and strutted forth in a mindless rhythmic stomp to Lisselton Cross, where we arrived about two hours later. To our surprise, we found that we had been beaten to it by a more famous visitor: a stone on the grass here bears an inscription dated Saturday, September 5th, 1998:

> At this cross, President Clinton walked;
> At this cross, there is no judgement;
> At this cross, all are cherished.

In view of such lofty and noble sentiments, we refrained from cracking any Monica Lewinski jokes. We stopped at the garage shop, The Lartigue Supermarket, for supplies. There, I spoke to Nolie Hegarty, who was fascinated with the map slung in a case around my neck. She was unaware of the OSI Discovery Series, and scrutinised the map in depth, picking out the local details and calling to the other customers that their home places were marked on it. I asked her if any traces of the old Lartigue railway remained, and she immediately pinpointed a place on the map, and phoned Michael Barry who lived a mile up the hill. He was not home, but his wife said we were welcome to come up and see the old railway carriage in the yard.

We headed up past the old ruined and ivy-clad church tower at Lisselton, and turned aside to Ballingowan. There we were welcomed by Mrs Barry and invited to examine the remnants of the railway. The Lartigue railway was one of the oddest railways in Ireland. It ran between Listowel and Ballybunion, from its opening in 1888 until it closed 36 years later. It was a monorail, designed by a Frenchman called Lartigue. The train ran on a single central rail supported by triangular trestles with a guide rail at a lower level on each side. The rolling stock was custom-made for the system, both carriages and locomotives being of duplicated pattern, like Siamese twins straddling the rail. The distance was about 15 kilomretres and the line was built in only five months, at a very low cost. However, operating conditions were difficult. Passengers sat back to back, facing outwards with the wheels on the elevated rail clattering and clanking behind them. Railwaymen had to ensure a balanced load, and access between the sides of the train was limited and awkward. Level crossings could not be accomodated, necessitating complicated draw-bridges and ramps. At farm crossings a section of track was swung aside like a gate. Like so many other lines, the Listowel & Ballybunion Railway was never profitable and was eventually forced to close in 1924. In the yard, we found a section of track with a single wooden carriage straddled forlornly across it. We studied the system of monorail and trestles, the construction of the carriage, and the bearing mechanism. It would have been possible for passengers on opposide sides to converse, or at least to shout above the wheel noise, as the upper half of the division between the sides was quite open. It was sad that this unique railway curiosity had gone.[7]

We continued over the eastern side of Knockanore until the Shannon came into view. We could see the high chimneys of the Moneypoint power station, with the smaller stacks of Tarbert to the east. We picked out the Round Tower on Scattery Island further downstream. The rest of the way

---

[7] Since our visit, a section of the Lartigue railway near Listowel has been restored.

was downhill on a straight road. Coming to the river bank, we found a causeway leading to Carrig Island. We walked out, disturbing some large waders which we did not identify until later. Before going to our hosts for the evening, we explored the island, which is about a square kilometre or 250 acres. At Corran Point, we found an old battery, like a square Martello tower, built in Napoleonic times, with walls about two metres thick. An old farmer living nearby told us something about this battery, which is

one of a series along the banks of the Shannon estuary. He took out a large plastic fertilizer sack, which he called his 'bag of tricks', and emptied the contents on the ground, a motley miscellany of *objets trouvé*: broken clay pipes, bottle tops, fragments of pottery, coins and bones. He picked out a fist-sized stone which he said was an ancient axe-head. We chatted to him for some time as, living in this isolated place, he was clearly glad of the company and conversation.

A cuckoo called repeatedly as we made our way back along the shore of this peaceful island to the bridge, where Anne and Donncha were waiting to collect Frank. He was returning home while Mark and I were continuing the Commodius Vicus to Tarbert next day. We stayed with Garrett and Patricia Dee in Castle View House, beautifully situated by the bridge, looking across the reed-beds to Carrigafoyle Castle. They told us there are just five families living on the island. The old man we had met earlier was Garrett's uncle. After a meal we walked around by the mud-flats listening to a chorus of bird-song as darkness fell.

Stage 40: Carrig Island to Tarbert

We crossed the bridge to begin the final Kerry stage of the ramble. There was a group of large waders feeding along the shore. All but two of them rose in alarm as we approached. The remaining birds we recognised as curlews. The more timorous ones were the black-tailed godwits that we had failed to identify the previous evening. Black-tailed godwits (*Limosa limosa*) have long legs and long straight bills, black tails, white rumps and white wing-bars. The birds we spotted had predomi-nantly greyish backs, with lighter underparts. With a length of about 16 inches, they were large, but a good deal smaller than the curlews with which they were feeding before they fled. They have become more common in Ireland in recent years, but are very shy and hard to get close to, so we were delighted to have seen them.

Carrigafoyle Castle is a five storey castle, with a spiral staircase leading up to the battlements. It stands out in the water, in the channel between the mainland and Carrig Island, and is surrounded by a bawn which serves as a dock for boats. As we approached, a raven perched on the high battlements squawked angrily and flew off to a nearby tree. We explored the ruin, climbing over 100 steps to the battlements. Near the top, Mark spotted the raven's nest in a recess in the inside wall, not five feet from where we stood, but completely inaccessible. The views from the top were spectacular, although standing on the unprotected roof was a vertiginous experience. In a tower of the bawn below we found a series of square slots in the wall, a honeycomb structure, which must be the remains of an old dove-cote.

Carrigafoyle Castle was built by Conor O'Connor in 1490. On Palm Sunday ninety years later it was besieged by Elizabethan forces under William Pelham and when the occupants were overcome they were all massacred. Pelham sent all the valuables, which the Earl of Desmond had stored here, to the Queen. It would not surprise me if they are still in the Royal collection. The castle was finally wrecked by Cromwellians in 1649. Relaxing by the peaceful river bank, it was hard to believe that this tranquil spot was the site of a more recent atrocity, which has inspired a series of dramas. Elizabeth Healy tells the story in her beautiful book *Literary Tour of Ireland*. John Scanlan, a local man of aristocratic parentage, eloped with Ellen Hanley, a young and innocent beauty of more humble origins. After living with her for a while, he tired of her and decided to get rid of her. He took her to Carrigafoyle Castle one fateful night in 1819 and, with the help of his servant Stephen Sullivan, murdered her and threw her in the Shannon. Her body was found some months later, washed up on the opposite bank near Moneypoint. Both dastardly murderers were caught and hanged. The event was used as the basis of a novel, *The Collegians*, by Gerald Griffin, who moved the action to Killarney. This in turn inspired Dion Boucicault to write *The Colleen Bawn*, an instant box-office hit which is still staged occasionally. A popular opera, *The Lily of*

Killarney, was also based on the story. One of the main characters in *The Colleen Bawn* was Myles na Gopaleen, who gave the comic writer Brian O'Nolan, or Flann O'Brien, his other pen-name.

We walked along the shore of the inlet towards Ballylongford. At a church, now gone, near the village, Kitchener of Khartoum was baptized in 1850. Horatio Herbert (Lord) Kitchener, the British Field Marshal prominent in World War I – he may need you, but you don't need him – was born in Gunsborough a few miles to the south. In the village we popped into Kennelly's Bar. This was the home of Brendan Kennelly, one of Ireland's most popular poets and Professor of Modern English Literature at Trinity College in Dublin, and is run by his brother. On the wall of the bar hang a series of large reproductions of old photographs of Ballylongford, from the Lawrence collection. There was also a drawing of some noted writers from the district, John B. Keane, Maurice Walsh, George Fitzmaurice, Bryan McMahon and Brendan Kennelly himself.

Ballylongford stands at the head of a small inlet, Ballylongford Creek. On the eastern shore of the inlet stand the ruins of Lislaughtin Friary. The first monastery here was founded by St. Laughtin in 622. The Franciscan Friary, founded in 1477, was built by John O'Connor and two O'Connor chiefs are buried within its walls. Kennelly wrote of it in his poem 'Lislaughtin Abbey':

> *Ignoring green Lislaughtin where*
> *Subtle shadows pass*
> *Through shattered altars, broken walls,*
> *The blood of martyrs in the grass ...*

The friary was destroyed by Elizabethan troops in 1580. The structure of the elegant three-mullioned east window is still intact. Near the altar on the south wall is a sedilia, a series of three canopied seats. We left the ruins, in pensive mood, for the last stage of our journey, recalling Kennelly's final lines:

> *Restless at the gate, I turn away*
> *Groping towards what can't be said*
> *And know I know but little*
> *Of the birds, the river and the dead.*

There was little to see on the road around to Tarbert, save the huge power station at Moneypoint across the water and a few freighters plying the river. We saw a few wild arum lilys, also known as lords and ladies. Mark also noticed a curious plant by the roadside, called spurge, which is used by poachers as it has the effect of stunning fish. We considered picking some to send to the 'mad-about-dawks' woman in Ballyduff, to help her to keep salmon on the menu, but we doubted that she would approve or appreciate the gesture.

So we arrived in Tarbert on a Saturday afternoon to find a hive of inactivity. Hardly a movement was evident in this sleepy village overlooking the Shannon estuary. We had five pounds between us, insufficient for a bus back to Tralee where the car had been left. There was a bank but, of course, it was closed and had no hole-in-the-wall or automatic cash dispenser. It did not matter: there were no buses on Saturday; there were none on Sunday; and there were none on the following Monday, a Bank Holiday! What to do in a crisis? We headed for the nearest bar where, learning of our plight, the affable owner urged us to sit and offered us a free drink. He happily cashed a cheque for us. Now comes the boon of a mobile phone: Mark's brother John and his wife Fiona were journeying from Ennis to Ballyduff that very day and had earlier indicated that they could give us a lift back to Tralee if it suited. It certainly suited now, so we were happy when my little phone rang and John told us they were about to board the ferry at Killimer. We met them at the bottom of the town and drove to Listowel for a delightful meal in Casa Mia. Afterwards, John showed us an electronic fish-counter on the Feale, which he had been involved in installing, and then drove us to Tralee, where we parted company.

Chapter 10

TRACKING THE WEST CLARE RAILWAY

You may talk of Columbus's sailing
Across the Atlantical sea,
But he never tried to go railing
From Ennis as far as Kilkee.

'Are Ye Right There, Michael?' – Percy French

BEFORE ME LAY CLARE, HOME OF traditional music, land of rock
and rolling surf, endowed with a multitude of Megalithic monuments, Bronze Age forts and Early Christian remains. The county is also
famous for the West Clare Railway, immortalized by Percy French in his
witty song 'Are Ye Right There, Michael?' in which he lampooned it mer-
cilessly. I planned to follow the course of the railway from Kilrush as far as
'Sweet Corrofin', walking at least some sections. On previous experience,
I anticipated that it would be passable only in spots, and that alternative routes would have to be found where the line was blocked. But that
would give me a chance to visit some of the magnificent sandy beaches,
and explore the rocky Burren.

Stage 41: Tarbert to Kilrush

I stood outside Tarbert Gaol on a cold, bright January morning. It was
better than being inside: the politician Liam Lawlor had just spent
his first night behind bars in Mountjoy Jail in Dublin, guilty of contempt
of court for failing to co-operate with the Flood Tribunal. I was kitted
out in a new jacket and boots, ready for a week's walking in any weather

the turbulent Irish atmosphere could throw at me. I was also equipped with a Dazer, of which more anon. Starting in low gear, I strolled at a leisurely pace out to Tarbert Island to catch the ferry across the Shannon. Big waders were feeding at the water's edge, and a clutch of small ducks which I took to be scaups. I passed the gates of Tarbert House, described on a notice as a seventeenth century heritage house. A star-shaped fort marked on Sheet 64 might have diverted me, but the 11:30 ferry was just arriving at the pier as I crossed the bridge, so I did not detour to the fort.

The twenty-minute trip across the river on the Shannon Dolphin cost £2.50. As I sat on the upper deck soaking up the weak winter sun and admiring the broad canvas of the majestic Shannon, I chewed on a lump of marzipan. This greatly interested a young rook, who repeatedly swooped dangerously close to me. He would have snatched the prize had I not used my Hillpig to deter him. The twin towers of Moneypoint on the Clare bank dwarfed the Tarbert power station behind me. Moneypoint burns vast quantities of coal, producing large amounts of carbon dioxide (3.4 million tons per year, in fact). To meet international requirements to limit emissions, the government planned to close this power station, but the alternative source of electricity was not yet clear. Arriving at Killimer, I found an attractive sculpture inscribed with the name Jim Connolly, 1987. It was a bust of a beautiful young girl, representing the Colleen Bawn who is buried in the nearby cemetery. Her body was washed up here, having been thrown into the river over at Carrigafoyle some weeks earlier by her murderers.

I took a small road north to follow a quiet roundabout route to Kilrush. At a crossroads I passed a row of about fifteen long sheds, like Nissen Huts covered in black plastic sheeting, presumably used for growing mushrooms. On a hillock ahead I spied what looked like a miniature village of thatched cottages. They turned out to be tombs, built in the shape of small houses a little over two metres high with grass-covered roofs; this was Molougha Cemetery. Just beyond I noticed a triangulation pillar behind a wall; this was a curious position, as usually they are located on prominent hilltops. Checking the map I found it marked at 69 metres on Sheet 64. A few yards further on, I followed a sign down through a field to

St. Senan's Well. This is reputedly the birthplace of the Saint, who lived from 488 to 544 AD and was Bishop of Scattery Island. The well was surrounded by an elaborate super-structure on which devotees of St. Senan had placed a variety of statues and holy pictures. I tasted the water, praying for peace in the world — well, you never know!

Continuing, I came to a farmyard where I was pestered by a border collie. I had thought these dogs to be mild-tempered, but this one was aggressive and persistent. I took out my Dazer and pressed the button. The dog stopped, looking confused, then turned on his heels and ran into a barn. I was delighted with the effectiveness of this simple device. The Dazer is a little electronic gizmo, the size of a computer mouse, powered by a small battery. It emits an ultra-sonic screech, inaudible to humans but very irritating to dogs. This was my first use of the dog-zapper, and it performed completely in accordance with specifications. I had earlier tried it on the ferry rook, but without effect. So, entrepreneurs, there is an opportunity to develop and market a rook-zapper.

Heading back to the river bank at Moyne Bay, I carried on westward to a point where Scattery Island and the smaller Hog Island came into view. Scattery Island, or Inis Cathaig, is the island of Cata, a horrible monster who dwelt there until he was defeated by St. Senan. The Saint founded a monastery at Scattery in the early sixth century. The Vikings invaded it several times, and occupied it until Brian Boru re-captured it in 975. The monastery was destroyed in Elizabethan times. There are remains of several churches dating from the ninth to the fifteenth century, but most obvious from the mainland is the Round Tower, 120 feet in height.

At Aylevarroo Bay I walked along the rocky shore, frightening various small birds, stonechats and pipits as well as waders. Then at Cappagh Pier I found a Pilot Station. Entering, I introduced myself to Richard Glynn, who was on duty, 'keeping an eye on the river'. He showed me the radar display of the estuary, and explained the system of pilotage and navigation. Before leaving, I asked him about the West Clare Railway, which I knew had terminated here at Cappagh Pier. He pointed out the window at a circle of stones at the pier-head. This was the remains of the base of an engine turntable, the bitter end of the line. Little else remains, but the platform of the old terminus is still to be seen.

In Kilrush Creek a yachting marina has been developed. Indeed, the whole town had a lively go-ahead air. At Merchant's Quay, I came to the pre-fab headquarters of Nowcasting International. This company provides a computer-based system for mariners, giving them detailed and up-to-the-minute forecasts of sea conditions. A ship's captain only has to tap into an on-board PC to get the latest forecasts of sea conditions for his route. Andrew Jarocki, the Senior Software Engineer, showed me around the office, demonstrated the system and explained how it is used.

Kilrush is an estate town, more spacious than most Irish towns, with the broad and elegant Frances Street leading up from the marina. At the top of the street stands a statue of the Maid of Erin, erected in 1903 by public subscription to commemorate the Manchester Martyrs – Allan, Larkin and O'Brien – whom we had come across in Ladysbridge. The inscription described them as having been 'judicially murdered by a tyrannical government' in 1867. It is difficult now to understand the depth of feeling that followed their executions. They were hanged because a police sergeant had been shot while they were freeing their leaders from a Black Maria. Irish Nationalists argued that this was just an accident, overlooking the fact that the sergeant's widow might not see things the same way. At all events, the three executed men became powerful symbols of the Nationalist cause, and many statues to commemorate them were erected over the following decades. I stayed at The Grove B&B, looked after by Bridie Kiely. The evening was rounded off with a good meal in Kelly's Bar and visits to some of the town's other watering places – Buggle's, Crotty's and of course the Percy French Bar.

Stage 42: Kilrush to Kilkee

Before leaving the town, I had another quick look around Kilrush. Noticing that the door of Katie O'Connor's Hostel was ajar, despite my publicity brochure indicating otherwise, I entered and asked the proprietor if the hostel was open. 'Well, 'tis open and 'tis shut!' Hmmm, a quantum hostel, in two states at once, like Schrödinger's cat, I thought, but did not give utterance to my musings. 'Where are you from?' asked the owner. I gathered from this that, although the hostel might be closed, if I wanted a shakedown he would furnish one provided I hailed from a suitable place. He told me that the Kilkee Hostel was closed, that is, 'not open at all, at all'.

At the marina, several information notices had been erected by the local council, but the frost was so thick on them this crisp morning that I could not read them without the help of an ice-pick. A sculpture of a group of dolphins overlooked the creek. These delightful creatures have become regular visitors to the waters of south-west Ireland, and dolphin-watching trips are now a popular pastime. The most celebrated is Fungi, who frequents Dingle Bay, but there are now a number of others. Perhaps their presence indicates some change in climate not evident in the instrumental records.

The narrow-gauge West Clare Railway from Ennis to Miltown Malbay, taking a circuitous route through Corrofin, Ennistymon and Lahinch, opened in May 1887. In 1892 it was extended, technically as the South Clare Railway, to Kilkee and Kilrush via Moyasta Junction, also with a direct service between these two towns. Just four years later, Percy French set out from Ennis to give a concert in Kilkee. He was so badly delayed that he was too late to give his performance. He successfully sued the railway for loss of earnings. When his song, about 'railin' from Ennis as far as Kilkee', came out, the directors of the WCR filed a suit against him for libel, but withdrew it when it became clear that the case would be laughed out of court. By all accounts, the WCR provided a valuable asset to the people of the county for seventy years. But funding for maintenance of the track-work and rolling stock was inadequate, so the service was patchy. Still, it outlasted all other narrow-gauge lines in the country, being the last one to close in 1961.

I passed the old red-brick station house of the WCR and walked out along the creek. For a while, the course of the railway was clear but then I reached an impenetrable bramble barrier and had to make a wide detour through farmland. I met the friendly owner, and we talked for a while. He recalled travelling to hurling matches on the train. I asked if it was a good service. 'Not at all. Sure, 'twent all round the county, and took half the day to get there!' This was consistent with Percy French's experience. He told me where I could pick up the line again, and his information turned out to be sound. At a gate lodge, a woman warned me to avoid a section which served as a slurry pit, and to go through a small coniferous wood instead. But she said that after that the way to Moyasta was clear. I walked through the wood, looking down on the line, which was in a short cutting completely flooded with greenish-brown sludge. I was glad of the advice to avoid it. Further on, at a long causeway on the shore of Poulnasherry Bay, with Illaunaclaggin offshore, I rested and listened to the cries of the waders. The air was fresh and sharp, but a shallow fog made the opposite shore of the bay indistinct.

Near Moyasta the line was covered with long, thick, uneven grass and I fell several times, once nearly breaking my Dazer. Then, tumbling down the bank, I snapped my Hillpig at the joint. I concluded reluctantly that Hillpigs are not for serious walkers. At Clancy's in Moyasta, I savaged two pints of rock shandy; the walk had left me dehydrated, despite the cold weather. The bar-owner pointed towards the nearby station, where the line from the north branched to Kilrush and Kilkee. There I met Jackie Whelan, who was restoring a five-mile stretch of the WCR. Two carriages and a loco stood at the platform. The carriages are replicas of the originals, none of which remain. Passengers sat at either side, facing each other, more sociable than the back-to-back arrangement of the Lartigue Railway. The diesel locomotive was originally built for use in the construction of the Channel Tunnel. It will be replaced later by an original WCR engine, the Slieve Callan, which stood for many years outside Ennis Station and was currently undergoing refurbishment in Wales. Jackie told me of his plans to renovate more of the line. He said that the Kilrush–Kilkee section could easily be brought back into use if money could be found for the work. I asked if Síle de Valera, the Clare TD and Minister for (amongst other things) Heritage and Culture, had supplied any funding but he indicated that, so far, efforts in that direction had been fruitless. It is sad that so many people still fail to see the old railway system as a priceless part of our heritage.

West from Moyasta the line was clear for a mile or so, thanks in part to Jackie's efforts, and I strode across the bridge and along the firm ballast with ease. But it didn't last, so I took a path to the water's edge and followed the shore around to Blackweir Bridge. The going was mostly easy but near the bridge I found myself in reed-beds over two metres tall and had to take careful notice of the direction. To my surprise, I spied two seals playing in the water nearby, and watched them for a spell. Then, crossing the bridge, I followed minor roads by Termon, past an old ruined national school, and picked up the line again for the final mile to the old station at Kilkee.

A popular summer resort, undergoing rapid development, Kilkee had a slightly lugubrious feel this gloomy winter evening. Most of the hotels were shut (i.e., closed and not open) but I found a haven at the Bay View B&B, where Mary Hickey gave me a nice room with a sea view. The only other guest was a retired English priest. I sat by the window, watching the waves lapping on the crescent beach and resting my weary bones.

Stage 43: Kilkee to Quilty

I set out from Kilkee after a leisurely breakfast. Mary didn't like to rise too early in the winter, so I had breakfast at half-past nine. It was inauguration day for George W. Bush; numerologists might read volumes of significance into the repeating date, 20-01-2001. I took a small road eastward, following a sign for St. Senan's Altar. At the back of Kilkee, vast acres were covered with shabby caravans and mobile homes, all deserted until the sun's return. It was dull, featureless countryside, but at least quiet and traffic-free. At one point, a pack of dogs harried me. Two were particularly persistent and I could not shake them off. I pressed the trusty Dazer, which confused them greatly. Each one seemed to think that the sound was a signal from the other, and they snarled and snapped viciously at each other. Glaring at me with beady, translucent eyes and bared fangs, they worried me until their owner, alerted by their barking, arrived on his Honda and called them off. So I realised that the Dazer was no panacea; it seemed useful for a single dog, but dangerous when there was more than one. It definitely increased their aggressiveness, so I resolved to use it with discretion in future, and cut a stout stick to replace my broken Hillpig.

St. Senan's Altar is a recently constructed altar on the site of an old Mass Rock, where mass was celebrated in Penal times. A full-length statue of the Saint, in robes and with cross and staff, stands beside the altar. It is inscribed Sionán Naofa; I wondered if the Shannon River, An tSionáinn, is named for the Saint. A plaque mounted on a nearby wall showed him receiving a bell from heaven. In the graveyard down the hill were more curious house-like tombs, dating back to the early 1800s, and another holy well attributed to St. Senan.

I turned north and then east through a large marshy area. A local man stopped his car and offered me a lift, which I politely declined. We talked for a while: he was an amateur twitcher, and told me that this area was a wildlife reserve. He said I should look out for white-fronted geese and also might spot a hen harrier. He said he was going to Blackweir Bridge to look at the seals and was interested that I had seen them the previous day. He asked if I would like to join him, but I explained that I planned to go up through Doonbeg. When he heard that, he told me he had been watching some otters feeding near the bridge there. When I got to Doonbeg, I had a sandwich in the Igoe Inn and then sat by the river, opposite the ruined castle, hoping to spot the otters, but without luck.

Crossing the Creegh River, marked on the map as the Skivileen, I left the N67 and headed for the southern end of the White Strand, crossing the path of the West Clare Railway on the way. Behind the dunes a new golf links was under construction. I crossed over to a magnificent vista: the dark brown sand stretching northward for miles, with lines of huge aquamarine breakers tumbling towards the shore. A dozen surfers were out trying to ride the waves but the strong offshore breeze was steepening the wave-fronts too much for comfort. I sat eating a fried-egg roll and marvelled at the glory of the breakers. Despite the crescent shape of the beach, the waves always approached parallel to the shore. From the high dunes, I could see that the incoming surf had a profile similar to the arc of the beach itself. The reason is simple, though not obvious. The waves slow down in shallow water so, if waves initially approach obliquely, the part further out and in deeper water travels faster, catching up on the part further inshore, and the angle gradually diminishes. Of course, the detailed dynamics of the breakers are subtle and complex; I imagine that surfers could enlighten physicists about some aspects of wave behaviour.

The rain came down as I crossed the headland of Carrowmore Point to another beach or, more accurately, a long stoney ridge. As scrambling on the loose rocks was tough going, I followed the edge of Lough Donnel on the landward side of the ridge. The last four miles to Quilty were on a small coastal road, in pelting rain and under darkening skies. Mutton Island, a few miles offshore, was barely visible. As I turned the corner at Seafield, a Round Tower loomed up, a modern replica at the church in Quilty. I headed on to the sole pub in the village, the Quilty Tavern, where I got a meal and a bed for the night.

Stage 44: Quilty to Ennistymon

When I rose at 9.00 o'clock there was no one about. I knocked on a door marked 'private': the owner was stretched out on a couch watching TV-AM. He said he would get someone to make me breakfast, but I didn't want to wait an indefinite time, so I paid him £15 and left. It had rained so much that I didn't fancy the prospect of following the railway in such windy, soggy conditions. Trains of the WCR were vulnerable to the strong winds sweeping in from the Atlantic. In 1911 an anemometer was installed at Quilty. All trains had to cease operation when the winds were gusting to above 80 miles per hour. Non-ballasted trains could not run when gusting to above 60 miles per hour was measured. It was so windy this morning that I decided to move away from the coast. I took a side road to the Crosses of Annagh and then northward to Miltown Malbay. A man leaning on a gate, smoking a cigarette, told me I could get a good breakfast in Cogan's. 'Tell them Paddy Mack sent you,' he added. His word was good: I got an enormous breakfast, with a second pot of tea, all for £3.25. Miltown Malbay is a long street with numerous pubs; without counting, I reckoned that there were about twenty pubs in this small town, even more than the usually high average.

Northward from the town is a network of tiny winding roads. The landscape changes here from flat to rolling country with drumlins, hillocks formed during the ice ages. The fields are divided by dry stone walls made from split limestone slabs, almost like tiles, which can be stacked easily and neatly, quite different from the rough rock walls of Connemara. As I reached the top of the hill at Ballyvaskin North, the glorious vista of Liscannor Bay opened up, with the coastline from the sands of Lahinch to the cliffs at Hag's Head on its northern shore. I sat on a wall listening to the booming of the Atlantic breakers crashing on the rocks more than a mile away. At Toor Hill, the road was darkened by the sheer limestone cliffs flanking it on the right. Passing a ruined castle, I came to a little church at Moy Beg. It was so peaceful to sit there meditating, alone. I took a green road or, more accurately, a mud track, across the Moy River to a megalithic tomb. From here, the remainder of the journey was on minor roads and lanes along a hillside overlooking Lahinch and the Inagh River, with the cloud–capped mountains of the Burren to the north.

At Ennistymon, I was struck immediately by the opportunities: so many shops with wonderful traditional designs, but most in a poor or even dilapidated condition. The town has great potential to be a really beautiful place, but only if the owners will invest in a few pots of paint. I passed under an arch down to the splendid cascades on the river and followed a path downstream to a small ruined hydro-electric plant. This once provided power to the Falls Hotel, but looked as if it had been out of use for some years. Further on, I came to the hotel itself, where I bargained for a room at a knock-down price, knowing that in January they would be glad to get customers. This hotel, greatly extended and modernised, was totally different from the draughty place I had stayed in years ago. I learned that the Dylan Thomas Bar is named for the famous Welsh poet because the hotel had once been the family home of his wife Caitlin McNamara, and he had occasionally visited here.

Stage 45: Ennistymon to Corrofin

I left the Falls Hotel and strolled down the main street of Ennistymon, admiring the many old shop fronts again. The ruined church at the top of Kilcornan Hill has a curiously dominant influence on the atmosphere of the town. The main road (N85) took me to the site of the old railway station, now a modern B&B. Then I turned left to a small pathway, the beginning of a whole series of grassy paths and farm tracks leading eastward. I planned to follow the West Clare Railway where possible. The air was fresh and clear after a frontal passage, and Slieve

Callan stood as a sentinel to the south. At Cullenagh, I climbed up the embankment at a bridge, and followed the course of the railway for a mile or so until it expired. Back on the road, I passed an old lime kiln at Moanreel Bridge. I turned aside along a forest track hoping to find the tiny Loughnagowen in the woods, but lost the way and returned to the road for a rest and a snack. At Boola Bridge I joined the old line again, and was able to follow the course of the railway for a few miles to Annalabba Bridge, with only minor digressions around blockages and negotiation of several barbed wire fences. It followed a shelf along a gently sloping hillside, then a low embankment through flat fields and finally a tree-lined grassy avenue.

At Annalabba I had to clamber over a rusty corrugated fence, arriving on the other side with bloodied hands. A route northward from here brought me towards Clifton Hill and across the Fergus River, which flows out of Lake Inchiquin. Actually, this stretch of the Fergus is the result of an artificial cut, made to provide power to a mill near the lake. Coming to the grotto at the northern end of Corrofin, I sought the nearby house of my friends Mick and Lorna Kelly, who had invited me to stay with them, and received a warm welcome on my arrival.

After five days of solid walking, it was time for a break and a chance to do some touring with Mick, so I declared the following day an 'official rest day'. We drove north to Killinaboy where, over the door of the old church, we found a good Sheela-na-gig. I didn't miss the opportunity to photograph her. Nearby is the stump of a Round Tower, about ten feet high, like a huge barrel bulging outwards as a result of the pressure of vegetation within it.

We then headed for Mullaghmore, a limestone hill of extraordinary interest and beauty. It comprises many discrete strata, gently contorted in elegant folds by ancient tectonic upheavals. The differentially eroded strata provide a stunning record of millions of years of geological history, from when the whole region lay below a shallow ocean. We visited the site of the Interpretative Centre which was to have been built near Mullaghmore. Construction commenced some years ago but was halted when a major controversy broke out about the advisability of building in such a unique and sensitive environment. The issue was highly contentious, generating much anger and resentment in the locality. Finally, a decision was taken to abandon the project, after considerable funds had already been invested in it. But the restoration of the site to its original state, estimated to cost about a million pounds, caused further controversy, unresolved at the time of my visit.

From here, we drove along a small track, lined with hazel woods. Continuing northwards, we passed the house of Father Ted, where the popular television programme was filmed. The sudden and tragic death of the actor and writer Dermot Morgan had put an abrupt end to this series, which is destined to be remembered as classical TV comedy. Crossing a pass to Carron, we headed to the Cistercian Abbey at Corcomroe, a fine twelfth-century ruin. The monks gave it the name Sancta Maria de Petra Fertili, or Saint Mary of the Fertile Rock, and it stands in a lush limestone valley. A sign outside the abbey warns against littering under pain of a fine of £1,500, converted by an over-enthusiastic bureaucrat to €1,904.61.

After lunch in Kinvarra we took a stroll around the little harbour, admiring the Galway hookers tied up at the quay, and Dunguaire Castle across the water. Then we drove westward through Ballyvaughan to Black Head and, at Fanore, took a mountain road, which brought us high up the slope of Slieve Elva, the western outpost of the Burren. The climb from the road to the top was not far, but the mountain was covered in thick blanket bog and the going was tough and very wet. As we neared the top, a piramidal frustum loomed indistinctly ahead; this was the triangulation pillar at the summit of Slieve Elva, the height being 344 metres, the highest point in the Burren. My rest day had turned into a stiff exercise. We should have had a splendid view, but visibility was poor, and the Aran Islands appeared only as ghostly shadows in the mist.

Stage 46: Corofin to Seanaglish

I visited the Heritage Centre in Corofin and picked up a few information leaflets. Then I popped into the church next door for a dekko, to find a bevy of 'oul' wans' saying the rosary. As one group approached the half-way point of the Hail Mary, the other group burst enthusiastically into the Holy Mary, thereby achieving a breakneck speed of about one decade per minute. Our Blessed Lady must have been mightily pleased with such a blistering pace. I walked south from the town to take a quiet minor road to Ruan, where I stopped at the Dalcassian Inn. At the time of Brian Boru, one thousand years ago, this region was called Dál Cáis. Later, it had the name Thomond, or North Munster, with the Cork and Kilkenny regions being Desmond and Ormond, South and East Munster respectively. Later still, Clare was included in Connacht by Cromwell, in his scheme to drive the Irish out of the rest of the island, and suffered greatly as a result. At the Restoration it was included once again in Munster. The land border between Clare and Galway is not marked by any obvious geographical feature – the natural geographic border is at the Shannon – so from this perspective, and also considering the geological similarities, the county belongs in Connacht.

The Angelus bell rang out as I left the village of Ruan. Coming to a school, another evocative sound emerged: 'nine times five are forty-five, nine times six are fifty-four, nine times seven ...'. The children were learning their tables in the old reliable way. Soon I came to Dromore Nature Reserve, a varied habitat of woodland and wetlands, and a habitat for the pine marten. I looked around for a while hoping to spot one, but without luck. The path was sign-posted as the Mid-Clare Way. Crossing the Fergus River again, I continued along by the Castle River, until it disappeared into a hillside. The rivers of Clare have a pimpernel-like behaviour, disappearing down swallow-holes only to reappear elsewhere having followed an underground course through the limestone. The area is a hydrologist's dream and nightmare; a dream because of the fascinating behaviour of the waterways of the subterranean drainage system; a nightmare because of the complex pattern of flooding, with water spouting up unexpectedly and unpredictably, to the great consternation of residents in the lower-lying areas.

Soon I saw a castle near the road, Moyrhee Castle, and went over to explore. Climbing to the top on a spiral stairway of about a hundred steps, I had a good all-round view of the countryside, with its network of lakes and rivers inter-connected in complex ways. The castle was in good condition, with some excellently carved corner-stones. Returning to the road, I continued on to Tubber, where I got some supplies in Taaffe's and some refreshment in O'Grady's Pub. A few more steps brought me over the border from Clare and Munster to Galway and Connacht. Tubber is an interprovincial village, straddling the border. The other pub, The Burren View, is in Galway. Here I turned right and crossed the Limerick–Sligo railway, now disused, at the old Tubber Station, now a private home (in fact, I had once stayed here with Denis Bloomer, an old friend and previous resident). Another few miles brought me to the Garda Station in Seanaglish. The day's trek should have ended here, but I wanted to visit my brother-in-law, Step, and his family. So I had another hour's slog to get to their house in Gilroe, arriving there just before darkness fell. However, it was well worth while: Annette had a big bowl of stew waiting for me, and it was delightful to meet her daughters Esme and Madonna again, and hear all the latest news.

Stage 47: Seanaglish to Gort

Step gave me a lift back to the Garda Station at Seanaglish, where I had turned off the previous evening. I started down the road and soon came to a little church. Entering, I found an old priest saying mass to a non-existent congregation. I felt a twinge of conscience about abandoning him, so I remained, kneeling, standing and sitting at what I hoped were the appropriate times. After the mass, as I was lighting a candle for Cabrini, the priest came out from the sacristy and we talked for a while.

The next target was Kilmacduagh, whither I walked in persistent heavy rain. It is one of the most impressive monastic ruins in the west of Ireland, with a round tower, a cathedral, three churches and an abbot's house. The tower is in excellent condition, but is distinctly lopsided, leaning obliquely from the vertical; I guessed by inspection that it had a list of about three degrees. This may not sound like much, but a one-degree tilt in a 120 foot tower puts it two feet out of position at the top! Eventually, some remedial action will be necessary to prevent its collapse, though this may not be for some more centuries. The monastery was founded in the early seventh century by St. Coleman, son of Duagh, a local chieftain. Most of the ruins remaining today date from about 1200.

Large numbers of monasteries were founded in the sixth and seventh centuries. They became great cultural centres and repositories of knowledge, arts and crafts. Monks from them spread Christianity widely through Europe, re-introducing the classical learning that had been wiped out by the barbarian hordes. Later still, many of these monasteries suffered under Viking attacks. As I sat munching a sandwich, I imagined myself one thousand years back in time. The round tower stood in the centre, the other buildings being of timber and all surrounded by a wooden barricade. Large numbers of monks could be seen, some milking cows, some collecting honey from a hive, others gathering grain and milling it into flour. Two monks carried a tray of dough to a kiln. More scholarly ones sat in the scriptorium, busily illuminating the vellum folios of a sacred manuscript, the Gospel of Luke. Suddenly, the bell in the tower rang out urgently. All the monks scurried towards the tower and climbed up the wooden ladder, the last one hoisting it up after him. From the north came a band of Vikings on a lightning raid. They burned some of the buildings and stole whatever food they could carry. But their long-ships were in Kinvarra, about six miles away, and they felt uneasy when away from the water. After vain attempts to get into the tower, being pelted with heavy rocks, they retreated, leaving the monks shaken but still in possession of their lives, and their golden treasures, which were safely kept in the tower.

I headed northward, planning to walk through Coole Park, former home of Lady Gregory, a founding member of the Abbey Theatre. Nothing remains of the old house, but the grounds are now part of Coole-Garryland Nature Reserve. I found the entrance on the west side of the park and followed a trail marked on the map. Having noticed that there were two networks of paths, to the east and west of Coole Lough, I planned to cross through the forest between them. However, this proved to be impossible. Turloughs (the name means dry lake) abound in the karstic limestone of the Burren. They are fed and drain through swallow holes or *slogaide*, channels through the limestone linking them to other water bodies, sometimes several miles away. In times of heavy rain in one area, flooding in another region can result from water bubbling up through these swallow holes. Praeger described the hydro-geology elegantly in his book *The Way that I Went*:

> If you stay at Gort ... you find yourself in a region
> where the solid limestone which is everywhere in
> evidence is really but a honeycomb, a sponge filled,
> below an uncertain and fluctuating level, with water.
> The streams are as erratic in their behaviour as the
> turloughs, for they are continually appearing above
> ground, issuing from caverns in walls of rock or from
> deep well-like pools, flowing for a while in one direc-
> tion or another, and then vanishing again.

Coole Lough is an excellent example of a turlough, rising and falling with the seasons and with the level of the prevailing water table. The lake area indicated on the map is no guarantee of the extent of water at a given time. As I headed east on dead reckoning, I soon encountered an impassable body of water. Working around it, I came to the bound-ary fence of the park and discovered that Coole Lough and the lakes to the south of the park now formed one continuous body of water, or so it seemed. I spent about two hours exploring the terrain in a vain attempt to get through. The area was a dense forest of moss-covered oaks and the ground was a soggy mass of rotting leaves, completely blackened in places where it had recently been submerged.

I had to abandon the hope of getting through, and needed an exit strategy. I headed westward in an attempt to retrace my steps. But now finding water to the west as well, it was as if I were on an island. A group of swans, not the 'nine-and-fifty' that Yeats wrote of in 'The Wild Swans at Coole', but about a dozen, were swimming serenely on the lake. Coole Park, which inspired Yeats' poem, is home to all three of Ireland's swans – mute, Bewick's and whooper. They were too far away for me to be certain which type they were. They appeared to have yellow beaks, and were not large, so I guessed they were Bewick's. Eventually, after much floundering around, I came to a trail and made my way back to the point where I had entered the park. I had failed to find the 'autograph tree', an old copper beech on which many famous writers – Yeats, Shaw,

Synge and O'Casey among them – had carved their initials. So, after a four-mile slog along a road that was much harder now than earlier in the day, I came to the town of Gort. O'Grady's looked the most appealing of the pubs in the town square, so I went in for refreshment. Clare is known as the Banner County, for the role played by its countymen in the Battle of Ramilles, in Flanders, during the War of the Spanish Succession in 1706. My trip across the Banner County was now complete, and Connacht lay ahead.

Chapter 11

THE MARCH OF THE QUIET MANIACS

I've walked in my time across England and France,
From Spain to Greece and back by sea;
Met many a maid at many a dance,
But none had an airy grace like she.
If I had the power and the flower of youth,
I'd find her out wherever she'd be,
I'd comb all the coasts from Cork to Beirut,
To live with this gem from Bally-na-Lee.

'The Lass from Bally-na-Lee' – Anthony Raftery
(Trans. D. O'Grady)

IN THE SPRING OF THE YEAR 2001, a plague was visited upon Britain, and a murrain spread among the cloven-footed beasts. The Foot & Mouth disease was a catastrophe for farmers there. Many thousands of animals were slaughtered and, nightly, the television news showed huge mounds of burning carcasses. By swift, serious and sustained action, FMD was kept out of Ireland, with only two cases, one each side of the border and both due to the treacherous actions of smugglers. As a precautionary measure, all hill-walking was halted and farm lands were declared off limits. Fortunately, we managed to avoid a major outbreak in Ireland, thanks to the coordinated efforts and cooperation of all concerned. By mid-summer, the threat was much reduced and country walking was possible once again. But I decided it would be wise to stick to the roads as far as possible for the next stretch and avoid crossing farmlands until the final 'all clear'.

Frost's Dilemma had to be faced once more. Galway City has many attractions, and the land to the west is spectacular. A possible route would have taken me through the city, out to Oughterard and along the southern side of Lough Corrib, the largest lake in the Republic. The old Clifden railway might provide an opportunity for off-road walking. But I was anxious to avoid the drudgery of a slog through the city and its concrete suburbs, and was not confident that the railway would be passable. Lough Corrib, which splits County Galway down the middle, is a large lake stretching north from Galway city and reaching westward into the hills of the Joyce Country. Around its shores are a number of interesting castles and other antiquities. I chose the alternative route east of Lough Corrib, following a network of minor roads via Athenry and Headford to Cong. I was interested to visit Cong, never having been there, and the narrow strip of land between Lough Corrib and Lough Mask would give easy access to the mountainous region to the west.

Frank McKenna joined me on this section of the Commodius Vicus. We were provided with a lift to Gort by Frank's daughter Aoife, stopping just north of the town to visit William Butler Yeats' ivory tower, Thoor Ballylee or Ballylee Castle, a Norman tower house originally built by the de Burgos. It was renovated by Yeats who bought it for £35 in 1916 and he lived there for about twelve years. It fell into disrepair after he left in 1929 but was renovated around 1965 and is now a museum. It was also once the home of Mary Hynes, a local beauty much fancied by the poet Raftery, who described her as 'the shining flower of Bally-na-lee'. The tower has a picturesque setting by a stream, and there is a magical atmosphere about the place which must have appealed to Yeats' mystical nature. An oft-quoted saying of the Clare wise woman, Biddy Early, was that 'there is cure for all evil between the two mill wheels of Ballylee'. Biddy was renowned throughout this district, and when I worked in Shannon Airport in the 1970s, the older staff there would occasionally tell tales about her or quote her sayings. After climbing up to the flat roof for a view of the surrounding countryside, we watched an audio-visual exhibition about Yeats and explored the castle museum, which houses some first editions and a miscellaneous collection relating to the poet. On a tablet mounted on the outside wall, Yeats' words are inscribed:

I, the poet William Yeats,
With old mill boards and sea-green slates,
And smithy work from the Gort forge,
Restored this tower for my wife George;
And may these characters remain
When all is ruin once again.

A row of stepping stones leading across the stream by the castle provided a scene for *The Quiet Man* when Maureen O'Hara hopped across, followed by John Wayne. Frank tried the same trick but slipped on a loose boulder and had an unplanned paddle.

Stage 48: Gort to Ardrahan

From Gort we headed north, following the track of the railway which is all but disused. An occasional goods train runs on the line, but passenger services ceased many years ago. In the nineteenth century Irish railways were run by several different companies in robust competition with each other. Hostile buyouts and takeovers were common. The extension of the line northward from Ennis involved five separate companies, and completion of the link to Sligo took some 35 years. It was never profitable, Tuam being the largest population centre on the route, which passed through some of the poorest regions of the country. The engines and rolling stock were decrepit, with frequent breakdowns, and the operating companies were continually harassed by creditors. In 1870 the Sheriff of County Clare seized a train, allowing it to proceed only with a posse of bailiffs aboard, presumably with the intention of confiscating it upon its return to Ennis. But when the train reached Gort, just across the border, the County Galway Sheriff dispatched the bailiffs back to Clare and impounded the train. When the engine was put up for auction, the only bidder was the A&EJR, the Athenry and Ennis Junction Railway, which found itself buying its own engine back. Things improved in 1934 when the sugar beet factory opened in Tuam, but passenger traffic ceased in 1976, except for Sunday specials for Knock pilgrims. The sugar factory closed in 1985 and the only traffic now is an occasional goods train carrying cement or fertilizer.

At Kiltartan we left the track to see the Gregory Museum, but as it was now evening the museum was closed. Kiltartan figured in a number of poems of both Yeats and Raftery. A few miles further on a sign pointed to Lydacan Castle, another tower of the Hynes clan. Tullira Castle, once the home of Edward Martyn (1859–1923) author, poet and playwright, who was closely associated with Lady Gregory and Yeats, was also marked on the map, but we didn't digress as it is not open to the public. One wet afternoon, Martyn took his friend Yeats to see Lady Gregory. They talked about Irish drama, and about the lack of a theatre in Ireland where it might be performed. As the afternoon wore on, a dream became a plan, eventually leading to the establishment of the Abbey Theatre and to the Irish Literary Revival. The story is told in Elizabeth Healy's *Literary Tour of Ireland*.

We clambered down again onto the track at a bridge and followed the line to the village of Ardrahan, where we passed the ruined Anglo-Norman castle to come to The Old Forge. We had booked into the B&B of Maria Joyce but upon our arrival she told us her husband had already given the room to someone else. We went into the Ardrahan Inn next door, where we got a bed for the night.

Stage 49: *Ardrahan to Athenry*

After breakfast next morning, we talked with the owner, Áine Tarpey. She told us she had lived in Ardrahan for forty years and that, when she came, the village had a railway station, a co-op, a mart, a doctor and a bank, all gone now. Still, she was happy to live there as it was a quiet, trouble-free spot. As we set out, a row of swallows on a telegraph wire looked as if they were readying themselves for a journey south. We took a quiet road in the opposite direction, heading northward in search of Raftery's resting place. The blackberrys were plentiful on the hedgerow brambles and just ripening. Almost every house sported a maroon and white flag to support Galway, which had a chance in both the football and hurling All-Irelands. A monument by the roadside commemorated Liam Mellows and his comrades, who had set out from here to fight for Irish freedom in Easter week, 1916. Shortly afterwards we came to Killeeneen, the little graveyard, Reilig na Bhfilí, where Anthony Raftery the blind poet is buried, along with the Callanan brothers, two contemporary poets. Raftery's poems were taught in school until recently, and old fogeys will easily recall the following lines:

Mise Raifterí an file	I am Raftery the poet
lán dóchais is grá	Full of hope and love
le súile gan solas	With eyes without light
le ciúineas gan crá	And calm without torment
ag dul siar ar m'aistear	Going west on my journey
le solas mo chroí	By the light of my heart
fann agus tuirseach	Weak and tired
go deireadh mo shlí	To my road's end
Féach anois mé	Look at me now,
lem aghaidh ar bhalla	My face to the wall
ag seinm cheoil	Playing music
do phócaí folamh.	To empty pockets.

Frank O'Connor's translation is literal but prosaic, catching the rhythm but not the rhyme. With the help of Dinneen's Foclóir Gaedhilge agus Béarla and an unbridled imagination, I offer a more florid alternative:

The poet Raftery am I,
  My heart with hope and love is blessed,
Mine eyes are dark, but in my soul
  No grief abides, but blissful rest.
My way, upon a western road,
  Is guided by an inner Sun;
Though tired and weak, I travel on
  Till home at last, my journey done.
Behold me now: a wretched wraith
  With worthless eyes in vacant stare,
The crowds that throng to hear me play
  Are gaunt with hunger, pockets bare.

Continuing eastward, we stopped to talk to an old man who addressed us thus: 'Are ye strangers from another country?' We assured him we were Irish but he was clearly unconvinced. He offered to give us a lift into

Craughwell and when we declined, he told us of a back road to the village: 'Take the third road on the right,' he said repeatedly, as if doubting our ability to understand such complex navigation. 'It's the Greenwich Road and will take you directly to Craughwell.' I was perplexed by the reference to the prime meridian, until a look at the map showed a townland called Crinnage. Sure enough, it enabled us to avoid the busier main road to the town.

At Craughwell we had lunch in Raftery's Pub, The Blazers. The name is that of the famous County Galway Hunt, the Galway Blazers. The kennels of the hunt are just outside the village. Also nearby is St. Cleran's, once the home to the film director John Huston, and now a luxury hotel. The midday news on the pub TV told of another Foot & Mouth outbreak, the eighth in four days, in Northumberland; the danger was not yet past.

The railway again provided a direct, traffic-free route to our destination for the day, Athenry. We followed the line in the blazing afternoon sun, getting into the rhythm enforced by the alignment of the sleepers. They were generally regularly spaced but with a shorter gap every seventeenth sleeper, where the sections of rail were joined. As the joints are staggered on the left and right sides, the rhythm is eight-nine-eight-nine, rattling like a rickety train. In any case, walking the track demands constant attention to avoid a misplaced foot. Further on, concrete sleepers had been laid. These were much worse to walk on, with very irregular spacing which made it impossible to get into any sort of rhythm. However, we carried on with caution, stopping at one point under a bridge to rest and shelter from the hot sun and came at last to the junction at Athenry.

Athenry, Baile Átha an Rí, the town of the King's Ford, is an Anglo-Norman town, one of the oldest in Ireland, founded by Meiler de Bermingham. Ruins of the town walls, together with five towers, still survive and one of the town gates, known locally as the Arch, straddles a main street. The large de Bermingham Castle, with a three-storey keep and defensive outer wall, is in good condition. Meiler also founded the Dominican Priory (1241). It was wrecked by Cromwellian troops in 1652. After visiting the priory, we crossed to the park to watch an intrepid aviator operating his model helicopter. He was fiercely enthusiastic and, when we showed interest, was delighted to demonstrate its capabilities and describe its dynamics. The craft was about a metre in length with a main rotor of similar size, and ran on methanol. The radio-control panel was complex but he explained the action of the various switches and joy-sticks. He told us he also flies real helicopters, which are vastly more difficult and dangerous than fixed-wing aircraft. We talked about the helicopter crash earlier in the year that had claimed the life of Bertie Fisher, King of the Road Racers. Although the official investigation had yet to be concluded, it appeared that he had run out of fuel in foggy weather and crash-landed, killing everyone on board. After a 10 ounce steak in Keane's – locally pronounced Kane's – we had a sup in Thompson's Bar and retired to Mary Gardner's guesthouse in Old Church Street for the night.

Stage 50: Athenry to Corrandulla

A network of minor roads gave us a choice of routes north from Athenry. We chose the road via Turloughmore and Lackagh since it seemed to pass some interesting sites. We stocked up with food and drink as there were no towns on the route. After an hour we came to a curious monument, a large block capped by a pyramid, but whatever plaque or inscription it may have had was stolen or obliterated and we couldn't determine its purpose. A nearby pump provided a convenient spot for a rest and snack. A little further on, a roadsign read 'Road Liable to Flooding'; It was clear that we were still in turlough country, with karstic underground drainage. To the left of the road at Coolarne was a small cluster of buildings marked on the map as a school. It is now Cúan Mhuire, a rehabilitation centre for those who, unlike the model helicopter, run not on methanol but on ethanol. Frank's Hillpig was getting wobbly as the joint weakened. Luckily, we came to a woodworks where a friendly workman quickly fixed it up with splints and glue.

At the old ruined de Burgo castle at Lackagh Bridge we stopped for a corned beef sandwich and some Foxford Lunch. Just beyond that point is Knockadoe, the site of a battle in 1501. A local 'expert' told us the battle involved two brothers-in-law and was 'all over a woman'. He said it was the first battle in Europe in which guns were used, gunpowder having been introduced from China not long before this. Can it be true that the

Irish were first in Europe to start shooting each other? Considering that we are still so keen on it, perhaps this is so! We climbed the hill to find the ruin of an old house, the Teach Mór, and a triangulation pillar. To the north was a slightly more prominent peak, Knockmaa, significant for its isolation rather than its altitude.

We continued an uneventful journey to Cregg Castle, near Corrandulla, where we were to stay the night. Cregg Castle is a majestic house, the exterior clad with russet Virginia creeper, the interior having a somewhat jaded opulence. The castle was among the last fortified houses to be constructed west of the Shannon. It was built in 1648 by the Kirwan family, one of the famous twelve (or is it fourteen) tribes of Galway. It stands in a 165 acre site of woods and farmland. Richard Kirwan, the noted scientist and first President of the Royal Irish Academy, inherited the house in 1754. Kirwan was one of Ireland's foremost meteorologists. He anticipated the concept of air-masses, important in the twentieth century, and studied the general circulation of the atmosphere. However, he had an ardent, even burning, attachment to the phlogiston theory, and believed that the Aurora Borealis resulted from combustion of equatorial air as it approached polar regions.

The owners of Cregg Castle were Ann-Marie and Pat Broderick, who opened the castle to guests in 1990. They are both traditional musicians and most nights there is a seisiún in the drawing room, or Great Hall as they prefer to call it. We spent the evening chatting here with the other guests, who were all Americans, around a large turf fire. Although it was a mild August evening, the fire provided a friendly focus and a welcoming atmosphere.

Stage 51: *Corrandulla to Greenfields*

A notice by the reception desk read:

> 'We accept Access, Visa or Mastercard but (! !) we
> much prefer cash, cheques, sterling, $ or more-or-less
> anything else. So, if its convenient, change money,
> but otherwise your flexible friend is ok.'

In view of this notice, we were inclined to settle our bill in cash. We strode forth into a dull morning, the skies darkening steadily until a thick drizzle was falling. We decided to undertake a time-trial. I had marked out on a map a straight section of road just 5 kilometres in length and we noted the time at start and finish. It took just one hour, confirming that our speed was about 3 miles per hour. I was pacing at about 120 steps per minute; Frank at something less, being taller. So my stride had to be the number of yards divided by the number of steps: $(3 \times 1,760)/(2 \times 3,600) = 0.74$ yards, or about 0.7 metres. Maybe this would be useful data for estimating our progress, though I suspected both our pace and speed would decrease as the day wore on.

Shortly we came to a small enclosed area, an outdoor church with an altar covered with a limestone slab. It was Dabhach Cúana. We took Cúan to be a local saint, but didn't know what Dabhach meant. I looked in Dinneen's Foclóir. As usual, he told too much: it could be a vessel, a vat, a press, a well, a sand-hill or a land measure of four ploughlands. So I suppose it was Cúan's Pad, Plot or Patch. The next word in the dictionary, Dabhair, was also apposite as it means a downpour, and indeed the weather was worsening by the minute. Turning a corner we noticed a carved stone by the wayside. It commemorated Padraig Joyce, aged 31, a helicopter pilot who had crashed nearby in 1982, killing himself and his four American passengers. We thought of our aviator in Athenry, of road racer Bertie Fisher, and of the helicopter accident in Tramore a year earlier in which four Aer Corps members died. Flying helicopters is a hazardous business.

The two sections of Frank's Hillpig finally parted company as we approached Headford, so he dumped it and acquired a stout stick from the hedgerow. This was further evidence that the Hillpig is not all it is cracked up to be. I had bought two telescopic 'trekking poles', which were proving of great use. They take a great load off the legs; indeed, the little booklet coming with them claimed that they reduced strain on the knees by 250 tons in an eight-hour walk. Goodness knows how that figure was computed. At Headford we stopped for lunch. The town did not appeal to us and we headed on into the mist, avoiding the main road northward, to seek the ruins of Ross Abbey.

Ross Errilly Friary, on the Black River, is one of the biggest and best-preserved Franciscan friaries in the country. There is a wide variety of ruined buildings, in very good repair (if one overlooks the minor detail of their rooflessness). In the kitchen we spotted a circular recess in the floor which we took to be a well. But a notice informed us that it was a water tank where fish were kept until required for the pot. There was glass in the tower, which was locked. Presumably, OPW put it there to protect the interior. Ross Errilly was founded for the Franciscans in 1351 by Raymond de Burgo. Most of the remaining building is from the fifteenth century. Although the community had to leave several times, they returned repeatedly and the friary was not finally abandoned until 1765, more than four hundred years after its foundation.

We scouted around to find a way across the river but it was too deep and wide so we returned to the road and walked westward to Ower (which rhymes with flower). At the Post Office there, the postmistress gave us the number of someone who does B&B. We continued west but couldn't get a response so we asked two men digging a trench about accommodation. They directed us to the house of Micheal Walsh, whose wife told us she keeps guests only in the May-fly season, but offered to take us to Greenfields where her husband was due to return after a day fishing on Lough Corrib and where there was a small hotel. As this was southward, we would have to trample back the road the following morning so that acceptance of a lift would not involve any infringement of the sacrosanct rule: No Skipping. We happily accepted her offer and arrived soon at the Corrib Lakeshore Hotel, in an idyllic setting by the water with a panoramic view across to the mountains of Connemara.

Lough Corrib is perhaps the foremost trout and salmon lake in the country and Greenfields one of the most popular bases for anglers. Despite this, we were the only guests in the hotel that night and the only diners to enjoy the cuisine of the Swiss chef, Jules, who prepared a dish of beef and tagliatelli, or flat spaghetti as Frank insisted on calling it. As the weather had cleared, we worked up an appetite by strolling out the causeway to Inchiquin Island. In the bar later, a local informed us that just to the north was the only inland lighthouse in the country. I seriously doubted this, citing a counter-example: Conor Cruise O'Brien had once been unkindly described as being 'Like a lighthouse in a bog: brilliant but useless'. Of course, there must be many lighthouses on navigable inland waters.

Stage 52: Greenfields to Cong

We left Greenfields in a shower of rain to follow a small road north to Cross. After about forty minutes we arrived back to where Toni Walsh had given us a lift the previous evening. An uneventful but pleasant morning's walk brought us past a house with a cleverly engineered stream running alongside, whose miniature weirs ensured constant soothing sounds of lapping waters. Further on a notice reading 'Beware of the Cat' caused us to quicken our pace. The last few miles to Cross were on a road running directly parallel to the main road but completely traffic-free. At the village we went into the Riverside Inn. It had recently changed hands and the new owner kindly stood us a drink on the house. Good luck to him! Now there were only three miles to Cong, but my feet were badly blistered so we took our time. A large megalithic tomb stands just north of the road, the Ballymacgibbon Cairn. It is about ten metres in height, crowned by a stone cairn, and presumably contains a passage tomb. We climbed to the top of the cairn to rest and enjoy the view. There are a large number of ancient burial grounds and stone circles in this area, known as Moytura. It was here that the first great battle between the Fir Bolg and the Tuatha De Danann took place. Eventually, the Fir Bolg were defeated and, according to popular legend, driven underground where, as the Sídhe or Little People, they remain to this day, occasionally emerging to help or hinder us ordinary folks. Moytura House, just south of the road, was owned by Sir William Wilde, surgeon and antiquarian, and his son Oscar spent several summers there with his brother and parents.

Nearing Cong we passed the main entrance to Ashford Castle. A notice indicated that we could enter for a payment of £4.00 but we suspected that there must be a more economical modus ingresii. So we continued to Kelly's Cave. This small cave near the road takes its name from a fugitive who hid here during the '98 Rebellion. A padlocked iron gate prevented further exploration, so we returned to the road and came soon to the old canal cut, where two enormous limestone lock walls stand in testimony to one of the greatest engineering fiascos the country has ever known.

Were there a Guinness Book of Avoidable Catastrophes, the Cong canal would surely be featured in it. The canal was built to join Loughs Corrib and Mask, allowing navigation between Galway and Ballinrobe. It was built in the 1840s as a Famine relief project. There is no surface river joining these two large lakes, but the entire area is of porous limestone and drainage is subterranean. The engineers of the canal overlooked this crucial geological quality and, when attempts were made to flood the canal upon its completion in the 1850s, the water vanished through the canal bed. The four-mile cut through sieve-like rocks was never serviceable and indeed was a monumental failure. However, we may have some comfort that, at fourpence per day, the workers were able to avoid starvation in those difficult times. We walked up the course of the canal for a short distance and were impressed by the quality of the stone carving. It might have been possible to line the canal with pitch or concrete to make it water-tight, but with the progress of the railways this costly option was never seriously considered.

Cong stands in a strategic position on the narrow isthmus between Loughs Corrib and Mask. My first introduction to the place was an illustration in my junior school history book of a beautiful ornate cross, the Cross of Cong, now in the collection of the National Museum. More recently, Cong had been in the news when Pierce Brosnan (aka James Bond) had his wedding reception at Ashford Castle. An older association with cinema was the filming here in 1951 of *The Quiet Man*, John Ford's romantic classic, starring John Wayne and Maureen O'Hara. We were reminded of our stop in far-away Lisselton, in north Kerry, where we had overlooked the monument to Maurice Walsh. It was his story that so electrified John Ford when it appeared in 1933, and that was the basis of the film. Cong was celebrating the golden jubilee of the making of the movie. For six weeks in the summer of 1951, the normally sleepy village was abuzz with activity. The Electricity Supply Board advanced its programme of electrification to ensure adequate power supplies and the telephone connections were upgraded so that calls could be placed at any time. Prior to this, only day-time calls were possible. The film showed Ireland in technicolor for the first time and generated huge international interest in the country. It would be difficult to overestimate the benefit that the film had for tourism. Des McHale has written an excellent account of the film with minute details of every scene and his book, *The Complete Guide to the Quiet Man*, is a 'must' for all those whom he calls Quiet Maniacs.

After finding a B&B, we wandered over to the old Augustinian abbey, founded in the twelfth century. From there, a network of paths lead through the woods to the grounds of Ashford Castle. The castle, in an idyllic setting by Lough Corrib, was once the country estate of Lord Ardilaun of the Guinness family. This large castellated mansion has been a luxury hotel since 1939. We rambled freely around the grounds, which are kept in beautiful condition. We might not have had such an easy time if the 'Bond Wedding', was on. We were told that security was very tight then. A local man who had managed to breach security and get some photos was caught and had his film confiscated. *Hello* magazine had bought exclusive rights to the wedding and were determined that no-one else would get any sneak previews. The hotel itself, while impressive, is a bit of an architectural mish-mash in a mixture of styles. You can have your choice of 83 rooms and it costs only £383.35 (high season, breakfast not included), according to my *American Express Guide to Hotels*. Alternatively, you might prefer to stay for a month at The Quiet Man Hostel for the same price.

Before leaving Cong, we wandered around the Augustinian abbey and found a tiny ruin out on the river, the Friar's Fishing Hut. Here the monks could sit by the fire, watching their nets through a slot in the floor until they were full enough to be hauled in. We explored the woodland trails and in the woods about two miles west of the village we came to a megalithic burial place called Toberbiroge Cairn. On the return journey we came to the Pigeon Hole, a natural crevasse in the rocks, about forty feet deep, leading down to a small tunnel bored by a subterranean river. We climbed down the sixty steps to explore but without a torch we could go no further. The tunnel was dry when we visited but we guessed that it must flood during the winter.

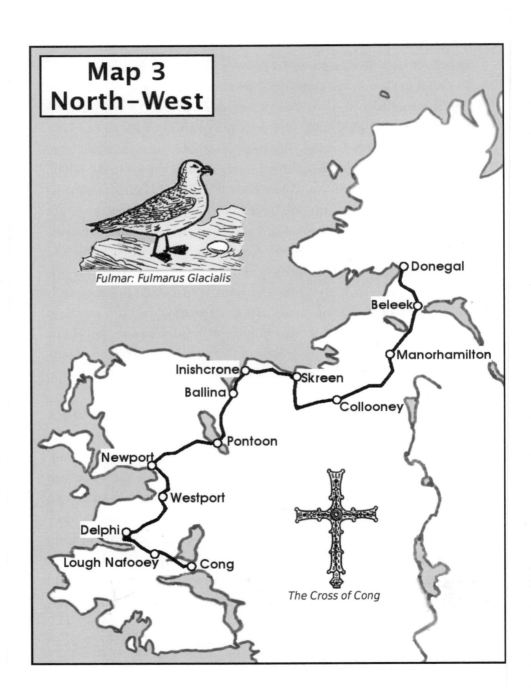

Map 3
North-West

Fulmar: Fulmarus Glacialis

Donegal

Beleek

Manorhamilton

Inishcrone

Ballina

Skreen

Collooney

Pontoon

Newport

Westport

Delphi

Lough Nafooey

Cong

The Cross of Cong

Chapter 12

MOUNTING MATER DIABOLI

'Woman, Ireland may be a poor country, God help us.
But here, a married man sleeps in a bed, not a bag!'

Father Peter Lonergan – *The Quiet Man*

IT WAS MORE THAN TWO YEARS BEFORE Frank and I returned to Cong
to continue the March of the Quiet Maniacs. In the interim, I completed a section of the route between Westport and Donegal, but that will be
described later. Our journey intersected the way-marked trail known as
the Western Way at several points, but we preferred to choose our own
route, rather than follow a trail mapped out by others. Indeed, the process of map gazing and route planning is one of the great delights associated with walking.

Stage 53: Cong to Lough Nafooey

We set out through the beautiful demense of Ashford Castle. The
grounds stretch for miles to the west of Cong and there is a network of glorious wooded trails. We were soon at the School of Falconry.
Here you may learn this ancient craft for just €55 a lesson (the Irish currency had by now switched from pounds to euros). Alas, a notice on the
closed gate read 'Gone Hawking', so our lessons would have to wait for
another occasion. Nearby is Ashford Farm, Squire Will Danagher's pile
in *The Quiet Man*. The field just beyond was where much of the fight in
the film was shot. Lasting over five minutes, this was the longest fist-fight
in cinematographic history. We came next to the School House, where

171

John Wayne and Maureen O'Hara sped away on a tandem to shake off the shackles of their chaperon. We followed a wooded trail near the lakeside. At a cross, a German girl stood, lost-looking, with a small-scale motoring map in hand, quite inadequate for walking. We were able to assist her by pointing out the way on Discovery Sheet 38. As we crested a hill, Frank noticed a wind farm on a distant hillside. There are a growing number of these in Mayo, with its open landscape, low population density and good wind climatology.

At Clonbur, we stopped at Brendan Lynch's pub for a sandwich. The locals gave us various titbits of inconsistent and contradictory advice. We stopped again at Ferry Bridge, where the road crosses a long neck of Lough Mask. We were in Mayo again for a few miles, and the scenery was growing more beautiful as we moved westward into Joyce's Country. The road followed the lake shore, with the Connemara mountains providing a splendid panorama before us. At the tiny village of Finny we stopped at the attractive church, painted yellow and white and slightly oriental in style. Buying provisions in the nearby store, we found a customer chatting in Irish with the shop girl: this is part of the Gaeltacht area of Connemara. The road climbed, giving us a nice view of Lough Nafooey and the tiny Finny River which links it to Lough Mask. At The Larches, an isolated pub, we made a final stop and were pleasantly surprised to find a full-size snooker table. Having misspent our youths, we misspent some middle age. My technique had deteriorated faster than Frank's, and he had no difficulty in dispatching me. At the western end of the lake, we came to Shanafaraghaun, where there is a small beach of coarse sand. Here my car was waiting where I had parked it a few days earlier, for reasons shortly to be explained.

Stage 54: *Lough Nafooey to Delphi*

The road from Cong to Leenane follows a circuitous route, so we had decided to travel as the crow might fly. But, not having wings, this involved a stiff climb over The Devil's Mother, a peak of 2,131 feet (645 metres). This mountain is named in both Irish and English on the Discovery Series Sheet 37. The Irish name is Magairlí an Deamhain, for which the best translation I can give is 'The Devil's Bollocks'. The story goes that when the surveyors were mapping the country, the local inhabitants were embarrassed to give the old name and so offered 'Mother' as a translation of 'Magairlí'. This inconsistency has continued ever since. The Irish name is more apposite, at least if interpreted metaphorically rather than anatomically. The English name may be euphemistic, but it poses an inscrutable conundrum about angelic genealogy.

We drove to the lake-head of Lough Nafooey and parked the car near the little beach. Since we were planning to leave it there for a few days, I spoke to a man staying in a caravan nearby and told him our plans. He was originally from this area but had lived in England for several decades. It was as well we took this precaution because, on our return three days later, he told us that another local resident had become anxious at seeing the car there overnight, and wondered if someone had been lost in the lake. Our caravan friend was able to reassure him that we were hiking in the hills.

The weather was middling, with slight drizzle and an overcast sky. Old Nick's Knackers was shrouded in cloud. It was evident that if conditions did not improve, we should not attempt to climb it. With such poor visibility there would be little point, and it would be reckless, as the peak is quite complex with some steep slopes nearby. A small side-road northwest from the main road brought us up the eastern side of the broad U-shaped valley of the Fooey River, along the flank of Knocklaur. Our plan was to climb to the col at the head of this valley and then decide whether to turn for the peak or head onwards down the valley to the Erriff River near Houston's Bridge. After a dry summer, the ground was firm underfoot and at first progress was easy. But the gradient increased and we soon found it tougher going. At one point, we had to cross a ravine gouged out by a mountain stream. We also climbed about half a dozen barbed-wire fences during the ascent. Frequent rests were needed and we lay down every five minutes or so to catch our breath and nibble on some Kendal Mint Cake. This confection was carried on the first successful ascent of Everest and was much relished by Sir Edmund Hillary and his Sherpa chum Tenzing Norgay, or so the wrapper informed us.

By the time we neared the col, the clouds had lifted and the peak of Lucifer's Liathróidí was visible. The wind was strong here, about force seven, being channelled by the terrain near the pass. We turned left and headed for the summit. The ground was really steep and we had to scramble up following close to a fence, the purpose of which was unclear. Fortunately the dry conditions meant that we could progress without sinking. Irish mountain-climbing often degenerates into swamp-wading or worse when the boggy ground is saturated, as is normally the case. After about another hour of stiff climbing, we reached the small cairn at the summit of the Ghastly Goolies. The effort to reach the top was rewarded by the most spectacular panorama. Before us was the silver ribbon of Killary Harbour, a fjord-like inlet at the mouth of the Erriff River. To the south-west were the Maumturks, and north-west were Ben Gorm and the Sheeffrey Hills. Further west loomed the massive bulk of Mweelrea, Mayo's mightiest mountain. Away to the north we could just see Croagh Patrick while behind us lay Maumtrasna and the Partry Mountains. Lough Nafooey sparkled in the valley below and, beyond it, Loughs Mask and Corrib.

To descend safely from the Daemon's Danglers, careful map-work was essential. The complexity of the terrain makes it quite hazardous and the ground west of the summit is so steep that it must be hellish in foggy weather. We headed north-west, avoiding the more precipitous slopes, and then NNW down a long undulating ridge until we were above the head of Killary Harbour. We clamboured down the last slope, zig-zagging all the way and grateful that we did not have to climb up here. We reached sea-level near a small church, climbing one last fence to gain the road. The nearby village of Leenane was where John B. Keane's play 'The Field' was made into a film, starring Richard Harris as 'Bull' McCabe. At a hairpin bend at the head of Killary Harbour are the picturesque Aasleagh Falls, where The Bull and his son slew the American blow-in.

From Aasleagh Falls, we headed west along the northern shore of Killary Harbour. Near the western extremity of the fjord is an An Óige Hostel, where in 1948, Ludwig Wittgenstein completed his magnum opus *Philosophical Investigations* or, in case you have read it in Latin, *Tractatus Philosophicus*. Lines of floats on the water marked the mussel fishery in the harbour. At the mouth of the Bundorragha River we turned inland and came, after another half-hour, to the Delphi Adventure Centre. We were planning to overnight here but it was full, so they directed us to the Mountain Spa next door. A room in this luxury establishment was €115 per person, so we had a drink and took a €12 taxi-ride back to Leenane.

Stage 55: Delphi to Westport

Reversing the procedure of yesterday, we took a €12 taxi-ride from Leenane to the Delphi Adventure Centre to continue the stroll. We set off towards the north, up the road between Ben Gorm and Mweelrea. This is a scenic valley, with steep mountains on both sides. Frank noticed three tiny coloured dots high up on the flanks of Ben Gorm. Some climbers were up before us, and had already reached about 1000 feet. Soon we came to Delphi Lodge, once the fishing lodge of the first Marquess of Sligo, whose seat was at Westport House. In 1811, he took the Grand Tour, during which he swam the Hellespont with Byron. He was particularly impressed by the Greek landscape and by ancient Greek culture. He was overcome with homesickness when the scenery around Delphi reminded him of his fishery at Lough Fin, so he adopted the name Delphi for the latter, and it has stuck ever since. Delphi Lodge now provides exclusive accommodation for wealthy anglers.

We soon reached Doo Lough, or Black Lake, looking sombre in the morning gloam (the lake, not us). By the roadside stands a memorial cairn, dedicated to the poor and hungry who died here in 1849. In that famine year a large group of destitute people trudged the trail from Louisburgh to Delphi Lodge in the hope of receiving some relief. No help was given, and many died there or on the way back. This region of Ireland has been one of the poorest for centuries. The area is beautiful, but the land is very poor and unproductive. The population density was much higher before the Great Hunger than today. This area of Mayo suffered some of the worst horrors of the Hibernian Holocaust at that time. Many thousands simply vanished, becoming The Disappeared. Whole communities vanished, the hillsides are dotted with numerous ruined houses, and the region is largely deserted today.

The trouble did not start with the Famine. Two centuries earlier, Cromwell's Parliament at Westminster passed the Act of Settlement ban-

ishing the Irish 'to Hell or to Connaught'. Oliver Cromwell, the Lord Pro-
tector, 1649–1660, is revered in England as the founder of parliamentary
democracy, but reviled in Ireland as a brutal and barbarous butcher. The
curse of Cromwell was the greatest in a long litany of Irish grievances
against English rule. The Act of Settlement, passed in 1653, decreed that

> Connaught and Clare shall be set aside for the habi-
> tants of the Irish Nation to which they must trans-
> plant themselves with their wives, children and such
> servants as will go with them before May 1st, 1654.

This gave the Irish people six winter months to abandon whatever
property and ties they had, and cross the Shannon to a greatly uncertain future. This was State-sponsored ethnic cleansing with a vengeance.
Those who moved west faced great hardship and suffering; of those who
declined Cromwell's 'invitation', some 50,000 were transported as slaves
to the cane-sugar plantations of Barbados or the tobacco fields of Virginia. A recent biographer has attempted a radical revision, claiming that
Cromwell was not all that bad. I claim no expertise in history, but see no
reason to doubt that he was a deeply evil man, a maniacal monster fired
by obsessive racial hatred and fanatical religious zeal. Should we forget
this, since it happened so long ago? Is forgetting a noble and generous
response or a timorous denial of reality? The latter, I think; you decide
for yourself!

The road north from Doo Lough, built by the Congested Districts
Board in 1896, leads to the coastal town of Louisburgh. Henry Browne, an
uncle of the First Marquess of Sligo – the Delphi Dude – took part in the
capture of Louisburgh in Nova Scotia in 1758. It is this that resulted in the
unusual adoption of an American placename for a location in Ireland,
the reverse of the usual practice. Grace O'Malley, or Granuaile, the six-
teenth-century Pirate Queen and chieftain of the Western Isles, had one
of her castles in Louisburgh. She married several times, divorcing under
the Brehon code. She controlled all the continental trade out of Galway.
Her methods were unscrupulous, but she became a folk-hero as she was
among the few Irish leaders to stand up to the English. Once, she sailed
up the Thames in London to parley with Queen Elizabeth I, and struck

an infamous deal that enabled her to pursue her freebooting frolics and privateering pranks under royal approval.

Our original plan was to travel north to Louisburgh and, the following day, traverse Croagh Patrick. But the weather was 'iffy', and we were tired after the assault on Beelzebub's Balls, so we decided to take a route direct to Westport. Thus, we turned eastward, up the Glenummera river valley south of the Sheeffrey Hills. This is a quiet road and the only people we met for the next three hours were a group of forestry workers. Much of the hillside is under coniferous forest, but it looks of poor quality, and is very unsightly where clearance has taken place. Above the pretty Tawnyard Lough we stopped at a picnic site to lunch, enjoying the mountainscape. The Hangers of Hades[8] loomed over the valley to the south, capped by a thin layer of cloud. At Barnaderg Pass the road bends sharply and the descent is cut out of the hillside. Near Sheeffrey Bridge, there was an option to follow the Western Way over the hills. But visibility was poor, and this route was very long, so we continued on the road. We passed through the tiny village of Drummin, where the children were at school in a pleasant-looking building. At Owenmore Bridge we left the bags in a churchyard and turned up a side road looking for Breslin's Bar. But not finding it, we returned, recovered the bags and continued. We learned later that the bar was not far up the road so we paid for our lack of persistence.

At Liscarney we crossed the N59, the Leenane–Westport road. There was nothing here but a Post Office which sold neither food nor drink. So, we continued straight on, on a road which is part of Tóchar Phádraig, St. Patrick's Causeway, a 25-mile pilgrim path from Ballintubber Abbey through Aghagower to Croagh Patrick, Ireland's Holy Mountain. The mountain, known locally as The Reek, is a beautiful cone of quartzite, towering over Clew Bay to the north, and dominating the landscape for miles around. At 764 metres (2,513 feet) it is no easy climb, yet up to 50,000 pilgrims make the ascent every year on Domhnach Chrom Dubh or Reek Sunday, the last Sunday of July. These devout multitudes, many in bare feet, perform rituals at strategic stations, or deiseal, where prayerful circuits of the stations are made. Traces of gold were found near Croagh Patrick some years ago, and a licence sought to extract the precious

---

[8] No more cracks about the Satanic Scrotum. That's a promise!

metal. The mining technique would have involved the use of highly toxic chemicals, and would have greatly despoiled the sacred mount. Mercifully, the Government refused permission for this. Let us hope for no reversal of that decision.

Long before Christian times, the mountain was associated by the Druids with worship of the Sun, and they called it Cruachán Aigli. They built a long causeway across the lowlands from far to the east giving access to the mountain. St. Patrick followed this route, Tóchar Phádraig, from Ballintober, prior to spending forty days and nights fasting and praying on the mountain top. It was from here that he banished snakes and reptiles and other venomous varmints from the island of Ireland forever (those who say it was the ice that did for the snakes are ignorant heathens, God help them).

Just north of Liscarney, at Boheh, there is a stone that, reputedly, lines up with the Reek and, at a certain time of the year, gives rise to a curious optical phenomenon, in which the Sun appears to roll down the side of the mountain. With a heavily overcast sky, there was no opportunity for us to investigate this further. There are several antiquities along the Tóchar, and signs placed by some thoughtful person or group indicate features of interest. A number of large standing stones were visible near the route. At Lankill, we turned north for the last few miles into Westport. Coming to the town, we crossed the remains of the old railway to Westport Quay, now converted to a pleasant walkway. We reached the Octogon at the town centre and had a meal in Wyatt's with our friends Denis and Audrey, who were kind enough to put us up for the night.

We broke our return journey at Cong to participate in an event of earth-shattering import, the annual meeting of the Quiet Man Film Club. The organisers were dumbfounded and incredulous to learn that one of us was a 'Quiet Virgin', an Irishman over fifty who had never seen the film. In an entertaining lecture, Des McHale described exciting recent research leading to the identification of the dog in one of the scenes. The day ended with a quiz on the film, which separated interlopers and impostors from true-blue 24 carat Maniacs.

Chapter 13

THE LAND OF HEART'S DESIRE

I call to the eye of the mind
A well long choked up and dry
And boughs long stripped by the wind,
And I call to the mind's eye
Pallor of an ivory face,
Its lofty dissolute air,
A man climbing up to a place
The salt sea wind has left bare.

'At the Hawk's Well' – W.B. Yeats

IN VIEW OF THE ATROCIOUSLY WET WEATHER that we had experienced throughout 2002, I decided to postpone the section from Cong to West-port. January was no time to climb the Devil's Mother,[9] with short days and saturated ground. So, the new year started with a ramble from West-port through North Mayo and Sligo. My friend Tom Murphy and I took the Westport train, scheduled to depart from Heuston Station at 08:05. It was SNAFU as usual for Irish Rail – Situation Normal: All Fouled Up.[10] The train pulled out half an hour late, the excuse this time being that the dining car had been vandalised during the night and had to be decoupled. Thus, we had no catering for the four-hour journey, not even a snack trolly.

---

[9] Having promised no more cracks, I am constrained to use the euphemism.
[10] 'Fouled' is another euphemism.

Stage 56: Westport to Newport

Westport is an estate town, planned by James Wyatt around 1780, a pleasant place with a tree-lined mall by the Carrowbeg River. There are a number of attractive Georgian buildings, and the town has a friendly and festive air; there was a lively atmosphere even on this mid-winter day. We had lunch with Denis Bloomer and his friends Jan and Connie, at O'Connor's in the Octogon, the unusual eight-sided main square, overlooked by St. Patrick on his pillar. Denis would join us on the walk for the following day.

The Western Way starts at Oughterard, winds through the Maamturk Mountains to Leenaun, on over the Sheeffry Hills and eastward, flanking Croagh Patrick, to Westport. Northward through Newport, it passes through the Nephin Beg Mountains to come eventually to the north Mayo coast at Ballycastle. Thence, it passes through Ballina and onward to The Gap, in the Ox Mountains. It is the longest way-marked trail in the country. At The Gap, it links up with the Sligo Way. The route we followed from Westport to Newport coincided with part of the Western Way. Had the days been longer, we might have continued on this trail, passing through the Nephin Beg range into north-west Mayo. But towns and villages were few and far between and we would have difficulty finding accommodation in the winter, so we chose another route from Newport to Ballina, via Pontoon.

We temporarily parted company with Denis at Matt Molloy's pub (Matt is the flute player with The Chieftans), setting out along the Castlebar road and turning north onto the Lodge Road after a mile or so, heading for Newport. As a light drizzle was falling, we put on waterproof trousers or, as Mark calls them, incontinence ganderbags. The drizzle soon fizzled out, and there was to be no more rain for ten days, with a settled spell of cold, dry weather, ideal conditions for walking. With our temperate, maritime climate, the weather in Ireland is rarely if ever too cold for walkers.

At the church in Fahy we snacked. Then we came to the Owennabraghy River, a little trout stream where a ruined castle stood by the road-side. The road climbed and fell repeatedly; this was drumlin country, with a myriad of small mounds dotting the landscape and reaching out to Clew

Bay where they form the putative 365 islands. Drumlins are elongated hillocks formed from material deposited by ice flows overloaded with sediment. It is similar to the way a fast-flowing river sweeps up stones and sand and deposits them when it slows up and cannot carry them further downstream. Typical drumlins are 50 to 100 metres high and up to a kilometre or more in length. The steeper of the two ends faces the direction from which the ice flow came. Groups of drumlins, called swarms, can be found in various parts of Ireland.

Passing a handball alley we came to the seven-arched viaduct that once carried the train from Westport to Achill Sound. This line opened in 1897 and was one of the earlier casualties of the railway system, closing in 1937. We crossed the viaduct, now converted to a linear park, and re-crossed the Newport River by the road bridge to the Gráinne Uaile, where we met Denis and his wife Audrey. Rory, Audrey's son, was giving us a shakedown for the night at his home, an old schoolhouse a few miles west of Newport. We ended the day with an enjoyable meal with Rory, Lucy and their three-year-old daughter, Sadhbh.

Stage 57: Newport to Pontoon

Denis was accompanying Tom and me for this ramble, to ensure that we didn't split our infinitives. We stocked up at Sheridan's in Newport and, after a mile on the Crossmolina road, veered off to a minor by-way running up Glenhest, parallel to the main road. As we left the Reek behind, the mighty quartzite dome of Nephin (2,646 feet) loomed ahead. A snipe rose in a rapid zig-zag, startled by our approach. At Cloondaff we stopped for a rest and a snack and then headed on to Lough Beltra. A small roadside shrine to St. Francis commemorates Mary McHale, the last native Gaelic speaker in Glenhest. At Beltra we reviewed progress. There were two options, an easy, flat route north of Farbreiga via Bofeenaun and Louth Levally to Pontoon, or a tough limb up through the Windy Gap and around the southern side of the mountain. With barely enough daylight remaining, we chose the latter route and took a small track over the hills. A farmer suggested a bog road alternative but, with so much recent rain, we didn't chance it and stuck to the way marked on the map.

The road to the Windy Gap was signed as Slí Humbert, or Humbert's Way. In August 1798, three French men-o-war entered Killala Bay, employing the crafty ruse of flying British colours. The French expedition of 1,100 men, under the command of General Humbert, had some initial success, being joined by Irish troops in various degrees of rabblement. They took Killala and Ballina and then marched south through the Windy Gap to Castlebar. They roundly defeated the British forces at Castlebar in what Thomas Pakenham, in *The Year of Liberty*, called 'one of the most ignominious defeats in British military history'. The engagement is popularly known as the 'Races of Castlebar'. Humbert continued through Sligo and Leitrim, with further successful military encounters, but was eventually defeated in September by superior British forces at Ballinamuck in County Longford. The French troops were taken prisoner and were sent back to France. The Irish rebels who were captured were all hanged.

The climb to the Windy Gap was strenuous and we stopped frequently to look back at the imposing contours of Nephin. Near the top, a dipper delighted us with his dapper dance along a stream. A marking on the road, KOH 200, told us we were nearing our goal: put there for a bicycle race, the Tour de Humbert, it indicated that the title of King of the Hills would go to the cyclist who covered the remaining 200 metres first. We reached the Gap just before 3.00 o'clock and, after a brief pause to soak in the splendid views, strutted onward. Time was now short and we still had miles to go. The route around the southern flanks of Farbreiga (395 metres) was circuitous and undulating and we took much longer than estimated. To shorten the road and improve our minds, we had a comprehensive lecture from Tom on the life-cycle of the salmon. Tom is an expert on fish diseases and soon we were up to our gills in fry and parr and smolts and grilse. The salmon's life-cycle is altogether fascinating. These fish leave their river homes for the Greenland Sea and return, as if by magic, after several years to continue the cycle. How do they find the way back to their river? Tom explained that the crucial factor enabling these creatures to perform their amazing navigational feats is 'pheremone imprinting during the smoltification phase'. In plain language, they sniff their way home!

A scene for The Quiet Man *at Thoor Ballylee, near Gort, where Maureen O'Hara hopped across the stream, followed by John Wayne*

Huge lock-gates of the canal at Cong, one of the greatest engineering fiascos the country has ever known

Ashford Castle in Cong

Frank at the summit of Magairli an Deamhain

Peter on Magairli an Deamhain, overlooking Killary Harbour

The pleasant riverside walk at Coolaney, County Sligo

The Roogagh Falls at Garrison, County Fermanagh

Belleek Pottery, an imposing building on the banks of the Erne

Cabrini guarding Derry's walls, with the Guildhall behind

Stained glass images of Saints Mark, Matthew and John in Raphoe, made in Sarah Purser's Tower of Glass studio

A sea cave on the glorious causeway coast (photo by Margaret Lynch)

Dunsaney Castle, home of the Plunketts for hundreds of years

The Lia Fail, or Stone of Destiny, that emits a roar when a King lays a hand on it

The 'wonderful barn', near Leixlip

Owen and Andrew by a lock of the Royal Canal

On the 16th of October 1843
Sir William Rowan Hamilton
in a flash of genius discovered
the fundamental formula for
quaternion multiplication
$$i^2 = j^2 = k^2 = ijk = -1$$
& cut it on a stone of this bridge

The plaque on the Royal Canal commemorating Hamilton's discovery of quaternions

The Jeannie Johnston on the Liffey, with the Convention Centre Dublin behind

Journey's end, at the Forty-foot bathing place in Sandycove, 29 November 2009

A friendly farmer wished us a Happy New Year, shaking our hands enthusiastically. He said we should reach Pontoon before nightfall. However, it was already dark when we reached the main road after passing Loughnambrackkeagh, and we had another half-hour in pitch blackness on a busy road. Fortunately, I had brought a powerful torch to signal oncoming traffic. We arrived in Healy's Hotel around 5:45 and staggered in, exhausted to varying degrees. As the salmon season was not due to begin for another two weeks, the hotel was quiet and peaceful. Frank McKenna was there to meet us as he was joining in for a few days. A delightful meal did much to revive our spirits and soon the four of us were laughing and joking, our aches and pains forgotten.

Stage 58: Pontoon to Ballina

It is surprising that the dates of earliest sunset and latest sunrise do not coincide with the winter solstice, the shortest day of the year, which occurs on or about the 21st of December. In our latitudes, the date of earliest sunset is around the 13th of December, while latest sunrise occurs around the end of December. This curious asymmetry is due to the discrepancy between clock time (or mean time) and sun time, since noon by the clock does not coincide with solar noon. Thus, sunrise and sunset are not equidistant in time from noon by the clock. The difference between local solar time and local mean time is determined by what astronomers call the Equation of Time.

The sun peeped over Lough Cullin at 8:56, a glorious sight that I photographed through the hotel window. We breakfasted in Healy's, enjoying the splendid scenery. Audrey arrived to collect Denis, leaving the three of us, Tom, Frank and myself, to walk to Ballina. The morning was crisp and clear and the roads were hazardous with icy patches. At Pontoon Bridge we stopped to capture the scenery on celluloid. This area is quite unlike much of the stark bog-land of Mayo, being more reminiscent of Killarney. A notice warned boatmen to take precautions against zebra mussels, recent arrivals that have spread rapidly and that can cause havoc. The name Pontoon does not sound particularly Irish. Presumably, a floating bridge once gave access across the narrow neck of water linking the twin lakes of Conn and Cullin, giving the place its name.

We ignored the turn-off for Foxford, a town notable for its woollen mills. Tom told us that, early in his career, he spent some time at the mills testing wool dyes. The dyes were to be added to sheep-dips to mark the animals that had been treated against sheep scab. However, the additional cost – about a penny per sheep dipped – was considered prohibitively steep by the farming authorities and the scheme was never implemented. We took a small hilly side road, gingerly crossing a treacherous ice-sheet. We had an animated debate as to whether 'gingerly' is an adjective or an adverb, concluding gingerly, or reaching a gingerly conclusion, that it is both. A multitude of small birds twittered in the morning sun, a goldfinch keeping us company for a mile or so. We bought food in Knockmore, including a Foxford Lunch of course, and stopped at an old ruined castle near Cloughans for lunch. Across Lough Conn we could see the ruins of Errew Abbey and, much further west, the cooling tower at Bellacorrick. There is a peat-fired power station there and also, more in keeping with good environmental husbandry, a large wind farm.

We turned eastward at Cloonygunnaun to follow a small trail to Greggaun. Nearing Ballina we came to a large cromlech, the Dolmen of the Four Maols. Soon we arrived at the level crossing just above Ballina railway station, the start of the extension to Killala. A set of open goods-wagons on the line above the crossing looked as if they had been long forgotten. We found lodgings at the Ridgepool Hotel, a room with three beds for €70. We had a forgettable Chinese meal at The Lantern and a few drinks at An Bolg Buí. There we narrowly escaped a fracas, after an ill-judged joke about the Mayo football team backfired. A tactical withdrawal averted catastrophe.

Stage 59: *Ballina to Inishcrone*

Sunday morning was again crystal clear, save for a thin cirrus veil indicating a front to the south-west. It looked as if the weather might break later but, in fact, the front moved away and high pressure intensified over Ireland keeping the weather dry for another week. Tom had to return to Dublin so Frank and I strode out from the Ridgepool Hotel, past

An Bolg Buí and over the Moy. We stopped for a quick look at St. Muire-dach's Cathedral. The plan was for an easy day, a short walk to Inishcrone, less than ten miles away. At the Waterside Meadow Wildlife Habitat, we stopped to watch a gull harrying a crow who was holding a piece of bread in its beak. The crow battled bravely, ducking and diving and swerving wildly to shake off its pursuer but, when a second gull joined the chase, gave up and dropped the bread.

Crossing the Brusna River, we took the coast road northward. The estuary provided rich feeding for a host of waders. A house called 'Emohruo', exercised Frank's crossword-doing mind. We considered a word for such a species of anagram, a word with letters reversed, and came up with retrogram. It was just as well that Denis was not with us; he would have been horrified at the mixture of Greek and Latin roots. Beyond Crocket's Restaurant a large wreck lies, long abandoned on a bank in mid-river, a ghostly, incredible hulk. For some mysterious reason, this prompted Frank to boast that his uncle had once driven a steam-roller from Cork to Dublin. With this revelation I came to appreciate the illustrious lineage of my fellow-rambler.

We stopped for a chat with a local farmer, who told us about the ruined castle visible down by the shore, once an O'Dowd stronghold. A little further on we crossed the county boundary into Sligo. A service was in progress at Killanley Church and Dean Ardis was praying for 'a better world down here'. Amen to that! Further on we found a large circular rath, surrounded by a ditch. In the centre was a corbelled enclosure, large enough to hold several people. There seemed to be an underground passage, but it was blocked up. A local resident told us that there was a tunnel leading to the enclosure from outside the fort, but we could not find any trace of it. The mound provided a fine aspect of the river-scape, with the ruined Rosserk Friary clear on the opposite bank and, further downstream, Moyne Abbey. A chimney in between must have been at the Asahi Plant, now closed. The railway extension from Ballina to Killala that served the plant is now abandoned.

Far to the south-west a large banner cloud clung to the summit of Nephin, where it remained all day. These clouds are triggered by mountains, which force passing air to rise, resulting in condensation. They remain in position, locked to the mountain peak like flags, while the air flows through them. So, unlike normal clouds whose moisture is carried along with them as they float on the breeze, these banner clouds contain different particles of moisture at different times, just like a waterfall. Sometimes the mountain sets off a series of waves downwind, and clouds called altocumulus lenticularis form at the wave-crests. These lens-shaped clouds are perhaps the most beautiful clouds of our latitudes.

The dunes of East Bartragh appeared ahead. Inishcrone Golf Links is there, and we decided to try for lunch. I rummaged in my rucksack for a tie, stashed there for just such a purpose – golf clubs are picky places – but we were out of luck; the chef was on holiday and no meals were available. So we climbed the dunes to the long crescent strand where para-gliders were exploiting the stiff breeze to zoom around the beach on carts. We lunched at the Atlantic Hotel and, as there was still an hour before Frank's bus, we strolled out the pier. Two large sighting obelisks here served to guide the fishermen into harbour at dusk. The boatmen got the correct approach bearing by lining up the two pillars against the horizon. An automatic beacon light has now been installed.

After Frank's departure, I went back down to Kilcullin's Seaweed Baths, a refurbished Edwardian bath-house, for 'the ultimate bathing experience'. I sat in a cedarwood box for five minutes, with only my head sticking out, pulling a lever to release blasts of scalding steam. Then into an enormous glazed porcelain bath with huge brass taps, filled with hot seawater and seaweed. The salt water is so buoyant that the lucky bather floats gently up and down with each breath. The final stage, a cold shower, was frankly shocking, but the overall effect was immensely exhilarating. I found lodging in a room over Walsh's Pub. Although I was the only guest in Walsh's, the landlady kindly lit a fire in the resident's lounge, where I sat in comfort, relaxed by the seaweed bath, writing up my journal.

Stage 60: *Inishcrone to Skreen*

The weather was holding fine: a front was stationary to the southwest, with a cold south-easterly breeze over Ireland. Listening to the traffic news for Dublin I experienced a certain schadenfreude, happy not to be amongst the masses struggling to work in a sluggish, metal stream. After a smoked salmon breakfast, I set out towards the north on the Easky road to the church at Kilglass. The sign there indicated that the Rector was again the Very Rev. E.G. Ardis, and Sunday Service was at 12:00, the same time as at Killanley. Had Rev. Ardis mastered bi-location or were these services on alternate Sundays, I wondered? Turning towards the morning sun, I left Killala Bay behind me. At Drinaghan there was another church, this time Catholic, with a Marian grotto and a bell-tower with a plaque commemorating 'our deceased children, born and unborn, baptized and unbaptized'. How refreshing, considering that in the past unbaptized children were refused burial in consecrated ground.

The ice on a roadside pool was over an inch thick. The stiff breeze accorded well with the forecast, which had warned of gales between Roche's Point and Slyne Head. The Irish sea-area forecasts are given in terms of headlands, always proceeding clockwise and mentioning three points where necessary to avoid any possible ambiguity. Thus, gales from Fair Head to Carnsore Point to Mizen Head refer to the east and south coast. If the west and north coasts were intended, one would hear of gales from Mizen Head to Bloody Foreland to Fair Head or something similar.

This region of Sligo seemed quite densely populated. Every house had a dog and every dog barked at me. My walking poles also served as powerful canine dissuaders, and the dazer remained in a rucksack pocket. At Bourke's Town I had some Foxford Lunch by the Leaffony River, then continued past Oghil House to a long forest trail. Climbing a gentle slope I saw the unmistakeable profiles of Knocknarea and Benbulben emerge over the horizon. Admiring their attractive contours intently, I stepped on an ice-sheet and crashed to the ground. Fortunately, no damage was done. Perhaps St. Catastravertus, patron of tumbles and spills, was guarding me. The Easky River flows down from Lough Easky in the Ox Mountains to the sea at Easky – very fishy! To cross it I had to join the main road, the N59, at Carrigeens. Here I sat at a picnic table outside Roger's shop to have lunch and reflect on the ghostly shell of the old Union Work House opposite. What luxury it was to be able to ramble around Ireland at my ease when, in times past, so many people were forced to tramp the country roads rather than enter the Work House. These were much-reviled places, with grim conditions, difficult to escape from once ensnared.

Leaving the main road again I found that a path marked on the map was completely overgrown and impassable, so I had to return to the busy, noisy N59 for another mile before turning aside again. There was a huge water tower ahead, like an enormous upturned trumpet. I passed this 'Satchmo's Tombstone' to gain the coast road, which led for many miles to Aughris Head and beyond. The road was dull but the views splendid, with the Ox Mountains to the south, Knocknarea and Benbulben ahead and Slieve League in Donegal far to the north. The cliffs at Slieve League are reputedly the highest sea-cliffs in Europe, although both Norway and Madeira would dispute this claim. The low profile of Inishmurray was just visible on the horizon. This island has impressive monastic remains, as I had found out on a visit earlier.

The sky was clear save for numerous jet contrails. Airliners heading west were using the aviation beacon at Eagle Island on the Mullet Peninsula as a waymark. As I sat on a bridge eating my last corned beef sandwich, I noticed a huge U-shaped contrail: a west-bound jet had turned back to the east. Was this a hijacking? Since the news later reported nothing unusual, it must have been a technical hitch, or something more routine. Or perhaps it was a military aircraft. The Americans were warming up for what seemed like an inevitable war in Iraq, and were operating through Shannon Airport, an activity that was generating considerable controversy.

I was to stay with Cíara, Mark's sister, and arrived in Skreen around 5:15, with just enough light to find her house. I was warmly welcomed and enjoyed the evening with her and her husband John Mark, who is a general practitioner. I asked John Mark about his view on various alternative medicines. The idea of homeopathic remedies is that the more dilute the medicine the stronger its action, but he was sceptical about their efficacy. They are diluted to such an extent that there is not a single molecule of the 'active ingredient' left in the dose. Thus, we hear about the homeopathic patient who died of an overdose when he drank pure water by mistake! Cíara and John Mark told me of their interest in kayaking and of an exciting encounter with a tornado in Ballysadare Bay. I recalled a book

I had read, called *Dances with Waves*, recounting the many adventures of Brian Wilson, who paddled around Ireland in a kayak. One particularly hair-raising escapade was his paddle through a sea-cave penetrating the Old Head of Kinsale. The bays at each end of the sea-caves are called, appropriately, Holeopen Bay East and West.

Stage 61: Skreen to Collooney

With a rucksack stuffed with freshly baked bread and home-brew honey, I set off, down a road known locally as Protestant's Lane, to Skreen. Skreen is hard to find: it is marked on the map, and well sign-posted, but there is so little there that it is easily missed. The name arises from the Latin word *scrinium*, a reliquary. It is said that St. Adhamhnáin, Columcille's biographer, deposited a collection of relics here. There is an extraordinary box tomb in the churchyard, depicting a gentleman in top hat, morning coat and cravat ploughing with a pair of horses. This excellent carving was done in in 1825 by Frank Diamond, first of five generations of monumental sculptors.

Skreen's most famous son was George Gabriel Stokes, the renowned nineteenth century mathematician. He was a son of the local Rector, Gabriel Stokes, who is commemorated on a plaque in the Church of Ireland that thanks him 'for twenty years of faithful intercourse with his flock'. Young George showed early mathematical flair, his first teacher commenting that he had found 'new ways of doing sums, better than the book'. He was Senior Wrangler – first place in mathematics at Cambridge University – in 1841. He went on to have a distinguished career, making major contributions in hydrodynamics, optics and asymptotics. For over fifty years, he held the Lucasian Chair of Mathematics, the position once held by Isaac Newton and occupied until recently by Stephen Hawking. Stokes drew early inspiration for his work in fluid dynamics by watching the Atlantic breakers on Dunmoran Strand, a few miles from Skreen.

From Skreen I took a long road south-west by Mullaroe, passing Holy Hill Hermitage, where a group of American Carmelite hermits have settled on land provided by the local bishop. By a curious coincidence, I had come across another of their hermitages in Colorado a

few year earlier, while working in Boulder. The road took me to Ladies'
Brae, a scenic route over the north-eastern flank of Knocknachree in
the Ox Mountains. Below Knocknachree, at the start of Ladies' Brae,
stands Ireland's youngest lake, Lough Aghree, formed by an earthquake
in 1490. No ladies were to be seen, nor any gentlemen either, as the icy
conditions made the road perilous and motorists were keeping to lower
ground. The wind strengthened as I climbed, reaching gale force at the
top of the pass. I made a brief stop to picnic and admire the view of
Sligo Bay and Knocknarea, with its huge summit cairn, the legendary
burial place of Queen Maeve. In school we learned Yeats' wonderful
poem 'Red Hanrahan's Song About Ireland':

> The old brown thorn-trees break in two high over Cummen Strand,
> Under a bitter black wind that blows from the left hand;
> Our courage breaks like an old tree in a black wind and dies,
> But we have hidden in our hearts the flame out of the eyes
> Of Cathleen, the daughter of Houlihan.

> The wind has bundled up the clouds high over Knocknarea,
> And thrown the thunder on the stones for all that Maeve can say.
> Angers that are like noisy clouds have set our hearts abeat;
> But we have all bent low and low and kissed the quiet feet
> Of Cathleen, the daughter of Houlihan.

> The yellow pool has overflowed high up on Clooth-na-Bare,
> For the wet winds are blowing out of the clinging air;
> Like heavy flooded waters our bodies and our blood;
> But purer than a tall candle before the Holy Rood
> Is Cathleen, the daughter of Houlihan.

I carried on to the southern slopes, where the land opened into a broad
glen with the plains of south Sligo spread out in the pale wintry sun. I
turned left onto a mountain trail, following the Sligo Way and guided by
the map, since there was no waymark at this crucial junction.

The impressive isolated mound of Knocknashee appeared ahead. A
fortified bronze age hilltop township was discovered here as recently as
1988 by OPW during a survey of Sligo. It is among the most significant

archaeological discoveries in Europe in recent decades. A deserted trail sloped gently down through a forested area to the village of Coolaney. I explored the beautiful riverside walk behind the town and then had soup in O'Grady's, the only one of the four pubs open.

Coolaney was on the rail route from Limerick to Sligo. Near the town I picked up the old line and followed it over a rusty bridge crossing the Owenbeg river. Ahead of me was Tullaghan Hill, also known as Hawk's Rock. This was an inspiration for Yeats' symbolic play, 'At the Hawk's Well', about Cuchulainn's search for wisdom. The gloomy conclusion of the play is that the seeker of wisdom must follow a difficult, tortuous track. The holy well on Hawk's Rock is reputed to have a most extraordinary property. The water level rises and falls in synchrony with the tides in Ballysadare Bay. Could this be true? The well is one hundred metres above sea level. It is tempting to dismiss such an idea as nonsense, but when I learned that the well is described in the *Book of Ballymote*, written in the fourteenth century, as 'one of the Wonders of Ireland', I decided to think more seriously about it. Remarkable as it may seem, there is a possible, if improbable, mechanism, akin to the action of a manometer, by which the well could oscillate in response to the tides. A simple analogy may explain the idea. The water in a toilet bowl may be caused, by pressure variations, to oscillate in response to a gusty wind blowing past the vent pipe. By a similar transfer mechanism, the well water might just be induced to move in sympathy with the tides. Or, perhaps, it's just a miracle.

The railway from Limerick to Sligo carried passengers until 1963, and goods trains continued to run until the section from Claremorris to Collooney Junction closed completely in 1975. The line, which is disused but not dismantled, was mostly clear, though I had to climb numerous barbed wire fences. Towards Collooney, some buildings have been erected on the line. I cannot believe that planning permission for these was granted. They seemed more likely to have been put up by latter-day land-grabbers. Lines like this have huge potential for development as walking and cycle ways and should be preserved against unprincipled opportunists.

Stage 62: Collooney to Manorhamilton

Frost's Dilemma arose again at Collooney. The nearest thing to a coastal route was north through Sligo town and round the western side of Benbulben to Donegal. But there was an alternative crescent route, eastward through Manorhamilton and touching Northern Ireland at Belleek. I chose the latter route to avoid the busy roads around Sligo town, and took the road for Dromahair, soon coming to the vast castellated gate of Markree Castle. I had phoned the castle the previous day but they were unwilling to negotiate a reduced price and I was unwilling to pay the asking price of €108 for a bed, and so had stayed at the more modest Chestnut Lodge in Collooney. Crossing the Unshin River, I took a track to Ballygawley. Slieve Daeane was away to the north. There is a large passage tomb near the summit of Slieve Daeane.

The road east from Ballygawley was designated as part of the Humbert Way. I stopped to photograph the ruin of Drumcondra tower house, south of the Slishwood Gap, with Killerry Mountain in the background. Slishwood is the Sleuth Wood of Yeats in 'The Stolen Child': 'Where dips the rocky highland / Of Sleuth Wood in the lake, / There lies a leafy island ...' The island is the tiny Lake Isle of Inishfree in Lough Gill, just north of Slishwood. This district is Yeats' Land of Heart's Desire, where he and his painting brother Jack found so much inspiration. Benbulben appeared through the gap, its profile almost identical to that seen from Aughris Head, like an Arizonan mesa. On the Ordnance Survey maps, the contours of Benbulben bear an uncanny resemblance to a huge dove flying westward. The dove's breast is King's Mountain, the wing is Benwiskin and the head is Benbulben itself.

At Ballintogher I stopped for a Lucozade and a chat with the publican in McGuinness's. He had spent many weekends tramping the mountains of Wicklow in all kinds of weather, and enjoyed recalling his adventures. At the Leitrim county border I picked up the trail of the Sligo, Leitrim and Northern Counties Railway (SL&NCR), closed since 1957, and followed it along a low embankment and into a shallow cutting. Flooded ground, with ice too thin to risk, and dense undergrowth forced me to leave the line and I lost my bearings. Distant power-lines marked on the map helped me to re-orient and locate the way again. Crossing the Bonet River, I came to

Dromahair, 'Seat of the O'Rourkes, Lords of Breifne'. The O'Rourkes were prominent in pre-Norman Ireland. It was from here that the red-haired Dervorgilla, faithless wife of Tiernan O'Rourke, eloped with Diarmaid MacMurrough in 1167 and 'brought the shtrangers to our shore'.

I watched the news while lunching in the village. The farmers were angry, as their incomes had fallen substantially in 2002, and thousands of tractors were converging on Dublin from all over the country, for a protest against government policy. The Dublin motorists would have one more trouble to add to their already-harried lives. Oh, what bliss to be a-rambling and a-roving, far away from the city noise.

Continuing towards Manorhamilton, I found Lough Nahoo about ten times larger than indicated on the map, another consequence of the recent torrential rains. A large flock of swans stood forlornly on the ice. Further on, Carrigeencor Lough looked beautiful in the late afternoon sunlight. At Gortgarrigan a small signpost in a hedgerow pointed into a field, indicating a Fulacht Fiadh, an 'Ancient Fianna Cooking Place'. At these bronze age cooking sites, stones were heated in a fire and then dropped into a large trough of water with 'meat and two veg.' to make an early variety of Irish Stew. In the field there was nothing but a nondescript mound, hardly noticeable to my untutored eye. Many of the archaeo-logical features marked on the maps are unspectacular to the uninitiated, and the guidance of an expert is required to provide interpretations and explanations of them. From here I followed a pleasant mountain trail over the side of Benbo (415 metres). The slanting sun lit up the russet bracken in a blaze of colour more typical of autumn in New England than winter in Old Ireland. This area was quite unfrequented, save for a few hippy-looking caravans.

Crossing the Bonet River once more, I took a side-road to Manorham-ilton. Darkness fell just as I approached the town. A large illuminated cross, erected for the millennium, shone on the hillside to the south. I found lodgings at the Central Hotel or, more correctly, the Central Bar. The room left much to be desired; indeed, it was the mankiest hotel room I have ever stayed in, but I was too tired to look for another place. I had an evening meal at Maguire's. Irish towns are often noted for their large number of public houses. Manorhamilton appeared to carry this reputation to an extreme. This tiny town has thirteen pubs, and little else. On this freezing January night it was a dismal place. The hotel owner told me that the social high point of the week is a disco on Saturday nights – at the Central Bar. I retired early.

Stage 63: *Manorhamilton to Belleek*

On a hill just south of Manorhamilton stands the ruin of Hamilton Castle. The town grew around the castle, built in 1634 by Sir Frederick Hamilton. During the Leitrim Plantation, Sir Fred was granted extensive lands that had been confiscated from the Irish; in other words, he was a fence, a receiver of stolen goods. During the Famine, the workhouse at Manorhamilton had one thousand 'residents'. The population of the town today is about 350.

The road to Rossinver runs over a pass between the many-streamed Dough Mountain to the east and Crocknagapple to the west. It is mainly a sheep farming area. A quiet hill trail runs parallel to the main road, and this was the route I took. I startled a cock pheasant, who rose with such clamour and commotion that he startled me back. As I neared Rossinver, Lough Melvin appeared ahead. The lake is about eight miles long, reaching from here to Kinlough (Ceann Loch, the head of the lake). At Rossinver Fisheries, ten small open boats lay on the shore, awaiting the opening of the angling season.

The bright green door of Sean Óg's Cottage sends a signal to those coming from the north: the cottage is the last house before the Kilcoo River, where I crossed the bridge to a new county, a new province, a new state. No sound of bombs or bullets, just 'lake water lapping with low sounds by the shore'. A notice erected by the Fermanagh authorities, with a list of instructions for boatmen using Lough Melvin, included a warning: "Foul Language is not Acceptable". This was Northern Ireland. Further confirmation was provided by a plaque in the village of Garrison, commemorating Bobby Sands, Óglaigh na hÉireann. Garrison originated when King William erected a barracks here on his way to Aughrim. Near the village, there is a beautiful walk by the river, leading up to the Roogagh Falls.

I had lunch at the Lough Melvin Holiday Centre, served by friendly staff with soft northern accents. The linguistic boundary – philologists call it an isogloss – is surprisingly sharp. Only a few miles back I had spoken to a farmer whose Leitrim brogue was totally different in character. Linguists draw lines separating regions where different words are used for the same things, for example, bucket and pale, or whin and gorse. A line like this is called an isogloss. If many such lines, for different word-pairs, come together, we have a dialect boundary.

From just north of Garrison, a dashed black line on the map leads almost to Belleek. I followed this leafy trail for about a kilometre, to a ruined house. Beyond this point, it became impossibly overgrown with holly and brambles and willow and ash trees. The wise course would have been retreat, but this is always unattractive, so I tried to find a way onward through adjacent fields. This was a risky strategy and, indeed, progress was equally difficult here. I was aided by the fact that the desired course was due north and the slanting sun cast long shadows ahead of me. I hacked my way through impenetrable undergrowth and eventually reached a clear track, badly scratched and exhausted. A distance of a half mile had taken over an hour. As daylight time was short, I completed the journey to Belleek on the main road. For the last hundred metres before the River Erne I was back in the Republic, so erratic is the border.

Belleek Pottery is an imposing building on the banks of the Erne. The pottery has been there for almost 150 years and Belleek porcelain is widely famous. I visited the pottery museum and bought a small gift in the showroom for Cabrini. Then I repaired to the Carlton Hotel across the road for a long soak. Belleek is a pleasant village with a wide main street and several attractive shops and pubs, vastly more appealing than my previous overnight stopping place. The day was nicely ended with a good meal at the hotel.

Stage 64: Belleek to Donegal

The mission statement of the Carlton Hotel is 'We say Hello as Strangers but Goodbye as Friends'. Having been treated with refreshing old-world courtesy, I bid the receptionist a friendly farewell and turned north, past the heavily fortified police station, into The Pullans, a region of small lakes and drumlins, with a maze of tiny roads bounded by dry

stone walls. Following the road by the Erne, I crossed back into the Republic and came to a wildlife sanctuary. I was now in County Donegal.
Care was needed to keep on the right track in this intricate network of
roads. The landscape was rolling and I had several brief but stiff climbs.
A notice pointed aside to the site where a Sunderland Flying Boat had
crashed during the Second World War; the date of the crash was August
12th, 1944. Since I had no way of knowing how far away the site lay, I
didn't turn aside. Soon I reached the tiny, beautiful Columcille Lough.
An anticyclone was centred over Ireland and, as there was not a puff
of wind, the lake surface was as smooth as glass, perfectly reflecting
the landscape on the opposite shore. Crossing the Behy River, I hopped
from Sheet 16 to Sheet 11. One drawback of the excellent OSI Discovery
Series maps is that they are edge-to-edge with no overlap. Thus, when a
road junction occurs at the map boundary, as here, map-reading errors
are easily made.

The church at Keiby came into view but there was not a stir in this
tiny hamlet. Two white geese flew overhead, honking loudly. To the right
of the road beyond Ummeracom there was a huge open basin under construction. I thought it was a reservoir but a local farmer, a Noel Purcell
lookalike, told me that it was a soak-pit for a landfill site. Just before Ball-
intra, the welcome site of Donegal Bay appeared. I stopped for refreshments at the Bay Bush Bar. An exceedingly drunken man, who was mut-
tering incoherently, fell off his high stool and smashed his head against
the floor. The other customers were unfazed, treating this as an everyday
affair. They picked him up and parked him in a corner where he had less
risk of falling, and he promptly fell asleep.

The road through Bridgetown to Laghy was without interest. The
name Laghy comes from An Lathaigh, a muddy place. I stopped at The
Seven Arches pub for a snack. The pub was named for the bridge opposite, which was on the mail-coach route between Derry and Sligo. Learning that the owner, Gerry McGirr, is known affectionately by his customers as The Quiet Man, I put on my best John Wayne accent when his wife
appeared and said, 'Mary Kate Danagher, where's me tae?' She didn't bat
an eyelid; in fact, she must have been chuffed, for she threw in a mince
pie and a slice of Dundee Cake with the tea.

The railway from Donegal Town reached Laghy in 1906. The bridge is still there, below the seven-arched road bridge. From here to Donegal, I followed close to the route of the railway, picking up its spoor in several places, once spotting a large single-arched viaduct in the woods near the road. I arrived in Donegal just in time to catch a bus to Sligo for my train home.

At Edgeworthstown the train was delayed, and the driver made the following announcement: 'Attention: We'll be here for a while, at least twenty minutes. There are two trains coming down. So, go ahead and have a smoke on the platform, or whatever.' The unfortunate lady opposite me was reading a book *How to Quit Smoking*. We arrived in Dublin about an hour late. The mission statement of Iarnród Éireann: SNAFU. At least the return leg of my ticket between Dublin and Westport was good for the journey from Sligo, something positive to say about Irish Rail.

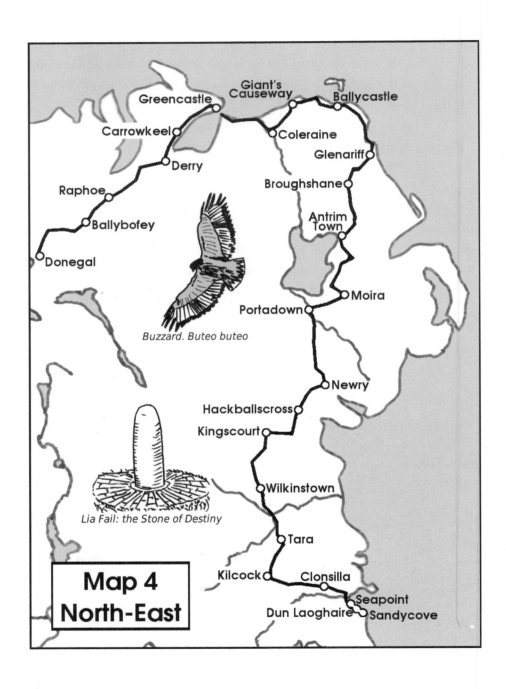

Giant's
Causeway
Greencastle
Ballycastle
Carrowkeel
Coleraine
Glenariff
Derry
Broughshane
Raphoe
Antrim
Town
Ballybofey
Donegal
Moira
Portadown
Buzzard. Buteo buteo
Newry
Hackballscross
Kingscourt
Lia Fail: the Stone of Destiny
Wilkinstown
Tara
Kilcock
Clonsilla
Seapoint
Dun Laoghaire
Sandycove

**Map 4
North-East**

Chapter 14

THE NORTH-WEST FRONTIER

There's freedom when you're walking
Even though you're walking slow.

'Homeless Brother' – Don McLean

MUCH HAPPENED BEFORE THE Commodius Vicus continued. Most no-
torious was the pig-headed decision of George Bush to invade Iraq, with
Tony Blair tagging along. Much can be written in praise of G-and-T, but not
this particular blend. The Olympic Games were under way in Athens, but
Ireland was having no luck. However, all this changed a week later when
Cian O'Connor won gold in the singles equestrian event.[11] Hurricanes Alex,
Bonnie and Charley had already strutted their stuff around Florida, and
Danielle was threatening to follow. Atlantic hurricanes that reach middle
latitudes can often have a major impact on the weather in Ireland. Charley
(the first) had brought dramatic storms in 1986, and its namesake was now
on the way. Already, torrential flooding had almost washed away the Cornish village of Boscastle, and there were landslides in Scotland and flooding in Derry. I was off to Donegal for the monsoon season.

Stage 65: Donegal Town to Ballybofey

A bus from Dublin dropped me at the Abbey Hotel in Donegal and, after a solid lunch there, I headed out past Donegal Castle along Tircon-
nel Road. Tir Conaill is the historical name of this region. More history was

---

[11] Later, the gloss wore off, when his horse, Waterford Crystal, tested positive for a prohibited
substance. The Olympic Board stripped O'Connor of his medal and disqualified the Irish
show jumping team.

revealed as I passed Railway Road. There have been no trains for half a century but, despite some forbidding terrain, Donegal was once served by an extensive rail network. I took a quiet side-road towards Lough Eask, coming soon to a wee hexagonal church (everything is 'wee' here in Donegal) where I lit a candle for Cabrini. Soon I came to the lake – Loch Iascaig or Fish Lake – and rested briefly by the shore. Then onward along a road lined with mountain ash laden with red berries. As I neared the crest of Barnesmore Gap I had to join the main road, the N15, and soon came to Biddy's O'Barnes where a rest and a refreshing drink made the world look rosy.

After a long climb on the hard shoulder, I reached the gap between Croagh Connellagh and Barnesmore Mountain. I looked wistfully across the wee Lowerymore River to a line on the hillside opposite. This was the line of the County Donegal Railway (CDR) which once crossed the gap between Donegal Town and Stranorlar. I imagined a lush green track stretching unimpeded for miles. In reality, it was probably more mush than lush, with barbed wire fences and miscellaneous other obstacles. After cresting the gap, I turned aside on the road towards Castlederg, a quiet route through a heathery bog. It crossed the old railway line, which was indeed waterlogged and overgrown. This is another golden opportunity to develop a long-distance walking way. I found a dirt track leading northwest over Lough Hill, overlooking Lough Morne. It was a delight to be away from the traffic noise, rambling along the quiet hillside. The track was easy going except at the hilltop, where it was flooded. It is a decidedly odd characteristic of Irish mountains that the summits are so often sodden, even in summer. The boggy soil just won't let the water go! The track led on through a large coniferous forest. I came to a notice, erected by Coillte, reading 'Unauthorised persons prohibited beyond this point'. As I had no intention of backtracking for a detour of several miles, I resolved to continue, and to apply for appropriate authorisation should I encounter a Coillte employee. The track eventually passed under a tiny stone bridge, just three metres wide, which once carried the narrow-gauge railway. It led me back to the N15, so the last few miles into Ballybofey were a beat against heavy traffic on a fast road with no hard shoulder.

I found a place to stay at the Roseville B&B. In the breakfast room there was an interesting print showing the CDR No. 1 Locomotive Alice heading for Stranorlar through the Barnesmore Gap. The artist was G. R. Hanan of the South Donegal Railway Restoration Society.

Stage 66: Ballybofey to Raphoe

I awoke to the twittering of swallows on the wires outside my window. I strode northward through the village of Ballybofey and crossed the bridge over the Finn to Stranorlar. What claims to fame have these twin towns? Finn Harps Football Club have their base here. Isaac Butt, founder of the Irish Home Rule Movement is buried in the local graveyard. All the churches and schools are on the north side of the bridge, allowing the citizens on the Stranorlar side to joke that their transfluvial neighbours are ignorant pagans. Stranorlar looked neat and clean in the early morning sun. I came soon to the churchyard where lie the remains of Isaac Butt. A notice mounted on the church wall read, 'A corpse may not be exhumed except on order of the coroner or other authorised officer'. In any case, I had neither a shovel nor the slightest intention of disturbing Old Isaac.

Near the tiny Lough Alaan, I passed the golf course, and continued through the townlands of Cooladawson, Corradooey and Blackrepentance. In a field I noticed starlings rummaging on the backs of the sheep. Presumably, there is a symbiotic relationship here, the birds getting their breakfast while grooming the sheep in the process. I crossed the Deele River, heading for Tops Hill, where the Beltany Stone Circle stands on the hilltop. It is one of the finest in Ireland, reputedly older than Stonehenge, with about 64 large slabs mounted vertically in a circle some fifty metres wide. A single stone about two metres high stands outside the circle to the south-east. The name Beltany comes from Bealtaine or Baal Tine, the Fire of Baal the Sun God. Bealtaine is one of the four great druidical festivals, celebrated near the time of the summer solstice, when the Sun God is at his most powerful. The stone circle must have been built for ritualistic purposes and the alignments may have astronomical significance, although hard evidence seems to be lacking. I was not alone on the hilltop. Three youths of New Age persuasion sat cross-legged in the circle, communing with the spirits. I forebore to disturb them and, after spending some time in contemplation, descended the hill by the leafy path and took the short road to Raphoe.

Raphoe is a pretty village, centered on The Diamond, a triangular 'square', a design not untypical of plantation towns. It has been described as the smallest cathedral city in Europe. Entering the town from the south, I passed the Masonic Lodge which bore the inscription Audi, Vidi, Taci. This means roughly 'Listen, Look and Keep Shtumm', a curious motto for an organization with nothing to hide. The tiny village of Raphoe was once an important ecclesiastical centre. There are several churches in the village in addition to St. Eunan's Cathedral. As a result of some local squabble, there are two Presbyterian churches and the congregation was divided for some seventy years. The cathedral was founded by Colmcille and is named for his follower St. Eunan, or Adamnan (627–704), who was at one time Abbot of Iona, and who wrote Vitae Columbae, a biography of Colmcille. The cathedral today is a mixture of styles with extensive rebuilding and alterations. The five windows depicting the four Evangelists and St. Eunan were made in Sarah Purser's Tower of Glass studio.

On a rocky hillock behind the cathedral stand the impressive ruins of the Bishop's Palace, a fortified house known locally as The Castle. Built in 1637, it was occupied until 1834 when the Diocese of Raphoe was united with that of Derry. The palace accidently caught fire four years later and was destroyed. I bought a little booklet, In and Around Raphoe, which contained interesting information about the history of the village and surroundings. The Royal School at Raphoe was one of five founded under royal charter, the others being at Armagh, Portora, Dungannon and Cavan. One illustrious past pupil of the school was Isaac Butt. A somewhat less illustrious one was John McNaughton, known as 'Half-hanged'. A Bushmills man and a gambler and wastrel, in 1761 McNaughton tricked a Miss Knox into marrying him and was challenged to a duel by her family. In the ensuing skirmish, the young lady was shot dead. McNaughton was found guilty of murdering his lover, and was sentenced to hang. He was hanged in Strabane, from a gallows constructed by the Knoxes. However, as they were carrying out the execution, the rope snapped, so they had to hang him again. The story goes that he was offered a pardon, but refused it, saying he could not go through life being known as 'Half-hanged McNaughton'.

I had difficulty finding a place to stay in Raphoe, as the hotel did not take guests! The local B&Bs were all closed, but eventually I found a room with the hospitable Mary McGranaghan, who had a house in The Diamond.

Stage 67: Raphoe to Derry

I awoke to the sound of eight chimes from St. Eunan's, across the Diamond. Mary treated me to a large omelette and an account of the many blessings and woes of family life. Asked whither I was bound, I told her I planned to walk to Derry and meet up with my wife. She advised me to try the City Hotel in Derry – some special offer had been announced in the papers – and she gave me directions to find the hotel.

As I strode forth from Raphoe, a small boy asked if I was going skiing: he had guessed this from the walking poles. I told him I was walking to Derry. 'What?' he asked incredulously, 'would you not get a taxi?' I explained that I enjoyed walking. 'You'll never make it. You're an eejit!' he said encouragingly and scampered off. Scamp is right. Disregarding his prognosis, I took a minor road past Oakfield Demesne. Here stood a castellated house, reflected like a postcard picture in a tiny pond. At White Cross I turned aside on a quiet wee byway over the northern flank of Binnion Hill and followed an uneventful path, interrupted only by occasional showers.

Approaching Saint Johnstown, the broad sweep of the River Foyle opened up ahead of me. I cut down through the churchyard of St. Baithin's. Baithin was another disciple of Colmcille and, like Eunan, an Abbot of Iona. I had lunch at The Trucker's Breakfast, a diner just beyond this pleasant village. Then, rested and refreshed, I carried on to Carrigans. A huge red and yellow sign reading CCCP, reminiscent of the former Soviet Union, was actually for Carrigan's Car Care and Parts. After the village, I followed the cycle track, which led down to the bank of the Foyle. Part of the National Cycle Network, this pleasant walk on a tree-lined path, away from the traffic noise, led all the way to the city of Derry. I heard a curlew cry far out on the mud-flats of the river. Then a passer-by greeted me with, 'Out for a wee dawnder, are yee?' The path followed the route of the old Foyle Valley Railway. From Milltown House to the city, the rails have been preserved and visitors can take trips from the city on a diesel railcar. Indeed, the path brought me directly to the Railway Centre, next to the double-decker Craigavon Bridge, where an ancient, rusting steam-engine stood on the line.

I arrived at the City Hotel stiff and foot-sore after an unchallenging three-day walk. It was clear that I needed to train before setting out, so as to be fitter. At the hotel I rendezvoused with my wife Cabrini, who had driven up from Dublin so that we could have a short break together. Enough has been written about the trials and turmoil endured by the citizens of Derry over the past thirty-five years, but the evidence is everywhere. Derry has a number of monikers, not all complimentary. One such is 'Stroke City' as, in a futile effort to keep everyone happy, its name is sometimes written London/Derry or Derry/Londonderry. Another name, the Maiden City, reflects the fact that the city walls have never been breached. Starting near the impressive neo-Gothic facade of the Guildhall, I took a 'wee dawnder' around the walls in pouring rain before returning to the hotel.

The next morning we drove a few miles to the Grían of Aileach, a spectacular circular fortification on the top of Greenan Mountain. Originally built, it seems, for some sun-worshipping ritual, it was the stronghold of the O'Neills of Ulster for several centuries. It was restored in the 1870s and is currently undergoing major repairs. The views from the hilltop over Lough Foyle and Lough Swilley are spellbinding. At the village of Burt, just below the mountain, stands a beautiful small church designed by the late renowned architect, Liam McCormack. Having worked for twenty-five years in another (leaky) building of his design, I was less enthusiastic than many about his renown, but this little church, its form inspired by the Grían, is unquestionably a gem.

We drove northward through Buncrana and Carndonagh to Malin Head and, after a brief visit to Martin Harren in the meteorological station, continued on to Banba's Crown, the northernmost point of the Irish mainland. Ten days later I resigned from my position as deputy director of Met Éireann to take up a new job, as professor of meteorology at UCD. This new responsibility kept me so busy that several months elapsed before the Commodius Vicus could be continued.

*   *   *

Stage 68: Derry to Carrowkeel

A new year, 2005, had begun. The world should have been full of hope, but it was hard not to be disturbed by both man-made and natural catastrophes. The Peace Process in the North was stalled again, over a demand for photographic evidence of decommissioning, but at least the shooting and bombing had stopped. Iraq was in an increasing state of turmoil, while President Bush continued to preach a fairytale that all would live happily ever after the coming elections. St. Stephen's Day had brought news of an earthquake off Sumatra, with one thousand dead. Next day the number was four thousand and a week later 300,000, most killed by the tsunamis generated by the sea-quake. Many more would perish from infection and disease. It was one of the worst natural disasters ever to have occurred.

I took the Derry bus from Busarus in Dublin, and my friend Frank picked it up at Slane. So we passed through Collon, Ardee, Carrickmacross, Castleblaney, Monaghan, Emyvale, Omagh, Ballygawley, Athnacloy and Strabane en route to Derry. After Omagh, the remnants of the Foyle Valley Railway were evident from the bus: embankments by the river, cuttings and vestigial bridges.

Emerging from the bus station, we passed the Guildhall and, at the Northern Bank, got some sterling notes from the 'hole-in-the-wall'. They were Northern Bank notes, the £20 depicting the renowned engineer Harry Ferguson. There had recently been a bank robbery in Belfast in which over £20 million, mostly in Northern Bank notes, had been taken. We wondered if eyebrows would be raised when we tried to spend the money.

The stormy, unstable weather was the aftermath of a particularly active cold front that had passed through the previous day. This was so intense that it had spawned a tornado in Clonee, ripping the roofs off several houses – not a pleasant New Year's gift for the owners. Braving the showers, we headed along the river path, passing a memorial to the many famine emigrants who took a one-way passage from Derry. After buying vittles in Sainburys we took the road northwards. We had just three hours of light left and eleven miles to go to Carrowkeel, so there was no time to waste. The road sticks close to Lough Foyle and it is possible to walk along the lake shore, but we were not keen to be stranded in the dark so we stuck to the road. Thus, we were on roadside paths or the hard shoulder the whole way, but the road was wide enough so this was not too uncomfortable.

Inishmore Peninsula is surrounded by several shipwrecks including a World War I German submarine, UB109, a Greek freighter called Argo Delos and the famous La Trinadad Valencera from the Armada, discovered by the Derry Diving Club in 1971. The Foyle broadens out in a graceful sweep below Derry, narrows again where the Foyle Bridge spans the river, and then opens out into broad Lough Foyle just below Culmore. Passing through the nondescript village of Culmore, we saw that the pillarboxes were still red. Then crossing the point marked on the map as Liberty Bridge, we were back to the freedom of the Republic. Here at the village of Muff, the former custom post had found a valuable new function as a Red Cross centre. A collection was underway there for the victims of the tsunami. With no spare time, we breezed through the village, not delaying for some sport at the Muff Diving Club. We passed several roadside pubs in our haste. First was the Ture Inn, not shrouded in mystery as the townland hereabouts is called Ture. Then came The Carman's Bar; and finally Mary Deeney's. So, we arrived at The Point Lodge by Quigley's Point near the village of Carrokeel just as the last of the daylight vanished from the sky.

Stage 69: Carrowkeel to Greencastle

Setting out from Carrowkeel, we took a path down to the shore of Lough Foyle. The shore, a sandy-rocky mixture, stretched north for many miles providing a wonderful means of progressing north away from the pesky traffic noise and fumes. The basalt block of Binevenagh stood sentinel on the far shore and soon Magilligan Point appeared ahead. This is the extremity of a huge sandy triangle on the eastern side of the lough. A number of streams enter the lough and at one we had to de-boot to cross. A large flock of brent geese were feeding on the lake.

The coastline here might be called the polychromatic shore: there is Whitecastle and Black Point and Redcastle and Brown Shoulder and Greencastle, whither we were headed. Near Drung, the sandy shore ran out and the lake water lapped against a sea-wall so, after buying something to eat and drink, we took to a quiet by-road that runs at a higher level parallel to the A2. A kind fellow stopped to offer us a lift but we explained to him that we were happy to walk. Near Moville, we made a short digression to see the early ecclesiastical site at Cooley, originally founded by St. Patrick himself. Here there is a tall Celtic cross with five perforations, the four as usual within the Sun-ring and a fifth in the upright above. There are also some monastic remains and many ancient tombstones. A drystone tomb in the form of a small church, and called the Skull House, is thought to be the resting place of St. Finian. Peeping in through the opening, we spotted some bones, thought they are hardly those of Finian, who was a contemporary of Colmcille.

At Moville we had lunch at The Town Clock and then took the shore walk to Greencastle. This beautiful lake-side path is a joy for ramblers, and gives easy access between the two towns. One of the houses along the shore is that of the renowned statesman and Nobel laureate, John Hume, another the residence of the playwright Brian Friel. Progress was easy, interrupted only slightly by diversions necessitated by the few house-owners who have put obstacles in the way of walkers. Presumably, they act without legal justification. There is certainly a case that the foreshore should be open to walkers.

Once again, we arrived at our journey's end just as darkness fell. It is one of the serious disadvantages of winter walking that daylight is so limited. At Greencastle we came to the Inishowen Maritime Museum, housed in the old coast guard station by the harbour. It is an attractive museum with an interesting collection of memorabilia, photographs and nautical equipment. There is also a small planetarium in the museum. I had visited it on an earlier trip here, but just now the museum was closed.

In front of the museum stands a memorial to all who have lost their lives at sea. A replica of the Cooley Cross is embedded in the ground, in front of a pillar bearing an armillary sphere, an ancient astronomical instrument used by navigators. An inscription on a nearby plaque reads:

There are no roses on a sailor's grave
No lilies on an ocean wave
The only tribute is the sea-gull's sweep
And the tear-drops that a loved one weeps.

There were up to fifty fishing boats tied up in the harbour. The National Fisheries College is situated in the town, so there is a constant flow of people with interests in fishing. We repaired to Kealey's Bar for refreshment and enquired about accommodation for the night. Hugo, who was enjoying a drink, offered to put us up at his B&B, just ten minutes away, and we accepted this offer. The house is in a townland with the curious name Eleven Ballyboes. A ballyboe, or *baile bó*, is one cow-land, or enough land to graze a cow. Just how they arrived at eleven, not ten or twelve, ballyboes is a mystery.

Stage 70: *Greencastle to Coleraine*

Strolling down through Greencastle to catch the ferry, we passed a Martello tower and Napoleonic fort built in the early nineteenth century and came to the ruins of the old Anglo-Norman castle that gave the place its name. The Magilligan–Greencastle ferry was inaugurated in 2002. We were carried across the mouth of the lough in the MFV Foyle Rambler, a mile or so in about fifteen minutes. Thus we came again into Northern Ireland, landing at Magilligan Point. Another Martello tower guarded the entrance to Lough Foyle and, beyond it, a modern look-out tower equipped with a radar scanner. I thought at first that it was a coast-guard tower but it is probably military. There is a prison nearby, for 'ordinary decent criminals', as opposed to the political variety, and there are several rifle ranges nearby. A large notice on the beach read 'Military Firing Range' and warned that access was prohibited when a red flag was hoisted. Luckily for us, no flag was evident this day, so we commenced a long walk along the beige strand. The whole area hereabouts is a nature reserve, and we enjoyed watching flocks of waders feeding along the water's edge.

On the ferry, I had noticed that the Moon, at its last quarter, was pointing upwards, even though the Sun was clearly at a lower elevation in the sky. That is, the line from the centre of the Moon, bisecting the visible semicircle, was angled upwards from the horizontal. The psychological tendency in extrapolating this line is to imagine it continuing to rise, in which case it cannot possibly reach to the lower level where the Sun was to be found. We ambled along, considering this Looney-Solar Paradox.

In Archimedean fashion, we drew pictures in the sand, trying to untangle the enigma. It is clear that the light from the Sun to the Moon must follow a straight line. Such a line drawn against the background of the sky may rise to a higher level, but it must ultimately descend again to intersect the horizon. Thus, if the Sun and Moon are at the same elevation, the straight line joining them does rise above the horizontal, so even in this case the Moon appears to tilt upwards. This could be further complicated by casting it in terms of lines projecting onto great circles on the 'celestial dome', but you are probably sufficiently baffled already.

The North Base Tower for the survey of Ireland stands in a field on the flat eastern shore of Lough Foyle, about three miles south of Magilligan Point. This area was chosen to establish a baseline for mapping Ireland, and fieldwork on the survey began in 1827. At the time the baseline was the longest of its kind and was measured to an accuracy never previously achieved. Measurement of the base commenced in September 1827 and was completed in November 1828. The length of the base, levelled and reduced to the adjoining sea level, was nearly 8 miles. The South Base Tower is at Ballykelly.

The earliest map of Ireland is that of Ptolemy, a Greek cartographer of Alexandria. His map, from the second century, shows the main rivers, and the tribes inhabiting different territories. Geraldus Cambrensis, or Gerald of Wales, in his *Topographia Hiberniae*, has a schematic map of Western Europe with Ireland marked and the main features shown. During the Tudor conquest, detailed mapping beyond the Pale began, mainly for land-grabbing reasons. In 1564 the Flemish cartographer Gerardus Mercator, mapped Ireland. The Ordnance Survey was set up in 1824 and the first survey of Ireland was completed in 1846. This required enormous effort, with mappers trundling up steep hills with heavy theodolites, dividing the land into ever smaller triangles. It is astounding that the results of their efforts are so accurate. Satellite imagery now available routinely shows that these surveyors achieved remarkable precision in defining the shape of the country. Until recently, the best series of maps covering the country comprehensively were the twenty five sheets at a half inch to the mile. While excellent in many ways, they were out of date and the scale was too small for the detail needed in cross-country walking. The new Discovery/Discoverer series of maps at a scale of 1:50,000 covers the country, North and South, with 89 sheets. I have found them to be of excellent quality and, apart from a few minor grumbles such as poor quality paper, can praise them enthusiastically.

We strode along Magilligan strand for about six miles, chasing plovers along the water's edge where a gentle swell was breaking. Eagle Hill comes close to the shore, where it ends in a cliff with a series of spectacular waterfalls. At a broad stream we had to de-boot and de-bag to cross. The railway follows the coast here to the tiny spot called Downhill, where it enters a series of tunnels to reach Castlerock. Passing Downhill Hostel, which was under renovation, we climbed the steep hill to Lion's Gate, opposite Dunboe Church and entered the grounds of Downhill House. After exploring the ruins, we headed for Mussenden Temple, perched precariously on the cliff-top. This tiny rotunda, an architectural gem that once served as a library, was modelled on the Temple of Vesta at Tivoli. It was built in 1785 and forms part of the estate of Frederick Augustus Hervey, the 4th Earl of Bristol, Bishop of Derry. The cliff below has been stabilized to prevent the loss of the building but, like the leaning Tower of Pisa, it must some day succumb to the forces of nature. An inscription on the building, 'Tis pleasant, safely to behold from shore / The rolling ship, and hear the tempest roar', from Lucretius, has an unsympathetic ring to it.

From the temple, we followed a rhododendron-lined path down through the scenic Black Glen to the Black Gate, and thence to the small resort of Castlerock. There we enjoyed refreshments in Crusoe's Coffee Shop. The remainder of the journey was uneventful. We followed Ballywoolen Road and Cranagh Road. This was technically part of The Ulster Way, but was one of the less interesting stretches. We came to Coleraine as darkness fell, and caught a local train back to Derry.

Chapter 15

THE CAUSEWAY COAST

Silent O Moyle be the roar of thy waters;
Break not ye breezes your chain of repose.
While murmuring mournfully, Lir's lonely daughter
Tells to the night star her tale of woes.

'Silent, O Moyle' – Thomas Moore

I TOOK THE ENTERPRISE TO BELFAST, heading for Coleraine to walk
the North Antrim Coast. As the train pulled out at 07:35, I looked forward to a nice breakfast. An announcement soon dashed my hopes: 'We'd
like to apologise for any inconvenience.' Some cook or waiter or wash-up
wallah had failed to show up and there would be no breakfast; SNAFU
again for Irish Rail. I thought of the starving hordes in Africa and followed mother's advice: offer it up! Sudoku had recently hit Ireland and
was in all the papers. I managed to finish the 'easy' panel by Belfast, not
exactly a Homeric accomplishment. Having just completed a book on
Lewis Fry Richardson and his weather forecast, I was in need of a break,
and planned to avoid TV and newspapers. But the giant screen in the
station blared out the news as I waited for the train for Coleraine: Avian
flu had reached Russia and was winging westward; huge forest fires raged
in Portugal (more effects of global warming, perhaps); England had won
the toss and had decided to bat first.

The train brought us out along the north shore of Belfast Lough then
through Mossley, Antrim Town, Ballymena, Cullybackey and Ballymoney
to Coleraine. Awaiting the passing of a heavy shower, I had an Ulster Fry
in Eileen's Diner – this would take about ten miles to burn up.

Stage 71: Coleraine to Giant's Causeway

I took a minor route between the Bushmills and Portrush roads, hoping it would be quiet, but there was too much traffic until I reached a junction at Islandmore. There I branched onto a quieter way that took me up a hill to a splendid prospect of Portrush on its promontory, with a string of islands – the Skerries – to the east, Binnevenagh away to the west and Inishowen Peninsula on the horizon. Soon I came to Dunluce, the ruin of a castle perched precariously on the cliff-top. Indeed, the castle kitchens fell into the sea, apparently during a banquet; no desserts that night! Far below, a sea-cave penetrates right through the promontory on which the castle stands; so, further collapse is ultimately inevitable.

The coast road soon brought me to Portballintrae, an attractive if slightly dull village resort at the head of a beautiful circular cove with a crescent of sandy beach. Here I rested on a bench, watching the gentle waves lapping the shore. As the large rollers entered the mouth of the cove they spread out, refracted by the geometry of the seabed so that, by simple energy conservation, their height decreased and they reached the shore much diminished. On a hill above the village are two curious circular embankments, the Rissanduff Earthworks. Heaven knows what role these structures, known locally as the Cups and Saucers, played in the remote past. Perhaps they had a function in some exotic pagan ritual. More likely, they had some prosaic, utilitarian purpose. Onward I went, crossing the little River Bush by the 'Three-quarters Bridge', to reach the route of the tramway. This was the world's first hydro-electric tram, operating from 1883 to 1949. It ran from Portrush through Bushmills and on to The Giant's Causeway. It was powered by a generating station at Salmon Leap waterfall on the Bush River. It enabled visitors, who had taken the train from Belfast to Portrush, to visit the causeway, and greatly helped in popularising this site. A narrow-gauge railway now runs along the route for about two miles, the Giant's Causeway and Bushmills Railway, and is popular with tourists. A path winds along beside the track, behind the dunes above Bushfoot Strand, and it soon brought me to the railway terminus, where I had tea and scones. Then I walked the final mile or so inland to The Smuggler's Inn, where a room and bath awaited.

Stage 72: *Giant's Causeway to Ballycastle*

Leaving The Smuggler's Inn after a hearty breakfast, I came to the Giant's Causeway Tourist Centre around 09:30 and so had a half hour to wait until opening time. I was anxious to book a room in Ballycastle as it was the Bank Holiday weekend and the Lammas Fair was on. Indeed, the friendly lady in the tourist centre had to ring a half dozen places before she managed to get a room for me. A tiny bus brings visitors from the centre down to the main causeway sights but, as I had been here a year earlier, I headed straight for the cliff path. The North Antrim Cliff Walk is about as good as it gets for walkers in Ireland: a good surface, well away from traffic, with constantly-changing views, all spectacular, and the surging surf providing a soothing acoustic backdrop. There is a good range of bird-life to be seen, and a rich fauna. But before all this comes the extraordinary geology. The 40,000 or so hexagonal prisms of basalt were formed in an uncertain volcanic maelstrom some sixty million years ago. They are arranged in many exotic formations with popular names: the Giant's Chair; the Amphitheatre; the Organ. Some of the basalt columns are more than a hundred feet tall. The area makes a lasting impression and prompts speculation as to how the causeway was formed. Discounting the usual stories about Finn McCool, the most popular theory is that the molten lava underwent intense convection or thermal overturning, with the molten rock rising in some places and sinking in others. Such convection can spontaneously arrange itself into hexagonal patterns called Benard cells. They can sometimes be seen in a pan of water that is gently heated on a stove. But it is a delicate process, which easily degenerates into more chaotic motion and it is difficult to see how this process could be maintained for a long time and over a wide area. The causeway is an Area of Outstanding Beauty and an Area of Special Scientific Interest, and has recently been declared by UNESCO as a World Heritage Site.

At Spanish Point, the wreck of the galleass La Girona was found in the 1960s. It was one of many Spanish ships wrecked on the Irish coast after the disastrous Armada of 1588. Some of the treasures recovered from the wreck are now in Belfast Museum. Following the lunetted path, I came to Benbane Head, the most northerly point on the Antrim coast, and the northern extremity of the Commodius Vicus. A mile or so further on are the ruins of Dunseverick Castle, which stands on the site of the early capital of the kingdom of Dal Riada that extended from Antrim across to Scotland. The castle was destroyed by Cromwellian forces, the last occupant, an O'Cahan, being executed in 1653. There is little left now but the ruins of a sixteenth century gateway. Continuing, I came to a headland where the path climbed sharply and veered inward towards the cliff. Reading the terrain, I could see no way through and dreaded a long retreat and a circuitous detour. Suddenly, there was White Park Bay, framed in a tunnel through the headland. I continued through the short tunnel with great relief, and reached the charming little fishing village of Portbraddan. The waves were smashing against the white chalk cliff beyond the village, so I had to take the road around to reach White Park Strand, a mile-long crescent of gold. Beyond the beach, progress was by clambering over slippery rocks. The coast was full of interest, with many twists and turns and rocky islets just offshore. The tide was just low enough to allow me through to Ballintoy Harbour. I explored a cave here, going in about 40 metres until it was too dark to continue. Then I climbed the hairpin road to Ballintoy to have some lunch.

Beyond Ballintoy, the Ulster Way is marked on the maps but it is a cheat: the way is nothing other than the main road. I detoured up Glenstaughley Lane to avoid the traffic, but the last few miles to Ballycastle were on the busy B15. Rathlin Island was away to the north and, further in the distance, some Scottish isles.

Stage 73: *Ballycastle to Glenariff*

There was a lively atmosphere in Ballycastle, with the Lammas Fair about to begin. The fair takes place on the last Monday and Tuesday of August, and is famed for having an unbroken history, taking place annually for the past 300 years, with its origins going back to much earlier times. I headed from The Diamond up Ann Street towards the sea. Beside McLysters Newsagents was an old shop-front, McAuley's where once lived John Henry McAuley noted as the writer of a song that is 'world famous in Ballycastle':

At the Oul Lammas Fair, boys, were you ever there?
Were you ever at the fair in Ballycastle-oh?
  Did you treat your Mary-Ann
  To Dulse and Yellow-man,
At the Oul Lammas Fair in Ballycastle-oh?

Dulse is an edible seaweed and Yellow Man a rock-hard sugary, denture-destroying toffee confection of lurid yellow hue. My maternal grandfather was John Gregory McAuley from Ballymena, and I wondered if I could be related to the songster, John Henry. I bought a stick of Yellow Man to suck as I rambled along the road. At the tourist office on the sea front, the assistant, Tierna, made great efforts to find a B&B for me in Cushendun or Cushendall. She had no luck, but she did find a bed in Glenariff, a few miles further on.

Ballycastle is the terminus of the Rathlin Island Ferry. Another point of interest is the monument to Gugliemo Marconi. In 1898, Marconi carried out an experiment here, transmitting signals across to a lighthouse on Rathlin Island. Some locals claim that this was the first successful wireless transmission.

Eastward I headed, up through Ballyvoy. Just beyond the village, I took a 'short cut', which involved negotiating a barbed-wire fence and a stream. The road led on through open moorland, mile upon mile and, to sooth the journey, I mumbled the mantra 'Om mani padme hum' again and again. Mani is the jewel of divine essence in the lotus-flower (padme) of the heart. This mantra was the constant companion of the Lama in Kipling's masterpiece *Kim*. At last, reaching the top of a hill, I beheld Torr Head, the nearest point to the Mull of Kintyre, 13 miles away in Scotland. The Moyle – Sruth na Maoile – is the ancient Irish name for the North Channel, the stormy straits between Ireland and Scotland, or Erin and Alban. Thomas Moore's 'Song of Fionnuala' tells the story of the children of Lir, who were turned into swans and banished to the farther shore. The spell was only broken by the peal of a bell signifying the arrival of Christianity in Ireland.

The road continued around the steeply sloping shore, rising and falling precipitously with the corrugations of the terrain. The slog up Green Hill was particularly arduous. The final stretch into the village of Cushendun was along a sandy beach. Cushendun is a village of considerable character. It was designed around 1920 by the Welsh architect Clough Williams-Ellis, also know for the Italianate Portmerrion in Wales. After downing a pint of water and a pint of orange juice, I continued, via Knocknacarry and over Cross Slieve, to Cushendall. At the Pepper Mill, the friendly Yvonne (from Meath) gave me a hearty meal. Cushendall takes its name from the little Dall River, and lies at the foot of three of the nine Glens of Antrim, Glenaan, Glenballyemon and Glenariff, on the shores of Red Bay. In the centre of the village stands a tall red sandstone tower, built in 1809 by Francis Turnly of the East India Company as a monument to the Brotherhood of Man. Less romantically, according to the Rough Guide to Ireland, it was a 'place of confinement for idlers and rioters'. The village is an attractive place and a good base for exploring the Glens. I decided that I must return when I had more time to spend here.

Continuing southward along the coast road, I came to Waterfront. Just before the village there are caves in the cliff-face by the road, with the ruins of dwellings, reminiscent of the pueblos of New Mexico (but wetter). At last I came to the Glen Road, where Rose had a bed warmed up at her B&B, Lurig View. I had walked from 8.00 o'clock in the morning until 9.00 o'clock in the evening, and was very happy to crash out.

Stage 74: *Glenariff to Broughshane*

After a hearty dose of Rose's potato bread, I was away up the wee Glen Road on a windy overcast morning. At the head of Glenariff, the Queen of the Glens, I passed a stone carved with the message 'You are now entering a stress-free zone', and shortly arrived at Manor Lodge. Here I had some refreshments and headed into the Forest Park. The Glenariff river cascades down through the dense forest, with a multitude of magnificent waterfalls. There is a network of silvan pathways running through the park. I kept to the right, climbing all the while above the raging waters until I came to the Glenariff Tea Rooms. From there, a long driveway brought me to the A43, the Ballymena road. A few miles further on I found an old dismantled railway running beside the road.

The Ballymena, Cushendall and Red Bay Railway (BC&RBR) was the first narrow gauge railway in Ireland. It was developed to transport iron ore, as there was no coal to smelt ore locally. The first ore was transported from Cargan in 1875. The name belies the route, which never reached the coast at Red Bay, as the gradient was too steep. It extended from Ballymena to Retreat, the summit being at 1045 feet, the highest point of any railway in Ireland. Several mines were served and there were a number of branch lines owned by the mining companies. I followed the route of the BC&RBR for a few miles, overcoming some awkward obstacles, most of the way to the village of Cargan.

Cargan was a scruffy, unappealing village: many of the houses were neglected, with untended gardens. An inordinately large proportion of the houses bore 'For Sale' signs; it seemed that the hapless residents shared my lack of enthusiasm and wanted out. The only restaurant, a Chinese, was closed, so a cup of tea from the garage had to do. Taking the waterworks road, I followed the Glenravel Water and then bore south over Glen's Brae. After a stiff climb, I looked back hoping to spot Trostan which, at 550 metres, is Antrim's highest peak. But Slievenanee, only seven metres shy of it, intervened. Further west stood a cluster of windmills on Slievenahanaghan. I stopped at Pound Bridge for a rest and a snack. The remainder of the walk to Broughshane was uneventful, the monotony broken only by the striking profile of Slemish, with its huge dome-like crown. It was here, as we learned at school, that the young Patrick, enslaved to a farmer called Miliuc or Milchu, tended sheep and dreamed of escape back to his patrician family in Wales.

The lamp-posts in Broughshane were festooned with Union Jacks. The obsession in parts of Ulster with flags and symbols can be nauseating. The atmosphere of the town was not particularly welcoming; stopping for a drink in 'The Thatch', I found myself sitting beside two men who were discussing various circumstances in which they would shoot someone. I took a hackney to Ballymena. There I visited the War Memorial, as I had heard that my mother's uncle was remembered there. Sure enough, Bertie J. McCann was among the unfortunates who lost their lives in Belgium and France in the First World War. Perhaps he died a hero; more likely, disease or some festering, gangrenous wound did for him. In any case, like millions of others, he never made it home. There was another wall of names for those lost in the Second World War. I thought that the stonemasons would be busy again when the Iraqi mess was finally sorted out.

Chapter 16

IN THE STEPS OF KING BILLY

Now it being on the 12th day of July
Our music so sweetly did play
And the Protestant Boys and Boyne Water
Were the tunes we played marching away.

'The Aughalee Heroes' – Traditional Orange March

DURING THE FOLLOWING YEAR I WAS too busy to escape so it wasn't until the beginning of 2007 that I could resume the Commodius Vicus. Over ten years had now passed since the first step of the CV had been taken. Technological advances in the interim meant that now the entire surface of the planet was available at a click, through Google Earth – this was unthinkable when I first set out. The Northern Peace Process ground on painfully, with Sinn Féin agonizing about support for policing and the DUP posturing about whether to govern with them. Tony Blair had just broken off his holiday to settle the latest crisis. Dr Paisley was ranting, but less volubly, the Celtic Tiger's roar was less virile. The Iraq war raged more violently following the execution of Saddam Hussein, while George W. Bush continued to utter vacuities.

My second stay at the Adair Arms in Ballymena would be my last. The price had been hiked by 50 per cent since my previous stay only sixteen months earlier. In my hotel room, I watched a programme on BBC2 called When we were Scouts. I had fond memories of my days in the 17th (St Begnet's) Troop in Dalkey and, earlier, in an unofficial scout patrol, The Kestrels, founded and run by my next-door neighbours, the Ellises. It occurred to me that a dedication of this book to them would be an appropriate, if overdue, acknowledgement of their inspiration, and so it is dedicated to John, Brian and the late David Ellis, with thanks.

Stage 75: Broughshane to Antrim Town

I set off from Broughshane into a stiff headwind, dressed for the heavy rain that was forecast. This did not arrive until late afternoon, so most of the walk was in dry if dull and overcast conditions. I took the Crebilly Road, avoiding the heavy traffic. A sign at a farmhouse offered Potatoes for Sale: Blue or White. Blue spuds didn't sound too appetising: there are surprisingly few blue foods, for good reasons no doubt, and blue steak is not to my liking. Once asked did I want my steak 'rare or ruined' I could only reply 'well ruined, please'. *Chaque à son gout.* I crossed the Deerfin Burn, turning from Kennelbridge Road in the townland of Crebilly to Wardlow Road in the townland of Dunnyvadden. At Waterwheel Cottage, the owner had cleverly diverted a stream to drive some toy mill-wheels. At Ballymarlagh, I crossed the busy Ballymena-Belfast Road.

Passing on through Liminary, I came to the remnants of a railway bridge. This was on the Ballymena & Larne Railway, which connected these towns and allowed the transportation of minerals to the coast. The railway went out of use in 1940. Shortly afterwards, I crossed Kells Water, one of numerous rivers feeding Lough Neagh, and came to the "Ancient Monastic Town" of Kells. There were no pubs in the town, and no restaurants open, so a sausage roll in the local supermarket had to do. Continuing southward, I followed a dull minor road, as the predicted rain finally arrived. The monotony was lifted by occasional glimpses of Lough Neagh, Ireland's Lake Superior, the Ladoga of the West. It was my first sight of this, the largest lake in these islands. I stopped under the M2 to finish a last banana and trudged the final mile or so to Antrim town, taking a short cut at Holywood Hospital. The Round Tower came into view, a well-preserved basalt tower, 93 feet in height, in the grounds of Steeple House, now a public park. Beside the tower is a large 'bullaun stone'. The monastic settlement of Antrim dates from the late fifth century. After photographing the tower, I sought out the guesthouse of Dougie and Sylvia McAuley, and was welcomed with a delicious cup of tea. I told them my mother was a McAuley from Ballymena, but the name is quite common and they thought it unlikely that we were related. The evening was rounded off with a nice grilled salmon at Viscount O'Neill's.

Stage 76: Antrim Town to Moira

The cost for B&B was £30 so I handed Dougie two pictures, one of Harry Ferguson and one of John Dunlop. Ferguson modernized farming by designing a revolutionary 3-point linkage: the plough was coupled directly to the tractor rather than being towed behind. He is featured on the £20 note of the Northern Bank. The £10 note has an illustration of Dunlop, famous for his development of the pneumatic tyre. The £100 has a picture of Sir James Martin with one of his designs for an ejector seat.

I bid goodbye to Dougie and Sylvia and set off southward on a bright clear morning, ideal walking conditions. With the sun setting so early, I left Antrim before nine, crossing the Six Mile Water at Muckamore. Shakey Bridge Walk skirts the river south of the town and more than twenty mills once tapped energy from this stretch of water. With a world energy crisis, maybe we should reflect on this. A robust bridge has replaced the wobbly one that gave the walk its name. After Muckamore National School, I kept straight on at a roundabout, but the road layout had changed since my Sheet 14 was printed (in 1989) and I went astray. Good job I had a compass! I soon managed to find the route I sought, skirting the southern edge of Belfast International Airport. The airport was quiet, with just a few executive jets taking off. At Aldergrove RAF Base, I turned sharp left (no hope of getting through the base, I thought) onto the Randox Road. With BIA behind me, the old Nutt's Corner airport was to my left, and a small military airfield, Langford, far off to the right. The latter is associated with the manufacture of Martin-Baker ejector seats, which have saved many lives. This Martin is the same Sir James we observed on the £100 note.

At Crumlin I passed under the bridge of the railway line that closed just a few years before. It provided an alternative route from Antrim to Belfast, via Lisburn. It occurred to me that this might have been a better walking route than the road. After a snack at Bush's Home Bakery, I continued, enjoying intermittent glimpses of Lough Neagh. There is a popular myth that the lake was formed when Finn McCool scooped up a lump of earth and hurled it at some rival. The lump landed in the Irish Sea, forming what is now the Isle of Man. Geologists have a more credible if less colourful theory. They believe that the lake formed when the Earth's surface subsided some 40 million years ago. The lush tropical vegetation that grew then is the source of the lignite that has been mined in recent times. The lake is rectangular, about 15 miles north to south and 12 east to west with an area of some 180 square miles. It is the biggest eel fishery in Europe. I recalled seeing Lough Neagh eels on sale in Holland some years ago. It is amazing to reflect that they were born in the Sargasso Sea, drifted 4000 miles across the Atlantic Ocean, and swam up the Bann to the Lough, only to be caught before they could go west again to breed. In World War II, flying boats operated out of Lough Neagh. The water level has been lowered several times, most recently in 1959. The level is now managed by flood gates in Toome. The lake is fed by numerous rivers and is a vital source of fresh water for Northern Ireland. The Lower Bann drains the lake, entering the sea below Coleraine.

Public houses in rural areas are marked PH on the Discovery/Discoverer maps. Noticing two PH marks, my hopes were raised and then dashed. The first, Eddery's beyond Pigeon Hill, was in a dilapidated state. The second, with a huge serpent sign, was closed. In any case, it had the look of a Country Club that might not welcome a rambler. Unlike Groucho, I wouldn't have anything to do with a club that would not have me as a member. I passed through the tiny hamlet of Roses Lane Ends, the highlights of which were an Orange Hall and a derelict bicycle shop. Partmore Lough, a circular lake and Nature Reserve, could now be seen to the west.

At Cock Hill I got some refreshment at the Horseshoe Inn. Then onward through Lower Ballinderry, where many new houses give hope that the railway may again become viable. I soon reached the small village of Aghalee, which is memorialised in the Orange song 'The Aughalee Heroes':

> *You Protestant heroes of Ireland*
> *Give ear to these words I write down*
> *Concerning those Aughalee heroes*
> *That marched through the sweet Portadown*

The old Lagan Canal passes through the village. The canal linked the Lagan to Lough Neagh, giving a navigable route from the lake to Belfast. Work on this navigation began in 1756, on the stretch between Belfast and Lisburn. In the 1790s the canal linking the river with Lough Neagh was constructed. The canal was closed in 1954. It is remarkable that in the nineteenth century it was possible to travel by boat across Ireland from Belfast Lough to the Shannon Estuary. Perhaps this will be possible again sometime in the future. There is great work under way on restoration of these old waterways.

I had originally planned to head straight for Portadown, but the temptation of this old water-course was irresistible, so I digressed towards Moira. I followed a delightful walkway through Friar's Glen to where the canal widened out at Broad Water. An old lock-keeper's house just before the lake is now a private house. There were several fishermen, and wildfowl in abundance. But I had to hurry as the light was failing, and I reached Moira Station just as darkness fell. I found accommodation by the canal bank just beyond the station and Theresa, my hostess at Ballycanal Manor, rustled up an omelette and tea, which was most welcome after the long walk.

Stage 77: *Moira to Portadown*

The next piece of the route, from Moira to Portadown, was postponed, as I was keen to explore the Newry Canal during the last day remaining at this time. So, I returned later in the year to close the gap. My friend Mark and I set out from Moira railway station on a sunny August day. We had thought to go to the town to inspect the ancient rath and buy some of McCarthy's famous sausages, but were distracted by the swans on the canal. Heading down to the bank we beheld a family of ten mute swans, cob and pen and eight cygnets who appeared to be thriving. A little further on we encountered a less successful family story: a tiny moorhen chick was struggling to wade through the thick duckweed. There were much larger fledglings, so he appeared to be one of a second clutch. He was exposed in mid canal, his parent squawking noisily to try and encourage him to the bank. We thought his chances were slim.

Giant's Causeway

The 40,000 hexagonal prisms of

Basalt were formed in an underwater volcanic

Maelstrom sixty million years ago. (Volcano?)

The hex. patterns are called Benard cells.

Post-extraction Instructions

Bleeding: Some oozing following extraction can be expected and will cause blood-stained saliva. If slight bleeding occurs, apply pressure to the socket by biting down firmly on a piece of gauze or cotton-wool placed on the socket. When lying down, keep your head slightly elevated to reduce blood pressure at the area. If bleeding cannot be controlled, contact Dr. Nolan   087 9474719

Diet: On the day of the extraction, avoid hot liquids and hot foods, and alcohol. Select softer foods that can be chewed comfortably. Smoking should be avoided.

Rinsing: On the day of the extraction, avoid rinsing as this will wash away the blood clot. Do rinse, using salty mouth-washes, the day after the extraction and on subsequent days. This will promote healing.

Exercise: Avoid extensive physical activity for the remainder of the day of extraction.

Numbness: Avoid biting the lip or cheek whilst numb.

We came to a Church of Ireland with a trendy sign: CH••CH: What is missing? On the reverse of the sign was an even dafter message: Jesus Christ: the Rock who never Rolls. It is difficult to imagine that young people will be drawn to the church by notices of such limited aesthetic appeal. At Drumbane Road we passed Clenaghan's Pub, where an ancient petrol pump stands by the roadside. Turning aside, we came to a small house, the Colane Primrose R.B.P. Lodge No. 240. The Royal Black Preceptory is, I believe, an up-market version of the Orange Order. A dead swallow lay by the kerb. In the sky, a buzzard was circling and circling lazily, quartering the ground. Suddenly, he was gone, shooting down to catch some unfortunate prey. Was it the little moorhen chick in the canal?

There was a good variety of flora in the hedgerows. Oxeyes, like daisies on Viagra, hawksbit, yellow and purple vetch, and lords and ladies or wild arum. This last has bright berries that are mildly purgative. Mark explained that this ensured that an animal eating the berries would include a packed lunch when he dropped them elsewhere, increasing their likelihood of survival. The blackberries were just about ripe, and sloes too, with their curious astringent flavour.

Ahead there appeared a white radome, housing the weather radar at Castor Bay. This is one of three in Ireland, the others being at Dublin and Shannon Airports. Raindrops reflect the radiation from radars, providing an instantaneous picture of the weather. During World War II, this was regarded as a nuisance as the interest was in enemy aircraft and weather reflections were regarded as noise. But their use in weather forecasting was soon realised. A network of radars covering the British Isles now provides a continuous stream of information on the intensity, movement and development of frontal and convective rainfall.

Soon we came to the small industrial estate north of Lurgan, where Mark had occasionally worked as a veterinary officer at the meat processing plant. He informed me that cows are processed on the ground floor and sheep upstairs. You never know when this nugget of information may be of value. At Kinnegoe Harbour we planned to stop for lunch but the restaurant closed at 2.00 o'clock so a choc-ice and coffee from a machine sufficed. There are about 200 berths for small craft in this pleasant marina, and more of interest at the nature reserve of Oxford Island just beyond.

We rambled on, crossing the M1 for the fifth and final time. The remainder of the route to Portadown was on the National Cycle Network No. 9. This took us by the Craigavon Lakes, twin lakes, one each side of the railway, with attractive parkland and a variety of wildlife. There were a good number of people enjoying the facilities here, walking and biking and fishing and boating. At the Craigavon Water Sports Centre we had some haute cuisine in the form of burgers and chips.

Just beyond, we took a wrong turn. I recalled that, just a few days before, a young man who had been knocked down by a car hereabouts was then beaten up by local gurriers. The hostility of the neighbourhood was illustrated by the reaction when we asked a man for directions. 'Go forth and multiply' is one rendition of his response, a two-word phrase of four-plus-three letters, the terminal ones being unvoiced labio-dental fricatives. We soon found the path again with the help of a more pleasant resident, and reached Portadown without further incident. At Bann Bridge there stands a commemorative plaque outlining the history of the bridge. During the rebellion of 1641, many settlers were drowned off the bridge by Toole McCann, presumably because they could not recite the Hail Mary as Gaeilge.

We had anticipated a day slogging through mainly built-up areas but it had turned out to be a pleasant ramble on country lanes and cycle trails. We were happy that the recent outbreak of Foot and Mouth disease in Surrey seemed to have been confined and did not have any repercussions for ramblers in Ireland.

Stage 78: *Portadown to Newry*

A local train from Moira brought me to Portadown in about twelve minutes, a journey that would later take us eight hours on foot. The line crosses the Upper Bann just before the station and it was here that I set out to follow the Newry canal southward. Just as I stepped onto the riverside path, I was hailed by a man who told me that his wife was planning to climb Kilimanjaro in a few weeks. He had mistaken me for one of the organizers of this climb. We chatted for a while and then I set out on what a notice described as the Bann Boulevard.

The canal proper starts about a mile above the town at Whitecoat Point where the cut joins the Bann and Cusher Rivers. I crossed a distinctive tubular bridge onto an embankment. For much of the route, there is water on both sides of the path, giving it a delightful aquatic atmosphere. Conditions were ideal for walking on this sunny winter day; only the low sun in my eyes spoiled the perfection. At this time of the year, the sun gets little higher that 20 above the horizon, and I was walking straight towards it. For the first few miles, the path was lined by tall poplar trees which provided some welcome shade.

Soon I was at the first lock, Moneypenny Lock (numbered the fourteenth) which takes its name from the family that looked after it for 75 years. The Newry canal was the first summit canal built in the British Isles. It crosses a watershed, linking the Bann basin with Carlingford Lough. The source of water was Lough Shark (also known as Acton Lake). The impetus for building the canal was the discovery of coal in East Tyrone and the need to transport it to Dublin. There are fourteen locks in all, with three north of the summit level, some 25 metres above sea level, and eleven to the south, The canal was constructed between 1731 and 1742, the navvies being paid 3d per day for back-breaking work. The Newry Ship Canal, giving access to to Carlingford Lough and the Irish Sea, was finished in 1750.

The canal was a great success for nearly two hundred years. The locks are all derelict now and the canal has been disused since 1947, but the tow-path is well maintained, providing an attractive 18 mile route from Portadown to Newry. There is some talk of reopening the canal as a tourist amenity. Campbell's Lock, after Terryhoogan, brought me to the summit level and soon I reached the tiny village of Scarva. A canal basin was built here and the coal supply led to the growth of the linen industry in the neighbourhood. I crossed to the canal visitor centre, but it was closed, so a chicken and ham pie in the Park Inn had to do. A plaque in the village, erected in 1990, commemorates the encampment of King Billy here in 1690, on his way to the Boyne. A mock battle is held here each year in which William gloriously triumphs over the Catholic James (yawn). Followers of King Billy don't like to be reminded that the Pope celebrated a solemn Te Deum to give thanks for William's victory.

South of Scarva is a high embankment that forms part of the Dane's Cast or Black Pig Dyke. This is an ancient terminal marker, delineating the territories of Conal and Eoin who ruled the North in days of yore. It is said to be traceable right across the country, to Donegal. Soon I reached Lough Shark, the feeder for the canal, which was teeming with wildfowl. This is an Area of Special Scientific Interest and a flock of whooper swans roosts here each winter. There was another Visitor Centre here, also closed. A short time later I reached Poyntz Pass, another village that owes its existence to the canal. Ironically, the canal was of great use in transporting materials for the construction of the railway that runs beside it, the railway that ultimately led to the decline and demise of the canal itself.

Between Poyntz Pass and Jerrettspass, motor traffic has access to the canal-side path, which is a great pity. The canal makes a wide sweep to the west of the railway and passes under it again at Gamble's Bridge. Beyond the bridge, I spied an imposing and elegant building on the hillside. This is Dromantine College, originally the 'Manor of Clanagan', built in the early nineteenth century by Arthur Innes as a family home. It is now run as a Retreat and Conference Centre by the Society of African Missions. At Jerrettspass, I stopped for a snack, admiring the elegant arch that carries the railway over the Knockduff road. The remainder of the journey was featureless, and I was hurrying to beat the approaching darkness. For two reasons, there is more light after (clock) noon than before. One is the 'Equation of Time', mentioned above. More importantly, I was at 6 degrees west, so local time was about a half hour later than clock time (GMT). Thus, dawn was around 8:15 am and dusk around 4:45 pm, centred on 12:30 GMT, that is, local noon and not clock noon.

Darkness was falling as I approached Newry. The multiple arches of the Craigmore Viaduct that carries the railway across the Bessbrook river, appeared away to the right. The canal veered towards the left, away from my destination, so I climbed up the bank at the B&Q Warehouse and, after scrambling through a series of thorn bushes with some difficulty, found a roundabout on the Newry by-pass. I had to slog a mile or so up the busy Dublin Road to reach the railway station, and catch the train home.

Chapter 17

THE GREAT ANABASIS

Cassiopeia was over
Cassidy's hanging hill,
I looked and three whin bushes rode across
The horizon – The Three Wise Kings

'A Christmas Childhood' – Patrick Kavanagh

THE YEAR OF 2007 WAS WHEN CLIMATE change moved from the scientific to the political arena. The Intergovernmental Panel on Climate Change issued an unambiguous message about the severity of the problem, urging the international community to act with urgency. On a more local level, with the arms issue settled in 'Norn-Ireland', Ian Paisley and Martin McGuinness were giggling their way through life as First and Deputy First Ministers. In a former round, David Trimble and Seamus Mallon had been christened 'The Odd Couple' when they shared power. Paisley and McGuinness were joking and laughing so much that a Ulster Unionist dubbed them 'The Chuckle Brothers', after the British comedians Barry and Paul Elliot, best known for their children's television programmes.

Stage 79: Newry to Hackballscross

The three Hillpigs, Mark, Frank and myself, were together again for a two day hike through the Gap of the North. The new year had started cold and there was some snow lying as we went north on the Enterprise to Newry. But the sky was clear and we would have two days with continuous if weak sunshine. Newry Station is spartan, with only a coffee machine for comfort. So we set out immediately for the village of Cam-lough, along a busy road that is sometimes used as a race-track. A stone plaque commemorated Richard Hughes, aged 10, who had been 'killed by a drunk driver'. The death of a young girl was marked by a stone a little further down the road.

At the village of Camlough we had an Ulster Fry in the Riverside Cafe. There are four pubs in the village and I counted four hairdressers. 'How do they survive?' I asked the cafe owner. 'Oh, there are six hairdressers here,' she told us, but without any inkling of the secret of their viability. We climbed the hill southward, soon coming to the lake that gives the village its name. There was a variety of wildlife, including fieldfares and redwings, winter visitors to this region. Just past the lake we had an en-counter with wildlife of a more threatening kind. As we passed an open gate, a rottweiler menaced us, snarling angrily. We stuck in a bunch and I made sure he saw my walking poles, so we could withdraw without inci-dent. But our words for the reckless and witless owner of this dangerous animal are unfit to print.

The scenery was pleasant hereabouts, with the lake in the foreground and Slieve Gullion as a backdrop. We sought a chambered grave that was marked on the map but failed to find it. At Killevy Castle the air was split by constant percussion that we took to be a clay pigeon shoot. Bypassing Meigh, we took a busy road to Drumintee, and visited the churchyard to whisper a prayer for 'Uncle Tom', my wife's uncle who rests there and who was a very loveable character known to us all.

We passed The Three Steps, a pub infamous for being the last known whereabouts of Capt. Robert Nairac. He was spying, it seems, for the Brit-ish Government, to the dislike of certain local residents who arranged for him to disappear. In May 1977, Nairac visited The Three Steps, where he aroused suspicion by posing as a member of the Official IRA. He was ab-ducted and taken across the border to a field in Ravensdale. Following an interrogation, during which he was tortured, Nairac was shot dead. It was claimed that his body was destroyed in a meat grinder. This is unlikely, although the location of the body remains a mystery.

We considered it wise to continue on our merry way to Forkill, where we stopped at Larkin's for refreshments. This sleepy village was much as

I remembered it from earlier visits, except that the large and obtrusive army barracks had now been decommissioned and the snooping posts on the surrounding hills were no more to be seen. These were significant benefits of the peace settlement. We took what we expected to be a quiet road south, and crossed the border about a mile below Forkill. There was no visible evidence that we were now back in the Republic, but the density of heavy goods vehicles appeared to be a manifestation of illicit transboundary entrepreneurialism. Unmarked fuel tankers were particularly evident. The disparity in the levels of taxation on the two sides of the border makes smuggling a lucrative business. The heavy traffic on the tiny road meant that our journey was more endured than enjoyed.

But soon we were delighted by the dramatic sight of Castle Roche, a Norman castle standing on a rocky knoll. Once marking the limit of the Pale, it controlled passage through the Gap of the North. The story goes that around 1250 Rohesia de Verdun, who commissioned the castle, promised to marry the architect if she liked his work. But when his task was done she had him defenestrated, or chucked out through a castle window, to prevent him from building anything to rival it.

We came to Hackballscross, sometimes ironically called HBX, around four in the afternoon, just as dusk approached. There is little here besides the Garda Barracks, which is now manned only on a temporary basis. The key significance of HBX is its strategic proximity to the border. One of Ireland's funniest men, comedian Noel V. Ginnity, had a song about it, of which I can recall only a snippet:

> There were Frenchmen, there were Dutch, selling cabbages
>   and such,
> When the Common Market came to Hackballscross.

We were met by Johnnie (The Bear) Matthews, a good friend of Mark, who is a farmer nearby. He took us for a spin into Crossmaglen, pointing out various recently-built mansions. The owners must have considerable business acumen, but I need not speculate on the precise nature of the business. We were taken back to Johnnie's house where we enjoyed a sumptuous beef-steak, about 12 ounces of Hereford, and delighted in the company of himself, his wife Deirdre and their children. Afterwards, The

Bear took us to Dundalk, where we were accommodated at a B&B called Krakow, the name of which derives from its former function as the Parochial House. The association is with Pope John Paul II, Karol Wojtyla, who lived in Krakow for four decades before his assumption of the papacy. We were on best behaviour, as the landlord was a former Garda Sergeant.

Stage 80: Hackballscross to Kingscourt

The soldier and writer Xenophon led an army of 10,000 on a heroic journey through deserts and mountain passes, winning many battles on the way. Ultimately they arrived at the the safety of the Greek cities on the shore of the Black Sea, greeting the sight with their famous cry of exultation Thalatta, thalatta, 'The sea, the sea'. Xenophon relates his adventures in his book *Anabasis*, often used as a first text in Greek. Anabasis (Αναβασις) means an expedition from the coastline into the interior of a country. The Hillpigs might have followed the coastline down through Louth and Meath to Dublin, but we decided to embark on our own Great Anabasis, heading inland to Monaghan and Cavan, to follow an old railway and the Royal Canal, giving us traffic-free access to the capital.

Our kind landlord, the ex-sergeant, dropped us out to HBX for the resumption of the Commodius Vicus. 'They're a different breed out here,' he warned us. 'Won't come to the front door.' There was nobody about on whom we could put this hypothesis to the test. It was the sixth of January, the Epiphany. The twelve day Christmas season traditionally ends on this day. Epiphany means 'appearance' and the day is both a celebration of the incarnation of God and a commemoration of the coming of the Magi, the Three Wise Men. In Ireland, we speak of Little Christmas or Women's Christmas – Nollaig na mBan. This was the day on which Christmas Day was celebrated prior to the adoption of the Gregorian calendar.

Although rain was forecast for later in the day, the sky was clear and walking conditions were close to ideal. We set off towards Inishkeen, through a landscape dominated by drumlins. At a small stream, we met a farmer starting his day's work. Hearing that we had come from Hackballscross, he explained that the name derives from the execution of members of a secret society, perhaps the Peep-O-Day-Boys, by evisceration, that is, 'Hack-bowels Cross'. It was less likely, but more colourful, than the more obvious alternative, that the cross-roads was a popular place for gelding colts. Further down the road we startled a large cock pheasant, which rose noisily and flew away towards a huge pylon. This was part of the inter-connector, linking the electricity grids north and south of the border, and was often a target of Republican activists.

Approaching Inishkeen we passed under a bridge of the old railway that once ran from Dundalk all the way to Bundoran in Donegal. This line, familiarly called the Irish North, opened in the 1850s. A branchline led from Inishkeen to Carrickmacross. There was a through train from Dublin in the summer months, which carried pilgrims and pagans; the pilgims went to Lough Derg, Saint Patrick's Purgatory north of Pettigo; the pagans went to the popular seaside resort of Bundoran. Passenger services ceased in 1957 and the line closed completely in 1960.

Inishkeen is a pretty village, most renowned as the birthplace of Patrick Kavanagh, one of Ireland's best-loved poets, despite his notoriously irrascible nature. There is a steel silhouette of Kavanagh in the village, on which some lines of his poetry are inscribed. By the beautiful River Fane, in a quiet churchyard, stands the stump of a Round Tower, the door about three metres above ground. In the centre of the village we found McNello's, a watering place of the poet, but on this early Sunday morning it was closed. Also closed was a small museum devoted to Kavanagh, so we were disappointed that we could not savour a Kavanagh Cappucino.

Onward we trod, turning left at the new church. At the townland of Mucker we saw a sign indicating a nearby house as Kavanagh's birthplace. He lived here as a farmer, cobbler and poet until he moved to Dublin in 1939, after his father died. He wrote several books, the best-known being *Tarry Flynn*, an autobiographical novel. The position of the house was in conflict with the location indicated on my map, but an old gentleman out for a stroll confirmed that it was indeed the Kavanagh family home, and said he had often brought Patrick home, somewhat under the weather. 'What was he like?' I asked. 'An abrupt man,' he said, suggesting that Kavanagh was working on his grumpiness from an early age.

We continued on our way, the drumlins making the route to Essexford unduly undulatory. Allegedly, the Earl of Essex parleyed with Red Hugh O'Donnell, or perhaps with Hugh O'Neill, hereabouts, reaching a truce that angered Queen Elizabeth I. Like Margaret Thatcher, she did not believe in 'negotiating with terrorists'. After stopping for a snack, we continued our quasi-vertical oscillations through the drumlins, and spied a round stump-like structure on a hill-top. After much speculation, Mark won the Mycroft Medal by identifying it as an old windmill. Sure enough, we found Windmill Hill marked on Sheet 35. The (mythical) medal, named for Sherlock's smarter brother, we decided to award for the most astute, or most bizarre, observation or deduction of the day.

The way was on quiet back-roads and we had an idyllic walk, undisturbed by traffic on this quiet Sunday. A planning application on a gate indicated that we were in County Louth. Checking the map later, we realized that our route had crossed the Louth–Monaghan border seven times. The roadside was bedecked with gorse. Kavanagh, in his poem A Christmas Childhood, had identified three gorse bushes on the horizon with the Three Wise Men who arrived on the Epiphany. But he called the bushes whins, a term more prevalent in the northern counties.

We passed a limestone quarry, where a small lake of deep turquoise had formed, looking striking but sterile. Further on, Frank identified a large industrial structure to the right as the gypsum mine. Frank Mitchell, in his book *The Way that I Followed*, wrote of a big block of younger mesozoic rocks, dropped down in a fault in the older paleozoic rocks, forming the Kingscourt Basin. Their lowered position saved them from the erosion that stripped the mesozoic rocks from the rest of Ireland. In these rocks there are thick beds of gypsum (hydrated calcium sulphate), the raw material of plaster of Paris, essential in construction as the basis for making plasterboards. We came to Cabra Castle, just north of the town of Kingscourt, as dusk fell and heavy rain set in. This was fortunate, as a slog onwards to the town in darkness on a busy road was something to avoid. We took refuge in the bar of this luxury hotel, awaiting transport home.

Stage 81: *Kingscourt to Wilkinstown*

Opposite the entrance to Cabra Castle there is a small track leading into Dún na Rí Forest Park. We followed the trail through beautiful woodland, by the rippling River Cabra, working our way south. It was just Frank and myself on this stretch. Rejoining the road, we soon found the northern end of the old railway line. Once used to transport the gypsum from the mines, the line is now derelict. An old railway house with solid granite cornerstones and a huge ramshackle warehouse spoke of earlier activity, but all was deserted now. For the first section, the line was heavily overgrown, and progress very arduous and slow: we must have taken over an hour to cover the first mile. The 50 mile post is just south of Kingscourt, but we saw no sign of it in the dense undergrowth. Things got a little better further on, and we soon passed the Gypsum Industries factory. The line was a glorious splash of purple, with rosebay willow-herb in abundance and exploding into seed.

The line running north from Navan was opened to Kilmainham Wood in 1872 and to Kingscourt in 1875. Worked by the Midland Great Western Railway, it was connected, via Kilmessan, to the Galway line at Clonsilla. Passenger services to Kingscourt ceased in 1947, and there are no longer any goods services except on the short stretch from the Tara Mines just west of Navan.

We stopped for a break and I foolishly sat on an ant-nest. The ants grabbed their opportunity to infest my haversack and trousers, and a rapid extermination exercise was required to eliminate them. We stopped again for a more peaceful rest on the old platform of Kilmainham Wood Station. The track then led us along the shore of Whitewood Lough, which was curiously quiet, with little wildlife stirring. Indeed the only fauna we encountered was a pigeon on the track, literally on his last legs. He made a feeble attempt to fly away as we approached, but he looked all done in and we didn't rate his survival chance as very high. At one point near Nobber, the line became completely impenetrable, so we digressed through a farmyard to the road. We soon came to an old charcoal burner, a square structure about four metres high with a fire-box in front and large interior chamber where timber was kept to undergo incomplete combustion, producing the charcoal, a vital fuel in earlier times.

Nobber (An Obair – The Work) was a sleepy village, with little to indicate how it got its name. We bought some refreshments and sat on a bench outside the Garda Barracks to eat and drink them. We were surprised to learn that the renowned harper Turlough O'Carolan was born here in 1670. He lost his sight at the age of eighteen due to smallpox, but this did not stop him travelling the length and breadth of Ireland, composing tunes, some of which remain popular today. O'Carolan is commemorated by a bronze statue by the roadside in Nobber.

We returned to the railway line and followed the track. Two cows and a calf that had strayed onto the line ran ahead of us for a mile or so before we could stand aside to let them bolt back past us. The line crossed a bridge over the N52, although the map (Sheet 35) indicated the road on top. The vegetation was not too thick for the remainder of the journey, but was bad enough to slow us up. With this, and the uneven sleepers and lack of ballast between them, our progress was slow. It took us about eight hours to cover the fifteen miles from Kingscourt to Wilkinstown. We drove to County Meath Golf Club, where we polished off two prime fillet steaks. Then back to Frank's place for hot baths and sleep.

Stage 82: *Wilkinstown to Tara*

From Wilkinstown we continued on the derelict railway line. Again, the rate was about two miles per hour but, with the pleasant weather, we were not complaining. After about four miles we came to Randalstown, where we noticed a large mound west of the track. This is the tailings pond for Tara Mines, the largest zinc and lead mine in Europe. A security fence surrounds the pond, and large notices warn against trespassing. But we were curious, so we made a minor, non-destructive and reversable adjustment to the chain-link fence and climbed up the bank. A huge expanse of water, about a square kilometre in area, stretched away to the west. The map indicated another pond of similar size beyond this. Tailings ponds hold the waste products from mining, often toxic and corrosive material, covered with water to prevent the dust from blowing away. A large flock of waders rose from the sands, too far off to identify. Their presence reassured us that the ponds must be capable of sustaining insect or crustacean life. Our curiosity satisfied, we climbed down the bank and re-adjusted the fence, so no one is any the wiser.

We stopped for a snack around one o'clock, reflecting that in Beijing it was eight o'clock on the eighth day of the eighth month of the eighth year of the millennium. This was the auspicious moment when the Olympic Games were due to open, eight being a particularly lucky number in the

Middle Kingdom. Near the 32 mile post, we took the road into Navan. Descending Flower Hill, we came to the confluence of the Blackwater and Boyne, the two major rivers of Meath. At the Valley Cafe, we stoked up on quarter-pounders and chips, having first downed a jug of water each. Then, following the Boyne southward, we came to Kilcarn Bridge, where we branched off on a minor road. The M3 motorway was under construction here. The route had caused major controversy, with court proceedings before a final choice could be made. The area is rich in antiquities and, especially in the region of Tara, archaeological sites abound. But the road was going ahead and, judging from the activity we witnessed, it would not be long before traffic was whisking along this route.

We crossed the Boyne at Ballinter Bridge, and then the Skane River. Turning left at Royal Tara Golf Club, and then right, we climed the mile or so to the top of the Hill of Tara. At just under 160 metres, it is not an especially prominent hill. But it commands a wide panoramic sweep, from Slieve Gullion in the North, through the Plains of Meath – Ireland's Fifth Province – with the Slieve Blooms beyond, to the Dublin and Wicklow Mountains in the south.

Tara has been a site of primary importance in Ireland for millennia. Ancient Ireland was divided into five regions, with Meath as the central province and Tara as its capital. Here ruled the great kings Lugh, Conn of the Hundred Battles, Cormac Mac Airt and Niall of the Nine Hostages. Here were deadly struggles between the Fir Bolg and the Tuath Dé Danann, when Lugh slew Balor of the Evil Eye. Queen Maeve reigned here, and battled with Cuchulainn, and Fionn Mac Cumhail set out from here on many dramatic and heroic escapades with the Fianna.

From Niall of the Nine Hostages sprung the Úi Neill, who ruled Ireland for 400 years, up to the time of Brian Boru. Some forty of his descendents held the title King of Tara. One of his nine hostages may have been Patrick, sold into slavery in Slemish in County Antrim. The circle was closed when Niall's son, Laoghaire, was later out-manoeuvred by Patrick, and Christianity came to Ireland.

Chronological lists in ancient texts like the Book of Leinster and Book of Ballymote name about 150 kings, ruling for some thousands of years. They give colourful accounts of the magical powers of the druids and the heroic deeds of mighty warriors. The questionable historical veracity of these records takes nothing from their social and spiritual significance, and their impact on the national psyche. In many ways, we are not too far removed from the old druidic traditions.

On the hilltop, I put my hand on the Lia Fáil, the Stone of Destiny, Ireland's coronation stone, brought here by the Tuath Dé Danann. This large standing stone is said to issue a roar when a rightful king lays his hand on it, but there wasn't even a whimper from the rock in response to my touch. Nearby is the Mound of the Hostages, excavated in 1955 when more than two hundred human remains were discovered, dating back some 3,500 years. There is a large stone in the mound, with engravings that may have astronomical or spiritual significance. We still have much to learn about the goings-on in Tara long ago. In the shop nearby I bought *The Book of Tara* by Michael Slavin, who gives a fascinating account of Tara's mythology and history. He includes a song he has written, that ends:

> *Diarmaid, Gráinne, Cormac, Fionn*
> *'Twas here they loved and lost and won*
> *Their secrets lie 'neath Tara's soil*
> *Known only to the Lia Fáil.*

Stage 83: *Tara to Kilcock*

For the following week, dismal monsoon weather interrupted the Commodius Vicus, but a short break on the Feast of the Assumption allowed us to continue. Mark was with Frank and me for this stretch. We parked one car in Kilcock, opposite the illustrious emporium of 'Mick the Barber – New York, Paris, Kilcock', and drove to Tara in the other. Resuming the Great Anabasis, we came soon to a Holy Well, the Well of the Numbering of the Clans, Dark Eye, the Healer, the Well of the White Cow, etc., etc. Clearly, its waters had great power, so I tried a sample. A little further on, we found Maeve's Rath. Little remains of this hill fort, which was about 200 metres in diameter, just a large ridge near the road.

Onward we went to Dunsany village – Dún Samhnai – where, incongruously, there was a piano shop in a beautiful old stone building. We turned off on a minor road to find the ancient Dunsany Cross opposite the gate of Dunsany Castle. Just inside the estate stand the ruins of 'The Abbey', St. Nicholas Church, built by the First Baron of Dunsany in the fifteenth century. We found an impressive tomb in the church, with carved effigies of Christopher Plunkett and his wife Anna Fitzgerald. Another tomb took my interest, one of Thomas Joseph Lynch. There are several T.J.'s in my family, including my father. Perhaps there is some connection here: the nearby village of Summerhill is, in Irish, Cnoc an Linsigh, or Lynch's Hill.

We knocked on the door of the Big House and were received by Lady Maria Alice de Marsillac Plunkett, wife of Edward, 20th Baron of Dunsany. For a nominal consideration, she brought us in to see the house and gave us much fascinating information about its rich history. It is one of the oldest continuously inhabited houses in Ireland (overlooking a brief interruption due to the dreaded Cromwell) and is still a family home, but is open to the public for ninety summer days each year (optimistic, considering the weather of 2008). Originating as a twelfth century castle built by early Norman settlers, the Cusacks, the house has been the home of the Plunketts for hundreds of years.

The house has a wonderfully eclectic collection of art, most notably several old Dutch masters. A curious indentation in the corner of one of these caught my eye, like large Gothic lettering in reverse. I mentioned this to our hostess, speculating that it might be an impression stamped on the back of the canvas before the picture was painted by Van Dyke. We saw some manuscripts of Dunsany the Writer, the 18th Lord D., written with a goose quill. He published more than fifty books, his speciality being fantasy, and he had an influence on many later works of fantasy, from Tolkein's *Lord of the Rings* to the Harry Potter novels.

From the house, we made our way west across the grounds to a huge block-work gate, complete with portcullis. It was boarded up and we couldn't get through without causing damage; so, with great difficulty, three oul' fellas clambered over the eight foot wall to the road, just by the River Skane. Having polished off some Borg Marzipan and Kendal Mint Cake (maintaining the illusion of aristocracy), we headed over a bridge crossing the old Clonsilla-Navan line on a road busy with goods traffic.

Heavy lorries, transporting gravel to the M3 construction, were thundering by, about one a minute. After we reached the junction at Batterjohn Big, things were quieter.

At Collegeland, we came to the aptly-named Shank's Mare (a pub formerly called Cody's Forge) and Mark decided to rest here while Frank and I continued. We were soon at Moynalvy, where we got refreshments at Scut Fagan's. This ramshakle and disheveled pub achieved great fame as 'The Comanchero Lounge Bar, Grill and Art Gallery' in the RTÉ political comedy programme *Hall's Pictorial Weekly*.

There was little of interest for the remainder of the journey. We passed a large radio mast, from which RTÉ broadcasts on 252 kHz Long Wave. We spotted Larchill Arcadian Gardens, and an ornamental lake. We passed several stud farms. A couple of motorists stopped on the quiet road to pass the time of day with us. One of them told us we were on the very road that St. Patrick took from Glendalough to Tara. For all we knew, he may have been right. The rain came on heavy as we spied a large mound, a Ring Fort, at Rodanstown. Heavy rain had been falling for weeks, and there was extensive flooding of the land.

Reaching Kilcock around 7.00 o'clock in the evening, we drove back to Shank's Mare and joined Mark for dinner. We were well looked after by the delightful hostess, Orna. Then back to Tara to pick up the second car, and home. The Commodius Vicus was nearing its close, and the rest of the way would be downhill.

Chapter 18

THE FINAL NAVIGATION

But when we're quit of all our load,
'Now God be praised for that,' says she;
And back we go the homeward road,
Near bet we are, herself and me.
Och! Sure the thought of home is sweet
To thim that thravels on their feet.

'Blackberry time' – Winifred Mary Letts

THE YEAR OF OUR LORD 2008 WAS nearing its close. The state of the world in the new millennium was not getting any better. America had chosen its 44th President, who would soon take up office. His mission: to save the planet. The Hillpigs, Mark, Frank and myself, were joined by my two sons, Owen and Andrew, for a ramble along the Royal Canal. We were in the final stages of the Commodius Vicus. A few days walking would bring us, via our Nation's Capital, back to the Forty Foot.

Stage 84: Kilcock to Clonsilla

Breakfast rolls in Browne's Garage in Kilcock set us up for the walk. With a stable anticyclone over Ireland, the weather was fair and the sky completely clear. The early morning sun glistened on the water of the canal as we strode along. A heron rose and landed again repeatedly in front of us. A bird of little brain, he took some time to realise that his strategy of repeated retreat was not going to afford him undisturbed fishing so, finally, he took to the other bank, letting us pass and regaining his peace. Just below Jackson's Bridge we spotted the little Lyreen River flowing beneath the canal.

About a mile west of Maynooth we left the tow-path and scrambled over a fence and ditch, circumvented a slurry pit and passed by a farmyard to a back gate of NUIM, the Maynooth College of the National University of Ireland. St. Patrick's, Ireland's main seminary, was originally founded by Gerald FitzGerald, Ninth Earl of Kildare, in 1521 but was suppressed within twenty years. During the years of the Penal Laws, Irish priests received their education in France. At the end of the eighteenth century, with the French Revolution at its height, it was feared that Irish seminarians might be 'infected' with heretical ideas, so the authorities approved the re-establishment of the college. This renaissance, in 1795, was greatly assisted by the Irish statesman, Edmund Burke, a strong supporter of religious toleration. The second Duke of Leinster provided the lands for the college. In 1908, St. Patrick's became a recognised College of the National University of Ireland. In the late 1960s, after the Second Vatican Council, the college was opened to lay students – of both sexes. Pope John Paul II visited St. Patrick's in 1979, and a large bronze sculpture of him by Imogen Stuart commemorates the visit.

The farmer must have spotted us as we crossed the farmyard and alerted security to our irregular entry to the college grounds, because, as we ambled along in carefree fashion, a security man approached in his Chelsea Tractor. 'How did you get in?' demanded the man in blue. Hearing that we came via the farm, he did his best to order us back the same way, saying the college was closed and we had no business to be there. Now, rudimentary geometry indicates that progress is generally not facilitated by retracing of one's steps. One thing was sure to me: we were *not* going back. By a combination of grovelling humility and stubborn cajoling, backed up by a flash of my UCD staff card, I endeavoured to persuade him to allow us through. I resolved mentally that, if he continued to demand a retreat, we would all run, by diverging routes, to the college perimeter. However, he finally agreed to let us go on, so we continued, by way of the College Chapel and St. Joseph's Square, to the front gate.

The college is an elegant complex, with two large quadrangles. The design owes much to the Gothic-Revival architect Augustus Welby Pugin.

In a cloister of the College, there is a giant limestone head of St. Patrick by the Cork sculptor, Seamus Murphy. The museum of the College contains some early electric devices invented by Rev. Nicholas Callan, a Professor of Science at Maynooth, who discovered or co-discovered the principles of electrical induction and the dynamo effect; he used to administer high voltage shocks to the students, for educational purposes! But on this late December day, all was closed up, so we continued to the main gate, where the security man was waiting, key in hand to let us out. We thanked him, and he looked distinctly happy to be rid of us.

The ruin of an early Norman castle stands by the college gate. The original castle was built by Gerald FitzMaurice, ancestor of the Fitz-Geralds, Earls of Kildare and Dukes of Leinster, in the thirteenth century. Gerald FitzMaurice arrived in 1170 with the Norman invaders who were brought in by the 'arch-traitor' Diarmaid McMurrough. By the fifteenth century, the FitzGeralds had sizeable estates in Leinster, Munster and Connaught and were the most influential family in Ireland. By the time of Gearoid Og FitzGerald (1487–1534), the Ninth Earl of Kildare, Maynooth Castle, lavishly furnished and with an extensive library, was one of the richest noble houses under the English Crown. However, the FitzGeralds' loyalty to the crown was open to question: Gearoid's son, Thomas – known as Silken Thomas – led a revolution in 1534. Maynooth Castle was beseiged for ten days by the forces of Henry VIII and, eventually, Thomas was taken to the Tower of London and then executed at Tyburn. The castle was badly damaged in the seige. The influence of the Geraldines was greatly diminished following the defeat by the Tudors. The castle was burned during the 1641 Rebellion and since then has remained in a ruinous state.

Maynooth is a reasonably attractive town, with an air of genteel dilapidation. The closure of the Leinster Arms Hotel does nothing to help the image of the town, which is somewhat shabby at present but which has great potential for improvement. The main street leads directly from the university gate to Carton Avenue, the long drive to the stately Carton House. The grounds of the house are accessible to the public – which is wonderful – and there are many attractive walks in the 1000 acre demesne where the Rye Water, a tributary of the Liffey, broadens into a decorative lake. A luxury hotel has been built beside Carton House, hidden discreetly by a stand of mature trees, and there are two golf courses in the demesne. We crossed the bridge and climbed a short hill to admire the south-eastern facade of the Palladian mansion. Carton House was designed by the renowned architect Richard Cassels, who also designed several other stately houses: Powerscourt House, Westport House, Russborough House and a town-house for the FitzGeralds, Leinster House in Dublin. Carton House was completed in 1747. The Earl of Kildare rocketed to aristocratic stardom around that time, becoming Viscount in 1747, Marquis in 1761 and Duke of Leinster five years later.

We returned to a beautiful boathouse and took a path by the lakeside. Crossing a pretty bridge over a small cascade, we came to Shell Cottage, where Marianne Faithfull, a popular singer who was an icon in the 1960s and one-time girlfriend of Rolling Stone Mick Jagger, lived for some years. Peeping through the window, we saw that the walls and ceilings are covered in a variety of sea-shells. However, the cottage appeared to be occupied, so we did not linger.

We continued, by a beautiful tree-lined path, to the road leading to the main gate of Carton House and back to the Royal Canal. We kept an eye out for a glimpse of Carton Obelisk, better known as Conolly's Folly, which stands about a kilometre south of the canal. The 140 foot folly was erected in 1740 by Catherine Conyngham, William Conolly's widow. Conolly was an attorney, who enriched himself dealing in lands and estates confiscated from Catholics following the Battle of the Boyne. He was ten times Lord Justice of Ireland, and, according to Dean Swift, bought himself, for £3,000, the appointment of Chief Commissioner of Irish Revenues. He held the position of Speaker of the Irish House of Commons from 1715 until close to his death in 1729, giving him the title by which he is best known, 'Speaker Conolly'. The folly is visible from the Conollys' pile, Castletown House, a few miles from Carton House, providing a focal point for the vista to the north-west. It was built by local labourers who were paid a halfpenny a day, bringing them some relief following the famine winter of 1739/40.

The canal runs around the northern edge of Leixlip. About 1 kilometre south of the canal, just before Leixlip, is the Wonderful Barn, a five-storey structure shaped like a conical bottle, with an external stairway, another famine-relief project, built for Mrs. Conolly of Castletown House in 1743. Leixlip, Old Norse for Salmon Leap, is named for the fall of the Liffey that is now harnessed for electrical power. It was established by the Vikings more than a thousand years ago.

After Louisa Bridge we came to the Rye Water Aqueduct. The Royal Canal runs from the Liffey at Spencer Dock to the Upper Shannon near Termonbarry, a route of about 90 miles. The canal was said to have resulted from a quarrel on the Grand Canal Board. Construction was started in 1790, but the canal was expensive to build and was never profitable, running close to the Grand Canal for much of its route and failing to attract traffic away from the older navigation. However, although the active lifetime of the canals was not much more than fifty years, they had a major influence on the development of the regions through which they passed. The remains of many canal-side hotels, warehouses, mills and other industrial activities can still be seen along the canals. The Duke of Leinster, a man of considerable influence, wanted the Royal Canal to pass by his estate at Carton House, and this required the construction of the aqueduct across the Rye. Hundreds of navvys spent some six years building this massive aqueduct, which ran well over budget, almost bankrupting the entire project. A wooden step-way took us down to the valley floor, from where we could admire the fine masonry work of the aqueduct.

The canal was sold in 1844, at a knockdown price, to the Midlands & Great Western Railway (MGWR) Company. The original plan was to fill in the channel and run the Dublin–Galway railway line on top of it. Fortunately, this plan was not adopted, and the railway was built alongside the canal. The MGWR line was opened from Broadstone Station in Dublin to Enfield in 1847, reaching Mullingar the following year. The extension to Galway opened in 1851, and another line from Mullingar to Sligo was completed in 1862. Today the line carries commuter traffic to Maynooth and serves as the main Sligo line, the Galway trains following a more southerly route, via Portarlington.

The ruin of the Collector's House stands by the canal just beyond the aqueduct. At one stage the canal terminated here and tolls were payable by travellers. A notice displayed the tariffs. Liveried servants were permitted on deck only. Dogs could travel in comfort in the cabins, but at the full passenger rate. At the end of the eighteenth century it cost 8 shillings to travel from Dublin to Leixlip by coach, whereas the fare by canal boat was only one shilling. We continued by Confey Station; the town of Leixlip has spread north to the canal-side here. After a long straight run to Collins Bridge, the canal swung north again, and re-curved where the derelict Clonsilla–Navan railway line joined the main line. The bulwarks of the old railway bridge remain, and the course of the railway could be seen stretching away to the west. This is the same line we had crossed near Dunsany. There is some talk of reopening this line to Navan. We live in hope.

Stage 85: *Clonsilla to Seapoint*

Some health problems interrupted my ramblings for a few months but by summertime I was back to full fitness, with no permanent damage done. Alas, the so-called summer was wet once again, for the third year running, with more than double the average rainfall in many places. Not until early September did an obliging anti-cyclone build up over Ireland and remain for a few weeks, bringing a spell of wonderful warm and dry weather. Such blocking anticyclones have the effect of steering the rain-bearing depressions on a track far to the north, keeping the weather in Ireland fine. In winter, they can bring cold weather and snow, but it was still early autumn.

Mark and I travelled from Glenageary to Clonsilla by rail in about an hour, changing trains at Westland Row, aka Pearse Station. I had read that there is a stained glass window by Evie Hone, depicting St. Fiacre, in a church in Clonsilla. So, stepping north from the station we took a look in the nearby St. Mary's Church, but found no sign of the window. The church was locked and in any case we suspected that we might be in the wrong place, so we returned to the canal and set out eastward along the beautiful towpath. The canal is in a shallow cutting, with trees on each bank, so there was plenty of shade from the blistering sun. It was the beginning of one of the most glorious and interesting walks of the entire Commodius Vicus. Although the canal was undisturbed and unfrequented, there was little sign of wildlife in or about the water.

At Porterstown Bridge we crossed to the south side of the canal and came before long to Coolmine Station, between Carpenterstown to the south and Blanchardstown to the north. Soon we arrived at the first of three double locks within a mile or so, one of which gives its name to a restaurant, The Twelfth Lock. We stopped for some refreshments and then inspected the barges and cruisers tied up by the quay. They were available for hire, but we did not see a single boat moving during the entire trip along the canal.

After Castleknock Station we came to what is perhaps the largest Celtic cross in Ireland. The Sun-ring is formed by the huge, high round-about of the Navan road, which stretches its arms to the south-east and north-west. The upright of the cross is formed by the M50, perpendicular to the Navan Road and passing far below it. Between these, the railway and canal pass through the centre of the cross at an intermediate level. It is a junction of intriguing complexity.

From here, the canal route is close to the Tolka, which flows in a valley just to the north. Beyond the river is Dunsink Observatory, the oldest scientific institution in Ireland. Repeated reference to 'Dunsink time' is made in *Ulysses*: the observatory provided the reference time for Dublin from 1865 until 1937. Ireland's greatest mathematician, William Rowan Hamilton, spent many years here as Astronomer Royal for Ireland. He would occasionally walk from the observatory along the canal to attend meetings of the Royal Irish Academy in Dublin. On one such walk, he had a flash of inspiration, finding suddenly the solution to a difficult problem that had been taxing him for many years. He was trying to describe rotations in three dimensions, and had to find a means of multiplying the complex mathematical quantities that he called quaternions. Ordinary numbers commute: that is, if A and B are two numbers, then the product formed by multiplying A by B, or A times B, is identical to the the product formed by multiplying B by A, or B times A. For example, 2 times 3 is the same as 3 times 2. Hamilton had thought that the same rule must apply to his quaternions, and his flash of genius by the canal was that this does not have to be the case: for quaternions, A times B is not equal to B times A. Mathematicians call quantities like this 'non-commutative'. Hamilton's departure from the conventional rules of algebra was enormously liberating, and led to an explosion of new developments in mathematics.

Quaternion multiplication is easily illustrated by a simple example. Hold a book in front of you with the front cover facing north (this is easiest if you are also facing north!). Rotate it clockwise through ninety degrees (a right angle) about the line pointing north. Now rotate it clockwise through ninety degrees about the vertical. The cover should face west, with the spine at the bottom. Next, return to the original position and repeat the operations, but this time in reverse order: rotate the book clockwise about the vertical, then rotate it clockwise about the line pointing north. The cover should face upwards, with the spine to the north. We can denote the rotation about north by A, that about the vertical by B, and the first followed by the second by A times B. Then we see that A times B is not equal to B times A. These non-commuting rotations are a special case of quaternions. Hamilton hoped that quaternions would become a universal language of physics. That did not happen, but they have recently emerged again in the contexts of astronautics and computer graphics. This is but one of many cases in which mathematics developed for one purpose finds application in another, completely unforeseen, area.

At Ashtown, we crossed the canal again to the north bank. There has been enormous development here. The atmosphere of the new village was quite continental, and we agreed that it must be an attractive place to live, and very convenient with the rail link to the city. But the poor state of the economy was in evidence: hundreds of apartments in a long row of newly built blocks appeared to be unoccupied, and work on further developments had halted.

Near the eighth lock we found flowers at a gate, a ghetto-blaster, and other mementos to Bippa, a young man who had lost his life here in a drowning accident just a few months before. We met two girls who were friendly with Bippa's cousin and who knew all about the tragic circumstances in which he had died. At the bridge an angler told us that he had caught some roach and a few 'hybrids'. He described the hybrid as a cross between a perch and a roach; I thought that poach would be a better name. In any case, he wasn't poaching: he didn't keep the catches, but photographed them and returned them to the water.

At Broombridge, just north of Cabra, we came to the point where, on 16 October 1843, Hamilton had had his flash of insight. He was so delighted that he scratched the quaternion equation on a stone of the bridge. A plaque on the wall of the bridge was unveiled by Eamon de Valera in 1958. On it is carved Hamilton's marvellous formula:

$$i^2 = j^2 = k^2 = ijk = -1$$

Hamilton spent the remainder of his life working out the many consequences of this discovery. In fact, his earlier work on mechanics proved much more important for the development of science, providing a fundamental framework for quantum mechanics.

There was increasing evidence of industry as we approached the city. We passed under the railway close to Liffey Junction, where an old branch-line led down through Phibsboro' to Broadstone Station. Then we noted another line passing to the south under the canal, the loop line that runs beneath Phoenix Park to connect with the main line at Islandbridge Junction near Heuston Station. St. Paul's, the southern section of Prospect Cemetery, squeezed between two railway lines, came into view. The O'Connell Monument, a replica of a Round Tower, stood prominently further to the north in Glasnevin Cemetery, the setting for the 'Hades' episode of *Ulysses*.

Approaching Prospect Road we passed the Shandon Mill, now converted to apartments. Here at one time was the ironworks of John and Robert Mallet. The Victoria Foundry provided the steel for the railways during the mid-nineteenth century. Mallet's name can still be seen on the iron railings that surround Trinity College. Robert Mallet is known as the father of seismology. He coined that term, and made many contributions to the science of earthquakes. In a famous experiment, he detonated explosions on Killiney beach so that he could measure the time taken by the shock waves to travel through the ground.

We stopped at Cross Guns Bridge for further refreshment at Hedigan's, the well-known watering place also called the Brian Boru. Then we took the path on the south side of the canal, passing some new apartments to come to Mountjoy Prison, where Brendan Behan was once resident, and where 'the oul' triangle went jingle-jangle'. We found a statue of Behan sitting on a bench at the lock just below the prison. A plaque indicated the tragic brevity of his life, from 1923 to 1964. Several of the locks along this stretch are in flithers, and would benefit from 'an injection of capital'. Perhaps when the Celtic Tiger roars once more the canal will be made navigable to the Liffey.[12]

The next bridge, at Dorset Street, was marked as Binn's Bridge, 1793. Numerous ducks were found here, mostly black with yellow eye-rings. We suspected them to be scoters, the only all-black ducks, but later scrutiny of a bird-book suggested that they might be hybrids between pochards and tufted ducks. The enormous new stadium of Croke Park, which holds more than 80,000 people, loomed over the canal. This also provided the venue for international rugby matches while Lansdowne Road was being rebuilt. Most of the people we passed here were sitting alone or in small groups, quietly drinking.

At the North Strand Road the tow-path ends. We could have headed for the Liffey by the streets, but it seemed sad to abandon the canal just as it was about to reach its goal, so we went down Ossory Road and, flexing the law ever so slightly, hopped over the wall, dropping onto the railway. We followed a grassy bank beside the canal and came to a brand new railway station, Docklands, which seemed not to be yet in use. It was all locked up and we were unable to climb a high wall that blocked our way at Sherriff Street, so we went back and worked around to Church Road Junction. Here a large black gentleman, Nigerian we guessed, drove up in an even larger SUV and questioned us. We said we were lost, having tried to follow the canal to Spencer Dock and the river, but found our way blocked. The security guard asked if we were travellers. Of course we were, and are, but we thought it prudent to say no, suspecting that he had a particular variety of traveller in mind. He phoned his supervisor, who said we could exit by the gate near New Wapping Street. This was ideal, as it brought us soon to Mayor Street Upper, where we quickly returned to Spencer Dock.

---

[12] The Royal Canal has recently been reopened to traffic all the way from Dublin to the Shannon.

The Luas line was under construction at Mayor Street; the first test-run was made the day after we passed by. The entire area has been re-developed, with hundreds of new eight-storey buildings, many of them quite attractive. At Excise Walk we had some refreshment at the 'Seven Wonders', a café latte for Mark and a Tropical Dew for me. Reaching the Liffey, we were delighted to find the three-masted barque Jeannie John-ston tied up by the quay. It is docked here and open to the public. More than nine years had passed since we had seen this ship under construc-tion in Blennerville, and it was refreshing to see her shipshape and sea-worthy.

A new bridge, with graceful lines in the form of a huge harp, was un-der construction, but we couldn't risk a law-breaking dash across it as there were workers busy on the site. So we went upstream, crossed the Sean O'Casey footbridge and took a left along the south quays. We found a statue of Admiral William Brown (1777–1857), founder of the Argen-tine Navy. Across the river was the new Irish Convention Centre, dubbed 'the Cube with the Tube' because of its lopsided cylindrical form. Further downstream stood The O2, formerly The Point.

On Sir John Rogerson's Quay stands a large ancient diving-bell It comprises a broad-bore pipe mounted on a concrete chamber in the form of a truncated pyramid about two metres high, open at the bottom. The whole structure is about ten metres tall. The bell was designed in 1860 by Bindon Blood Stoney. Stoney was Chief Engineer of Dublin Port and oversaw the development of the Dublin docks. He devised a new meth-od of constructing dock walls using pre-cast concrete blocks. He con-structed the diving bell so that the workers could operate below the water level. The bell was lowered to the river bottom and the workers entered through the pipe. Air was continually pumped down to the chamber to enable them to work in hot and dirty half-hour shifts. Stoney's invention attracted considerable international interest at the time.

After inspecting the bell, we turned up Blood Stoney Road to Ha-nover Basin, where the studios of U2 were once located. Graffiti, mostly expressing love of the band, covered the walls. A yellow amphibious craft, filled with tourists, was plying the basin. These Viking tours are very popular. We came to Camden Lock, completed in 1790. Here three sea-locks connect the basin to the Liffey estuary, and mark the beginning of a watery way through Ireland from the east coast, via the Grand Canal to the Shannon and downstream through Limerick to the west coast. We crossed the bridge at Ringsend, aka Raytown, to enter the ancient region of Cuala and the home stretch of the Commodius Vicus. Strolling along by the Dodder, we met a man and woman from Waterford. As Mark's father hailed from Dungarvan, he had stories to swap. The couple were up for the Irish Derby which was on that evening in nearby Shelbourne Park. I later learned that the favourite, College Causeway, came from the rear to win from Oran Classic at 5/4; one of the greatest dogs of all time, the commentator enthused.

The new stadium at Lansdowne Road was changing the skyline ahead. We turned down Londonbridge Road to take a refresher in the pleasant pub of John Clark in Irishtown. Then we continued through Sean Moore Park, named for a former Lord Mayor of Dublin. A memorial stone commemorates the role of the Irish Mercantile Marine during the World War II, 1939–1946. I was not clear why our Emergency lasted beyond the point of Victory in Europe. Further on we found two standing stones, mounted in modern times. Apparently they have an alignment of some significance, but the meaning eluded us. But what a brilliant engineering achievement, to erect two stones in a straight line, with such precision that the deviation from linearity is undetectable.

We walked down onto Sandymount Strand, following the steps of Stephen Dedalus and Leopold Bloom in Joyce's 'dirty book'. Thalatta, thalatta, the sea at last. The Great Anabasis was over. An attractive modern sculpture, representing a wave, stood by the shore, a gift from the Mexican people. We passed the Martello tower, where someone had tried to open a restaurant, evidently without success. Then we came to the large derelict swimming pool that stands off from the shore. It is in a sorry state, but is still popular and many people, young and old, were enjoying the sunny weather there. We bumped into Conor Sweeney, my post-doctoral researcher, his wife Karen Gillece, a successful writer and their ten-week old daughter Rowan. Then we strolled onward, heading inshore to cross the little Nutley Stream on stepping stones.

At Booterstown, we crossed the foot-bridge and took the path to Blackrock Park. At Idrone Terrace, we crossed once again to the sea side of the railway and passed the old bathing places. Ahead stood the elegant twin granite towers of a foot-bridge constructed to appease Lord Cloncurry when the railway was built. The landowners saw their opportunity to hold the railway companies to ransom, and extorted the maximum compensation. There was a small granite harbour here, and a tiny bathing hut with Doric columns, also built for Cloncurry by the railway company. The hut was a landmark until it was completely vandalized some years ago. All we found were the round carved pieces of the columns – shades of Ozymandias.

We met two teenagers who showed us the best way to climb a high wall that stood in our path. There was a long drop to the rocks below and the transit was a mildly terrifying experience. Dropping down on the other side, we found another small harbour, and the remains of a red-brick summer house that once belonged to Blackrock House, now demolished. There was a large group of youths, who seemed to be very pleasant and good humoured, enjoying themselves here. We strode on, passing a large mound like a Norman motte, and then followed the ankle-snapping forty-five degree bulwark of the sea-wall to a footbridge. The bridge had a gate, but fortune smiled upon us, for it was not locked, so we came easily to the station at Seapoint.

Stage 86: Seapoint to Dun Laoghaire

We disembarked from the DART at Seapoint Station. On the platform wall are four or five large circular openings. Behind them is an elaborate tunnel, which once gave access to the stables of a nearby house, and was built when the railway was being constructed. Mark and I headed down Seapoint Road and took the short-cut across the railway to Brighton Vale. Seapoint Baths once provided swimming facilities here, but the property is now a private residence. Beside the Martello tower at Seapoint is a plaque commemorating the Prince of Wales and the Rochdale, which sank in 1807 with the loss of 400 souls. This tragedy provided an incentive for the construction of Dun Laoghaire Harbour. A path by the railway leads from here all the way to Dun Laoghaire. We passed Salthill, named for the salt works that were active here during the eighteenth century. The Salthill Hotel, an elegant and attractive building, once stood on the small hillock nearby.

Just to the south is Longford Terrace. Peter Pearson, in his book *Between the Mountains and the Sea*, writes that Longford Terrace was once described as 'an aristocratic and commmanding pile'. Naturally, I was bound to agree, as I lived in Number 2 for the first three years of my life. One of my earliest memories is of gathering pieces of coloured glass on the stony beach at the back of the small pier below Salthill Station. The beach is now filled in except for a tiny section, about five metres wide. This spot is popular as a launching point for windsurfers. A path on the sea side of the nearby industrial site was blocked by an iron fence bearing a notice 'Access Temporarily Closed', erected by Dun Laoghaire Rathdown County Council. The Council's idea of what is temporary does not concur with the commonly-held notion. The notice had been there for several years, and will probably be there for several more, if not in perpetuity.

There are a number of industrial units here, although most of the buildings seemed to be derelict. We swung around the barrier fence, and around another further on. The back of the West Pier is a good place to spot waders, but the tide was high when we passed. The den of the Sea Scouts, a Marine Activity Centre and the Dun Laoghaire Motor Yacht Club are in a cluster on the pier. The National Nautical College was here at one time but was relocated to Cork. E. McCormack's Soap Factory was was located near the West Pier and I recall the smell of soap in the neighbourhood. On the roof was written 'E McC', which always tempted me to climb up and modify it to '$E=MC^2$'.

Dun Laoghaire is one of the finest built harbours in the world. Its two magnificent granite piers enclose an area of about 100 hectares or 250 acres. A notice board gave some interesting information about the harbour. The East Pier was built between 1817 and 1823 and is 1300 metres in length. The West Pier, built between 1820 and 1827 is somewhat longer, at 1548 metres. The harbour mouth is about 230 metres wide. The Old Pier was built in 1767, and Trader's Wharf in 1855. There has been extensive development of the harbour in recent times, with the construction of two breakwaters and a large yachting marina.

A stone near the Old Pier indicated that Laoghaire, King of Tara and High King of Ireland, had his sea fort (or Dún) here in the fifth century. He was the one with whom St. Patrick had a run-in over the lighting of the Paschal Fire. Passing the old Coast Guard Station, we came to the attractive new headquarters of the Commissioners of the Irish Lights. The building has a form reminiscent of a large lighthouse lantern, with an extensive array of solar panels on the roof.

Public access to the foreshore is under constant threat from acquisitive yacht clubs and others. I recalled a miniature 'harbour within a harbour' hereabouts, which is now gone, perhaps obliterated when the Marina Office was built some years ago. The large HSS Ferry was coming in as we came to the end of the ramble at the Caffe Ritazza, where we revived ourselves with some strong coffees. With just one mile remaining, the Commodius Vicus was all but over.

Stage 87: Dun Laoghaire to Sandycove

For the final stage, a group of our friends assembled at the Ferry Pier in Dun Laoghaire on a stormy November evening, near the stainless steel sculpture, Gaoth na Sáile, made by Eamonn O'Doherty, which is in the form of wind-swept sails. The Town Hall clock read seven o'clock. The building now known by some as the County Hall has been refurbished and extended. The clock is occasionally called the Four-faced Liar, like that in Shandon in Cork and many others. Nearby is the reconstructed Victorian Fountain, destroyed some years ago by a group that Mark referred to as the 'local woolly-faces'. They had run a chain around it, hooked up to a van and driven away, completely shattering the original fountain. Across the road is the Pavilion Theatre, originally an Edwardian pavilion, later a cinema, where we were often admitted without payment in our youth by the manager, who was a neighbour; a belated 'thank you, Mr. Kinsella'.

Near Carlisle Pier, an obelisk stands on four great stone spheres. It was erected in 1821 'To commemorate the visit of the King to this part of his dominions ... when he graciously named the harbour the "Royal Harbour of George IV" and on the same day embarked from hence [sic].' Richard Colley, Marquis Wellesley, Lord Lieutenant of Ireland gets his name on the monument. He was a brother of Arthur Wellesley, the first Duke of Wellington. On the back of the monument, the laying of the first stone of the East Pier in 1817 is commemorated. John Rennie was the Directing Engineer. John Aird, another engineer named on the obelisk, was a relation of Mark. Some years ago another group of self-appointed liberators blew up one of the spheres supporting the obelisk but failed to topple it. The British Empire is made of sterner stuff! The renovations are now hardly noticeable.

The anchor of the RMS Leinster rests on a stone nearby. The Leinster was torpedoed near the Kish Bank by the Germans in October 1918, just one month before the end of World War I, with the loss of 501 passengers, crew and postal workers. Another memorial stone marks the loss of 15 gallant men when the Kingstown life boat went down in 1895.

As we passed the East Pier, the effect of the storm became evident. Huge rollers were thundering in, driven by the strong north-easterly wind, and smashing off the pier. The sight was a spectacular backdrop to our ramble. We passed the old sea baths, which have languished in a state of dereliction for several decades.

When we reached the Forty Foot there was a crowd gathered to witness the enormous waves breaking over Elephant Rock and Peak Rock. There was no question of going down into the swimming area with such raging surf, so we took some photographs and then repaired to Odell's Restaurant for a meal to celebrate the conclusion of the Commodius Vicus. I gave a short speech at the dinner, summing up the experience, and it is reproduced below.

Greetings friends, welcome and thanks for coming to join the celebration of the completion of our ramble round Ireland, the Commodius Vicus of Recirculation.

One of the great privileges of being a weatherman is that one has complete control of the elements. The thunderous waves that we witnessed on our short walk were planned some thirteen years ago, as a suitable finale to the ramble.

You may ask, Why? Why would anyone walk around Ireland? There are many answers. It was partly a pilgrimage, partly a travel adventure, partly an educational trip and partly a Zen Buddhist exercise. As Zen, it was a great success, because nothing really happened. It is wonderful when nothing happens: I was not robbed or mugged and no accidents or serious mishaps befell me. I didn't even lose my virginity. But it was enormously enjoyable, especially when I had the company of my friends and fellow-Hillpigs, Mark and Frank and Tom.

I was in no hurry. Just as well, since it took thirteen years. That comes to about half a kilometre per day, a truly blistering pace. Everywhere there was something of interest: the landscape, the wildlife, industrial heritage, archaeological sites and, of course, the people of the country. We take it for granted, but it is really marvellous that Ireland is a peaceful and friendly country and a pleasure to travel in.

We came across a variety of wildlife on our travels. We saw a bittern, now very rare, and black-tailed godwits – you are all familiar with them, no doubt – and the little egrets that have since become widespread; Egretta garzetta, what a name, what a dame! At the outset I could recognise very few wild flowers and learned that there is a rich variety in Ireland. Literary connections are everywhere: Joyce was a running theme for the walk, we visited Kilgarvan, where the Kerry poets are commemorated, Yeats's Castle in Gort, the Kavanagh Country in Monaghan, and Dunsany, whence hailed Francis Ledwidge. And we found evidence of the scientific heritage that is often ignored. Boyle nearly drowned in a stream in Waterford; if only he had, we would not have had to learn Boyle's Law in school. And Kirwan, an early expert in chemistry. And of course Hamilton, Ireland's greatest mathematician and a world-leading figure. Following the dinner, I will present a three-hour discourse on quaternions [groans from the audience].

Many hours would be needed to tell you everything, so I will just pick a few highlights of the ramble, a sample from our journey through Cork. In Ladysbridge, in Irish Droichead na Scuab or the bridge of the brushes, we were told in the local hostelry that the village was named for a heroic event when the Black and Tans were beaten off the bridge with brushes. And why Ladysbridge? 'Sure, 'twas de wimmin was holdin' de brushes.' We verified the scholarly integrity of this account with another local, who added that 'Der's no ladies here anyway, only a few oul' biddies'. We caught the Navy tender from Cobh to Haulbowline; you may not know it, but you owe your freedom to Mark and me: as members of An Slúa Maraí, we guarded the coast in the sixties, and not a single Soviet submarine was able to penetrate our defences. In Ballinhassig a woman learning that I was walking round Ireland remarked 'You must be a shkilled walker'. 'I learned when I was very young' was all I could think of replying. In Crossbarry we were treated with great deference by the local publican. 'The new monument is up. Would you like to see it? ' he asked. Perplexed, we agreed, and he drove us a few miles to see a Celtic cross commemorating some republicans who had recently been killed. We kept quiet, but I am convinced that he thought that we were 'down from HQ' checking that money had been used for the intended purpose.

The bishop and the actress were our constant companions. English is a delight: almost anything can be misunderstood, usually with a sexual import, if you have a dirty mind. Thus a simple question, 'What's up?' takes on a new meaning as, 'What's up? as the actress said to the bishop', or, 'I'm coming! as the bishop said to the actress'. You get the point (as the bishop ...). We were having a meal in Macroom chatting about wildlife, and in particular caterpillars, when Mark uttered the most memorable bishop-and-actress statement: 'I must look up the Hairy Molly.' And while I'm on the subject, Frank and I spent an hour or more in the village of Muff in Donegal, searching for the Muff Diving Club, but to no avail.

There were many curious incidents: one day I walked from Ballinglen to ... Ballinglen, in a great fog-bound circle; Lady Dunsany made a pot of coffee specially for Mark; standing astride an electric fence, I nearly lost more than my virginity; we saw ogham stones and sheela-na-gigs (always worth a detour) and Jimi Hendrix' death certificate.

After climbing the mountain euphemistically called the Devil's Mother, Frank and I went to a meeting of the Quiet Man Club in Cong, where this greatest-movie-of-all-time was made. The film was based on a story written by Maurice Walsh, Tom's uncle. The organiser, Des McHale, opened the meeting with the astounding revelation that he had managed to identify the dog that ran across shot when John Wayne was thrashing poor Maureen O'Hara. And he added, 'We actually have someone here today who has not yet seen the film!' He was referring to Frank, who must be the only Irishman over fifty who has not seen The Quiet Man.

We had a few run-ins with security on the ramble, but nothing to worry about. In Maynooth we were under threat of being forced to re-trace our steps, but I had a Plan B: to shout 'Run like hell', scarper for the front gate and scramble over it before the security man could do anything. Fortunately, it didn't come to that: we managed to persuade him to allow us through the college grounds. Near Spencer Dock we had another, more colourful, scrape. The towpath expires at the North Strand Road and, wishing to follow the canal, we hopped over the wall and crossed the rails. But soon a large Nigerian gentleman drove up in his 4x4 and asked us, 'How did you get in?' 'Oh, we came in by mistake, and we're trying to get out,' I said, not really answering his question. His supervisor phoned him at that moment. 'Deys com in by mistake, and deys tryin' to get out,' he said. He was on our side! He let us go out by New Wapping Street, just where we wanted to go.

We came to the Luas line, just being completed at the time. This was one of the many changes that happened in Ireland during the course of the Commodius Vicus. The completion of the Jeannie Johnston, tied up on the river nearby, was another. Mobile phones had arrived, iPods, the Internet, Google Earth, and GPS. The Y2K bug had come and gone without incident, and another bug too, Foot and Mouth disease. Euros had displaced pounds, and the Celtic Tiger had prowled for a while but was now nowhere to be seen. Finally, the Good Friday Peace Agreement had been signed, and was holding. Perhaps this was the best of all.

By the goodly Barrow, I saw a bittern, An Bunán Buí, a once-common bird in Ireland. A poet wrote: 'The yellow bittern that never broke out / In a drinking bout, might as well have drunk.' He urges us to make hay while the sun shines, and drink up while we can. He goes on: 'I was sober a while, but I'll drink and be wise / For I fear I should die in the end of thirst.' So, I urge you now to eat up and drink up and enjoy yourselves. Thank you.

Afterword – The 87 Stages of the Commodius Vicus

A Scout smiles and whistles under all circumstances.

Scouting for Boys (1908) – Robert Baden-Powell

Anyone can walk around Ireland. There was nothing heroic about the Commodius Vicus: I slept indoors every night, and suffered no hardship save a few blisters and several drenchings. I hope this account inspires some of you to try your own Hibernian circumambulation.

The stages of the ramble, and the dates they were walked, are given in the table below. But don't follow the route I chose, for there is an infinite variety of other possibilities. I missed much of interest: the Wexford coast, the Kerry peninsulas, most of Connemara, the Rosses of Donegal, the Mourne Mountains and much more. You should solve Frost's Dilemma in your own way, and according to your own tastes.

Just a few tips to end this tale: spend time planning – it's almost as enjoyable as the real thing; get good walking boots and wet gear; bring maps and a compass or GPS; take along something to eat and drink; let someone know where you are heading; it's more fun, and safer, to go with friends than on your own; and, finally, don't walk on live railways – only a half-wit does that!

The 87 Stages of the Commodius Vicus

1 The Commodius Vicus Commences

Stage 1	Sandycove to Killiney	Sunday 1 December 1996
Stage 2	Killiney to Bray	Sunday 15 December 1996
Stage 3	Bray to Greystones	Friday 27 December 1996

2 A Walk in the Garden

Stage 4	Greystones to Wicklow	Monday 21 July 1997
Stage 5	Wicklow to Rathdrum	Tuesday 22 July 1997
Stage 6	Rathdrum to Avoca	Wednesday 23 July 1997
Stage 7	Avoca to Woodenbridge	Thursday 24 July 1997

3 Into the Croghan Valley

Stage 8	Woodenbridge to Ballinglen	Saturday 2 August 1997
Stage 9	Ballinglen to Ballinglen	Sunday 3 August, 1997
Stage 10	Ballinglen to Rosnastraw Bridge	Saturday 6 September 1997
Stage 11	Rosnastraw to Bunclody	Sunday 7 September 1997

4 Up the Airy Mountain, Down the Rushy Glen

Stage 12	Bunclody to Borris	Monday 13 April 1998
Stage 13	Borris to St. Mullin's	Tuesday 14 April 1998
Stage 14	St. Mullin's to New Ross	Wednesday 15 April 1998

5 Through Norman Territory

Stage 15	New Ross to Arthurstown	Monday 20 July 1998
Stage 16	Arthurstown to Waterford	Tuesday 21 July 1998
Stage 17	Waterford to Carrick	Saturday 1 August 1998
Stage 18	Carrick to Clonmel	Thursday 23 July 1998

6 *Where the Stars are Big and Bright*

Stage 19	Clonmel to Glasha	Sunday 25 October 1998
Stage 20	Glasha to Cappoquin	Monday 26 October, 1998
Stage 21	Cappoquin to Clashmore	Tuesday 27 October, 1998
Stage 22	Clashmore to Youghal	Wednesday 28 October 1998
Stage 23	Youghal to Ladysbridge	Thursday 29 October 1998
Stage 24	Ladysbridge to Ballinacurra	Friday 30 October 1998

7 *The Rebel Heartland*

Stage 25	Marlogue to Cobh (in reverse)	Monday 5 April 1999
Stage 26	Cobh to Ballinhassig	Tuesday 6 April 1999
Stage 27	Ballinhassig to Bandon	Wednesday 7 April 1999
Stage 28	Bandon to Ballineen	Thursday 8 April 1999
Stage 29	Ballineen to Shiplake	Friday 9 April 1999
Stage 30	Shiplake to Ballingeary	Saturday 10 April 1999

8 *Into the Kingdom*

Stage 31	Ballingeary to Kilgarvan	Friday, 1 October, 1999
Stage 32	Kilgarvan to Kenmare	Saturday 2 October 1999
Stage 33	Kenmare to Killarney	Sunday 3 October 1999
Stage 34	Killarney to Faha Cross	Monday 3 January 2000
Stage 35	Faha Cross to Castlemaine	Tuesday 4 January 2000

9 *The Road from Ratass to Rattoo*

Stage 36	Castlemaine to Tralee (in reverse)	Tuesday 25 April 2000
Stage 37	Tralee to Ballyheige	Wednesday 26 April 2000
Stage 38	Ballyheige to Ballyduff	Thursday 27 April 2000
Stage 39	Ballyduff to Carrig Island	Friday 28 April 2000
Stage 40	Carrig Island to Tarbert	Saturday 29 April 2000

10 *Tracking the West Clare Railway*

Stage 41	Tarbert to Kilrush	Thursday 18 January 2001
Stage 42	Kilrush to Kilkee	Friday 19 January 2001
Stage 43	Kilkee to Quilty	Saturday 20 January 2001
Stage 44	Quilty to Ennistymon	Sunday 21 January 2001
Stage 45	Ennistymon to Corrofin	Monday 22 January 2001

| Stage 46 | Corrofin to Seanaglish | Wednesday 24 January 2001 |
| Stage 47 | Seanaglish to Gort | Thursday 25 January 2001 |

11 *The March of the Quiet Maniacs*

Stage 48	Gort to Ardrahan	Sunday 26th August 2001
Stage 49	Ardrahan to Athenry	Monday 27th August 2001
Stage 50	Athenry to Corrandulla	Tuesday 28th August 2001
Stage 51	Corrandulla to Greenfields	Wednesday 29th August 2001
Stage 52	Greenfields to Cong	Thursday 30th August 2001

12 *Mounting Mater Diaboli*

Stage 53	Cong to Lough Nafooey	Friday 25th September 2003
Stage 54	Lough Nafooey to Delphi	Wednesday 23rd Sept. 2003
Stage 55	Delphi to Westport	Thursday 24th Sept. 2003

13 *The Land of Heart's Desire*

Stage 56	Westport to Newport	Thursday 2 January 2003
Stage 57	Newport to Pontoon	Friday 3 January 2003
Stage 58	Pontoon to Ballina	Saturday 4 January 2003
Stage 59	Ballina to Inishcrone	Sunday 5 January 2003
Stage 60	Inishcrone to Skreen	Monday 6 January 2003
Stage 61	Skreen to Collooney	Tuesday 7 January 2003
Stage 62	Collooney to Manorhamilton	Wednesday 8 January 2003
Stage 63	Manorhamilton to Belleek	Thursday 9 January 2003
Stage 64	Belleek to Donegal	Friday 10 January 2003

14 *The North-West Frontier*

Stage 65	Donegal Town to Ballybofey	Thursday 19 August 2004
Stage 66	Ballybofey to Raphoe	Friday 20 August 2004
Stage 67	Raphoe to Derry	Saturday 21 August 2004
Stage 68	Derry to Carrowkeel	Sunday 2 January 2005
Stage 69	Carrowkeel to Greencastle	Monday 3 January 2005
Stage 70	Greencastle to Coleraine	Tuesday 4 January 2005

15 *The Causeway Coast*

Stage 71	Coleraine to Giant's Causeway	Thursday 25 August, 2005
Stage 72	Giant's Causeway to Ballycastle	Friday 26th August 2005
Stage 73	Ballycastle to Glenariff	Saturday 27 August 2005
Stage 74	Glenariff to Broughshane	Sunday 28 August 2005

16 *In the Steps of King Billy*

Stage 75	Broughshane to Antrim Town	Wednesday 3 January 2007
Stage 76	Antrim Town to Moira	Thursday 4 January 2007
Stage 77	Moira to Portadown	Wednesday 8 August 2007
Stage 78	Portadown to Newry	Friday 5th January 2007

17 *The Great Anabasis*

Stage 79	Newry to Hackballscross	Saturday 5 January 2008
Stage 80	Hackballscross to Kingscourt	Sunday 6 January 2008
Stage 81	Kingscourt to Wilkinstown	Thursday 7 August 2008
Stage 82	Wilkinstown to Tara	Friday 8 August 2008
Stage 83	Tara to Kilcock	Friday 15 August 2008

18 *The Final Navigation*

Stage 84	Kilcock to Clonsilla	Sunday 28 December 2008
Stage 85	Clonsilla to Seapoint	Saturday 12 September 2009
Stage 86	Seapoint to Dun Laoghaire	Sunday 20 September 2009
Stage 87	Dun Laoghaire to Sandycove	Sunday 29 November 2009

REFERENCES

The factual information in this book is based not on my meagre knowledge, but on a wealth of excellent books about Ireland. Some of those that I found to be most interesting and useful are listed here.

Brady, Jim, 1996: *The Irish Navy. What a Life!* Anchor Press, Dublin. 180 pp.

Bulfin, William, 1907: *Rambles in Eirinn*. Reprinted by Roberts Wholesale Books Ltd. 456 pp.

Cronin, Kevin, 1996: *Off the Beaten Track*. Appletree Press, Belfast. 191 pp.

Dinneen, P.S., 1927: *Focloir Gaedhilge agus Bearla. An Irish-English Dictionary*. Educational Co. of Ireland, Cork. 1343 pp.

Duffy, Sean, Ed., 1997: *Atlas of Irish History*. Gill & Macmillan, Dublin. 144 pp.

Fewer, Michael, 1992: *By Cliff and Shore: Walking the Waterford Coast*. Anna Livia Press.

Gilbert, Stuart, 1963: *James Joyce's Ulysses*. Penguin Books, Middlesex. 364 pp.

Greenwood, M. and H. Hawkins, 1996: *Ireland. The Rough Guide*. Rough Guides Ltd., London. 635 pp.

Harbison, Peter, 1970: *Guide to National and Historic Monuments of Ireland*. Gill & Macmillan, Dublin. 400 pp.

Healy, Elizabeth, 1995: *Literary Tour of Ireland*. Wolfhound Press, Dublin. 272 pp.

Killanin, Lord and M. V. Duignan, 1995: *The Shell Guide to Ireland*. Revised and updated by Peter Harbison. Gill & Macmillan, Dublin. 340 pp

MacHale, Des, 2000: *The Complete Guide to The Quiet Man*. Appletree Press, Belfast. 268 pp.

Mitchell, Frank, 1990: *The Way that I Followed*. Country House, Dublin.

Mulvihill, Mary, 2002: *Ingenious Ireland*. Town House, Dublin. 493 pp.

Nairn, Richard and Miriam Crowley, 1998: *Wild Wicklow*. Town House, Dublin. 236 pp.

Newby, Eric, 1987: *Round Ireland in Low Gear*. Picador, London. 308 pp.

Power, Frank and Peter Pearson, 1995: *The Forty Foot: A Monument to Sea Bathing*. Environmental Publishers, Dublin. 135 pp.

Pearson, Peter, 1998: *Between the Mountains and the Sea*. O'Brien Press, Dublin. 381 pp.

Praeger, Robert Lloyd, 1997: *The Way that I Went*. The Collins Press, Cork. 397 pp.

Reader's Digest, 2003: *Illustrated Guide to Ireland*. Reader's Digest Association, London. 352 pp.

Roche, Richard, 1995: *The Norman Invasion of Ireland* Anvil Books.

Rowledge, J. W. P., 1995: *A Regional History of Railways. Volume 16: Ireland*. Atlantic Transport Publishers, Cornwall. 280 pp.

Slavin, Michael, 1996: *The Book of Tara*. Wolfhound Press, Dublin. 173 pp.

Wilson, Brian, 1998: *Dances with Waves: Around Ireland by Kayak*. O'Brien Press, Dublin. 319 pp.

INDEX

Index